T0311491

Mega-Events, City and Power

This book examines the power relations that emerge from the convergence of the universe in which the sporting spectacle is produced and the universe in which a city is produced.

The book adopts Bourdieu's concept of field to explore the interests and disputes involved in the production of sports mega-events across different times and spaces, and the role of host cities in these processes. It aims to identify the bases that give these spectacles the power to produce disruptions in the social fabric of the host cities and countries and to enable the production of authoritarian forms of exercising power. By observing the historical constitution of the field of production of sport spectacle as an autonomous field, this book explores how sport mega-events create both an arena and a context for radical expressions of authoritarianism of neoliberal planning models.

The book will be of interest to students, scholars, and professionals in architecture and urban studies, urban planning, municipal governance, sport and leisure studies as well as those interested in the relationship between state and capital in the production of urban space.

Nelma Gusmão de Oliveira is a professor at State University of Southwestern Bahia in Brazil where she researches large-scale development projects. Her doctoral dissertation was awarded the 2012–2013 prize for best dissertation by the Brazilian National Association of Research and Graduate Studies in Urban and Regional Planning.

Routledge Critical Studies in Urbanism and the City

This series offers a forum for cutting-edge and original research that explores different aspects of the city. Titles within this series critically engage with, question and challenge contemporary theory and concepts to extend current debates and pave the way for new critical perspectives on the city. This series explores a range of social, political, economic, cultural and spatial concepts, offering innovative and vibrant contributions, international perspectives and interdisciplinary engagements with the city from across the social sciences and humanities.

Spatial Complexity in Urban Design Research
Graph Visualization Tools for Communities and their Contexts
Jamie O'Brien

Urban Neighbourhood Formations
Boundaries, Narrations and Intimacies
Edited by Hilal Alkan and Nazan Maksudyan

Urban Ethics
Conflicts Over the Good and Proper Life in Cities
Edited by Moritz Ege and Johannes Moser

Urban Art and the City
Creating, Destroying, and Reclaiming the Sublime
Edited by Argyro Loukaki

Housing Displacement
Conceptual and Methodological Issue
Edited by Guy Baeten, Carina Listerborn, Maria Persdotter and Emil Pull

Mega-Events, City and Power
Nelma Gusmão de Oliveira

For more information about this series, please visit www.routledge.com/Routledge-Critical-Studies-in-Urbanism-and-the-City/book-series/RSCUC

Mega-Events, City and Power

Nelma Gusmão de Oliveira

LONDON AND NEW YORK

First published 2021
by Routledge
2 Park Square, Milton Park, Abingdon, Oxon OX14 4RN

and by Routledge
52 Vanderbilt Avenue, New York, NY 10017

Routledge is an imprint of the Taylor & Francis Group, an informa business

© 2021 Nelma Gusmão de Oliveira

The rights of Nelma Gusmão de Oliveira to be identified as the author of this work has been asserted by her in accordance with sections 77 and 78 of the Copyright, Designs and Patents Act 1988.

All rights reserved. No part of this book may be reprinted or reproduced or utilised in any form or by any electronic, mechanical, or other means, now known or hereafter invented, including photocopying and recording, or in any information storage or retrieval system, without permission in writing from the publishers.

Trademark notice: Product or corporate names may be trademarks or registered trademarks, and are used only for identification and explanation without intent to infringe.

British Library Cataloguing-in-Publication Data
A catalogue record for this book is available from the British Library

Library of Congress Cataloging-in-Publication Data
A catalog record for this book has been requested

ISBN: 978-0-367-19698-1 (hbk)
ISBN: 978-0-429-24266-3 (ebk)

Typeset in Times New Roman
by Apex CoVantage, LLC

Contents

Figures

Tables

Foreword

In recent decades, the staging of mega-events such as world exhibitions, international conferences, and major sports competitions like the FIFA World Cup or the Olympic Games has become a justification to initiate large-scale urban transformations. Mega-sporting events are viewed as instruments of economic regeneration, stimulating domestic consumer markets while capturing mobile sources of capital. These spectacular events are entrenched in a complex political web shaped by the interests and desires of multiple actors, both internal and external to the city, whose irreconcilable demands and divergent viewpoints about policy orientations and development priorities can exacerbate local existing tensions. Apart from their obvious economic interests, actors covet mega-events as means to influence the decision-making process, to reprioritize the urban agenda, and to increase their power within local politics. The role of international sporting federations in the production of the event spectacle has not been fully scrutinized and sufficiently analyzed. Which is why this book is so important.

In 2009, after having spent 15 years researching the urban transformations of the city of Beijing in China and documenting the spectacularization process in the years leading to the 2008 Olympic Games, I arrived in Rio de Janeiro with the intention of testing whether my expertise could be applied to such a different social, cultural, and political environment. I spoke no Portuguese and only summarily knew the city, but the prospect of studying the city's transformation in the years leading to the 2014 FIFA World Cup and 2016 Summer Olympic Games was exhilarating. In what had become known as the country of social movements with the famous Porto Alegre Forum, I was expecting to find a very different environment in terms of criticism and resistance to the mega-event spectacle. I was not disappointed. Brazilian scholars turned out to be incredibly sophisticated, critical, and deeply involved in social movements in favor of social justice and state transparency.

After I gave a first lecture at the urban and regional planning department of the Federal University of Rio de Janeiro about my research in Beijing in January 2009, I was flooded with demands from professors and researchers interested in cooperation and partnership. Professor Carlos Vainer invited me to work with his research group at IPPUR (ETTERN) and rapidly introduced me to one of his most promising doctoral students, Nelma Gusmão de Oliveira. There started a long and prolific research collaboration that would last over a decade.

Nelma proved to be a brilliant and rigorous researcher, a very involved activist and a faithful collaborator. She spent several months at the University of Quebec in Montreal under my supervision, and we organized several international conferences together in Rio de Janeiro and other Brazilian cities as well as abroad in Montreal, Los Angeles, Buenos Aires, and elsewhere. Her reputation as a scholar was established when she presented her doctoral dissertation and obtained Brazil's highest recognition for the best dissertation in urban and regional planning. This prestigious prize was well-deserved because of the impressive quality of her work which painstakingly revealed the inner workings of a complex and secretive system where graft, corruption, and the merchandizing of power and influence is endemic. Her careful and enlightened study of Olympic files, legal documents, legal derogations, and behind-the-scenes agreements revealed information that was essential for the understanding of this system.

This book draws upon this exemplary scholarly work to deliver a detailed and sophisticated contribution to the understanding of the inner workings of mega-events.

It provides a rich addition to the current literature on mega-event and reveals with a rare clarity the complexities behind the production of the sports spectacle. Nelma Gusmão de Oliveira manages to retell in comprehensive terms the history of the institutions that are at the origin of sporting mega-events. Her exemplary documentation work, based on a careful and exhaustive study of several primary sources, convincingly back up her claims about the inner workings of the mega-event machine and highlights some the hidden realities she has managed to uncover. One of her greatest contributions lies in her analysis of the political role of mega-events, which are instrumentalized in the creation of consensus around mega-projects and policy re-orientations, for the benefit of a small political and economic elite and to the detriment of the common good. She convincingly argues that the state of exception that marks the production of the sports spectacle thrives upon a widespread depoliticization of the decision-making process in favor of a consensual, neoliberal view of public policy. She also reveals not only the authoritarian nature of these transactions but also the resulting disappearance of space for dissent and debate.

Nelma Gusmão de Oliveira's painstaking efforts to document the historical transformation of mega-events, to explain their political and legal implications, and to reveal their dark side will inspire many scholars, journalists, and other analysts. The book reveals little-known facts and information that are of immeasurable importance for the communities affected by sporting mega-events as well as for the activists, scholars, and others who are helping them fight for their rights. By uncovering important facts that various authorities in the sporting world have long striven to conceal, this book thus provides a great public service for various resistance groups around the world. The work also reveals Gusmão de Oliveira's achievements as a researcher and a scholar and her analytical talent for extracting enlightening meaning from complex and obscure data. The quality of the writing, the rigor of the research, and the sophistication of the analysis make this work an essential reading for those seeking to understand the Olympic system and its impact upon cities and their inhabitants. This is a book of exceptional pertinence in the contemporary political context, both in Brazil and around the world.

Anne-Marie Broudehoux
Université du Québec à Montréal

Acknowledgments

Portions of this book appeared previously in Portuguese. I am grateful to Editora UFRJ for their permission to reprint passages from my book *O Poder dos Jogos e os Jogos de Poder: Os interesses em campo na produção da cidade para o espetáculo esportivo* (2015).

The research presented in this book began during my doctoral studies in Urban and Regional Planning at the Federal University of Rio de Janeiro's Institute of Urban and Regional Research and Planning (IPPUR/UFRJ), which I concluded in October 2012. The institutional and financial support that I received during this time from the State University of Southwestern Bahia (UESB) was fundamental in allowing me to dedicate myself entirely to research. I thank IPPUR/ UFRJ for its institutional support as well as the *École de Design da Université du Québec à Montréal* (UQÀM) where I held a doctoral stay with the *Programme des Futurs Leaders dans les Amériques* (PFLA) supported by the Canadian government. I collected some of the data that served as the basis for reflections in this book during trips supported by the State, Work, Territory, and Nature Laboratory (ETTERN), the *Heinrich Böll Foundation*, and the Research Council of Norway. I would also like to thank Faye Leerink, Nonita Saha, and Ruth Anderson of Routledge for their patience and their interest in my work, as well as Helena Hurd for inviting me to submit a proposal for publication.

The challenge of studying two objects as complex as the production of sport spectacle and the production of the city would not have been possible without the collaboration of many of my friends and colleagues, to whom I am sincerely thankful. When I began my doctoral studies at IPPUR, I was already dedicated to studying theories and practices of urban planning that had become hegemonic in the field in which the city is produced, but I did not yet glimpse the possibility of studying the convergence between these ideas and the production of sporting mega-events. In order to study the production of sport spectacle – a research object that heretofore had been completely outside my area of knowledge – I relied on the unconditional support of my advisor, Carlos Vainer, as well as important contributions from professors Ana Clara Torres Ribeiro (*in memoriam*), Rainer Randolph, and Henri Acselrad. I must also thank Carlos Vainer for his confidence, incentives, and the clarity of his critiques and suggestions as my doctoral advisor. In his company I came to understand, in both theory and in practice, that transformation cannot exist without conflict. I would also like thank the rest of IPPUR's faculty for their teaching and support, as well as my fellow cohort members, especially Daniella Bonatto, José Ricardo Farias, and Krista Lillemets. I am also thankful to have had the opportunity to participate in ETTERN's research group into major urban development projects. I am grateful to Gilmar Mascarenhas (*in memoriam*), Helena Galiza, Fernanda Sánchez, Pedro Novais Lima Junior, Glauco Bienenstein, and Camila Lobino for their contributions, exchanges, and encouragement.

When the city of Rio de Janeiro was still a candidate to host the 2016 Summer Olympics and sport spectacle was an underexplored topic in Brazil, my first steps toward understanding this object of study came about through the support of companions from the Social Committee for the 2007 Pan American Games. I am especially grateful to Inalva Brito, Luiz Mário Behnken, Joylse Domingues, Maria Luísa Tamberllini, Alessandro Biazzi, Christopher Gaffney, and others who joined this group and its successor, the Popular World Cup and Olympics Committee of Rio de Janeiro. From City Councilman Eliomar Coelho, I learned a great deal about power relations in the city of Rio de Janeiro. Members of his staff – especially Denise Firme, Jorge Borges, and Andréa Cassa – gave me access to documents, as well as opportunities for intellectual exchanges that helped me understand the processes involved in producing laws and measures of exception in Rio de Janeiro.

Meeting Anne-Marie Broudehoux and James Freeman in 2009 marked the beginning of a relationship of intense intellectual exchanges, partnerships, and sincere friendship. I thank them both for the care with which they received me during my studies in Montreal, and especially Anne-Marie for her advising. With my colleagues at the PFLA in Canada, especially Glauci Coelho, Breno Pimentel, Luciana Ferrara, and particularly Anne Latandresse, professor at UQÀM, I had the opportunity to participate in valuable intellectual exchanges that contributed to the reflections I present in this book. From my friends John Horne (London), Stavros Stavrides (Athens), Alan Mabin (South Africa), Malte Steinbrink, Christian Russau, Thomas Jedlistschka (Germany), Charles Heying (USA), and Einar Braathen (Norway), I learned a great deal about the territorial repercussions of sport spectacle beyond Brazil.

The dialogue that took place during the defense of my doctoral thesis was also extremely valuable and marked a significant maturation for my research. I am very thankful for the contributions of the professors on my committee: Anne-Marie Broudehoux, Raquel Rolnik, Sonia Rabello, Michel Misse, and Pedro Novais.

Finally, I would like to give special thanks to some of the people whose help in publishing this book was instrumental. First, Alberto Olivera and Maxwell Canaverde for their encouragement and their contributions in creating a proposal for publication, and Raphael Soifer for his help with my limitations with the English language. Second are people whose affection gave me unconditional support in writing this text, especially my friends Laís Ferraz, Andrea Gomes, Débora Cardoso, Anete Viana, Caroline Vasconcelos, José Henrique, Sílvio Macedo. and Márcio Pedreira, and my nephews, Tales Oliveira and Victor Rodrigues.

Abbreviations

ABC	American Broadcasting Company
ACOG	Atlanta Committee for the Olympic and Paralympic Games
ANCOP	National Articulation of the World Cup Popular Committees
APO	Olympic Public Authority
ATHOC	Athens 2004 Organizing Committee for the Olympic Games
Atl	Atlanta
BBC	British Broadcasting Corporation
Bj	Beijing
BOC	Brazilian Olympic Committee
BOCOG	Beijing Organizing Committee for the Games of the XXIX Olympiad
BOPE	Police Battalion of Special Operations
BRT	Bus Rapid Transit
CAS	Court of Arbitration for Sport
CBS	Columbia Broadcasting System
CDDHC-ALERJ	State Legislature's Commission for the Defense of Human Rights and Citizenship
CDURP	Urban Development Company of Rio de Janeiro's Port Region
CEPACs	Certificates of Additional Construction Potential
CIU	Convergence and Union Party
COHRE	Centre on Housing Rights and Evictions
COOB'92	Barcelona '92 Olympic Organizing Committee S.A.
CRJ	City of Rio de Janeiro
Cth	Commonwealth of Australia
DCMS	Department for Culture, Media and Sport
DEM	Democrats Party
DHESCA Brasil	Brazilian Platform for Human, Social, Cultural, and Environmental Rights
EBU	European Broadcasting Union
EKS	Events Knowledge Services
ESPN	Entertainment and Sports Programming Network
FGTS	Severance Indemnity Fund
FIFA	Fédération Internationale de Football Association

FRG	Federal Republic of Germany
HR	Hellenic Republic
HRC – UN	United Nations' Human Rights Council
IAB	Institute of Architects of Brazil
IADB	Inter-American Development Bank
IAHRS – OAS	Inter-American Commission on Human Rights of the Organization of American States
IF	International Federation
IMF	International Monetary Fund
IOC	International Olympic Committee
IPP	Pereira Passos Institute
ISL	International Sport and Leisure
Jpn	Japan
LAOOC	Los Angeles Olympic Organizing Committee
LOCOG	London Organizing Committee for the Olympic Games
MAOGA	Metropolitan Atlanta Olympic Games Authority
NBC	National Broadcasting Company
NOC	National Olympic Committee
NSW	New South Wales
OAKA	Athens Olympic Sports Centre
OCA	Olympic Coordination Authority
OCOG	Organizing Committees for the Olympic Games
ODA	Olympic Delivery Authority
OEK	Workers' Housing Organisation
OGKM	Olympic Games Knowledge Management
OGKS	Olympic Games Knowledge Services
PC do B	Communist Party of Brazil
PMDB	Brazilian Democratic Movement Party
PPP	Public-Private Partnership
PRC	People's Republic of China
PSC	Socialists' Party of Catalonia
PSOE	Spanish Socialist Workers' Party
PT	Workers' Party
RDC	Differentiated Public Contracts Regime
RECOPA	Special Tax Regime for the Construction, Growth, Renovation, or Modernization of Football Stadiums
RE	Kingdom of Spain
RFB	Federative Republic of Brazil
Rio 2016	Organizing Committee of the Olympic and Paralympic Games Rio 2016
RK	Republic of Korea
RSA	Republic of South Africa
SOCOG	Sydney Organizing Committee for the Olympic Games
TCU	Brazil's Federal Court of Accounts
TOK	Transfer of Olympic Knowledge

Tokyo 2020	Tokyo Organizing Committee of the Olympic and Paralympic Games
TOP	The Olympic Partners
TUBSA	Tecnologies Urbanes Barcelona S.A.
UCLA	University of California, Los Angeles
UK	United Kingdom
UPP	Police Pacification Units (Rio de Janeiro)
USOC	United States Olympic Committee
WADA	World Anti-Doping Code
ZEIS	Special Social Interests Zone

Introduction[1]

On September 13, 2017, in Lima, Peru, the International Olympic Committee (IOC) officially announced Paris and Los Angeles as the respective host cities for the 2024 and 2028 Olympic Summer Games. The announcement followed a symbolic vote by the IOC Assembly, but in fact, the cities had already been confirmed as hosts following a period of negotiations between their Candidature Committees and the IOC.

The simultaneous announcement of host cities for two successive editions of the Summer Olympics was unprecedented in the history of the modern Olympics. The IOC proposed the agreement after five cities abandoned their bids to host the 2024 Games;[2] subsequently, out of the seven original bids, only Paris and Los Angeles remained. This situation repeated the selection process for the 2022 Winter Olympics[3] when, five out of seven candidates dropped out leaving only two potential hosts: Almaty and the eventual winner, Beijing. Cities' arguments for abandoning their candidatures included high costs, the IOC's impositions, and the resulting lack of popular support for their bids. This loss of interest in hosting the Games runs counter to the IOC's expectations of its institutional power. Furthermore, it calls into question the current selection process and has led to different strategies for organizing the event.

A very different scenario took place in Copenhagen on October 2, 2009 – eight years before the IOC Assembly in Lima – when Rio de Janeiro was announced as host city for the 2016 Summer Games. Mainstream media throughout the world showed parties on Brazil's streets; after all, Rio had won a fierce contest that included rival bids from Tokyo, Madrid, and Chicago. In Brazil, agents acting across a variety of different scales – and representing a diverse coalition of interests – celebrated together. Images of these celebrations synthesized the symbolic expression of a "consensus" through which hegemonic groups in Brazil joined forces with the goal of inserting Rio de Janeiro into an international circuit of production of sport spectacle.

The focus given to Rio de Janeiro's bid for the 2016 Olympics was not an isolated occurrence. Throughout the world, competitions to attract mega-events – which present themselves as timely strategies for implementing an agenda determined by contemporary theories and practices of urban planning driven by the market – were intensifying.

The Olympic Games, which are intrinsically linked to a spectacular production that reaches half of the planet's population (IOC n.d.), are an expression of the universalist and moral ideals of Baron Pierre de Coubertin, whose dedication led to the establishment of the modern Games. This expression of de Coubertin's ideals – along with appeals to contemporary values of solidarity, or of "saving" the planet – also features in all other events organized by institutions affiliated with the Olympic Movement.[4] Since the 1990s, when market-oriented logic became a dominant benchmark in city planning, the strong symbolic weight of mega-events has been a key ingredient in the convergence of production of this type of event with the production of urban space in accordance with a neoliberal framework.

How, then, does a strategy so convenient to the market begin to become unattractive to some cities? To what extent does this indicate radical changes in relationships between the production of sport spectacle and the production of the city? Any attempt to answer these questions must first address other, earlier questions that have guided the reflections in this book.

What circumstances have led to the current scenario? How, historically, have sporting events been produced? What interests and disputes are involved in their production across different scales of space and time? What role do host cities play in these processes? What are the bases that give these spectacles the power to produce such deep disruptions in the social fabric of the cities and countries in which they take place? Finally, to what extent and in what way does the execution of sport spectacle enable the production of authoritarian forms of exercising power and organizing public administration?

Exploring overlaps between the execution of mega-events and market-oriented urban policies has been a recurring subject in contemporary urban studies, both from supportive points of view and from more critical perspectives.[5] Most existing research investigates the effects of these overlaps through an approach focused on the production of urban space. However, there is a paucity of research examining the convergence of these two systems of production – namely, the production of sport spectacle and the production of urban space – from a perspective that considers the how the former operates.

As Bourdieu (1993) suggests, we can consider the existence of a space of production in which "sports products" are created. This space – endowed with a specific hierarchy, a particular history, and with its own logic – tends to function as a field of disputes. In writing this book, I have carried out my research in accordance with this perspective.

My research utilizes Bourdieu's concept of field as an analytical tool to explore power relations that involve the convergence between the universe in which sport spectacle is produced and the universe in which the city is produced. This approach privileges the understanding of *modus operandi* of hegemonic groups that command the production of the planet's two biggest events: the Football World Cup and the Summer Olympic Games. As such, I focus on disputes between – and coalitions built by – individual and collective subjects who take control of sports mega-events so as to develop projects and strategies that are intended to maintain or bolster their positions in the social space.

Authors including Žižek (1998, 1999a, 1999b), Rancière (2001), Swyngedouw (2010), and Vainer (2017) have elucidated the authoritarian nature of the consensus proposed by the neoliberal project. Agamben (2005), on the other hand, affirms that a state of exception tends to assert itself through the paradigm of government in contemporary politics, even in so-called democratic regimes. Similarly, Stavrides (2008) defends the idea that sport mega-events create conditions for the existence of "emergency cities," while Vainer (2017) identifies a "city of exception."

In my own attempt to contribute to this debate, I argue that the production of sporting mega-events creates both an arena and an appropriate context for the most radical expressions of authoritarianism inherent in the neoliberal planning model, thereby facilitating the existence of "cities of exception." I show how this is made possible through the growing political and legal autonomy that the field of sport spectacle has gradually conquered over the course of a century through its relationship with the field of economics. The main protagonists in this conquest have been and continue to be the International Olympic Committee (IOC), the Fédération Internationale de Football Association (FIFA), and the interests that these institutions represent. In other words, while the production of sport spectacle constitutes an autonomous field in relation to legal and political fields, it has gradually submitted to the field of economics. As such, it also allows the city to be submitted to the same field through interactions that combine articulated interests on different scales of power.

I begin my study by observing the constitution of the field of production of sport spectacle and by taking as my primary object of study the rules that have guided its operation throughout history. I begin this historical overview with the original Olympic Charter,[6] published in 1908, and continue through the present-day tangle of rules and laws that govern the relationship between this field and the city. Based on these documents, other official publications, and narratives of agents working in the field, I have observed the historical contours of the relationship between the field of production of sport spectacle and that of production of the city, including intra- and inter-scalar disputes between individuals who work within these fields as well as their relations to other fields of disputes.

This work culminates with an analysis of ruptures and realignments produced in the political and institutional dimensions[7] of countries that host mega-events. I analyzed candidature application files from the last two decades as well as reports issued by Organizing Committees and other international institutions responsible for producing mega-events. I have paid special attention to Brazil and, especially, to the city of Rio de Janeiro over the course of its candidature for and organization of the 2014 Football World Cup and the 2016 Olympic Games. However, although the study focuses on Rio de Janeiro, the other countries that hosted mega-events since the 1990s were also studied.

In observing ongoing disputes at any given moment, I have sought a perspective that shifts between macro- and micro-scales of observation. As such, my research always takes into account collective subjects and their subspaces. I have also sought to note the relevance of individual agents who have played significant roles in existing disputes within a given field or subfield and to offer some context regarding their trajectories.

Finally, the objective of this book is to unravel truths regarding relationships, between sport spectacle and cities, which are often hidden under the aegis of passion, Olympism, and urban development. Next, I will explain some of my methodological choices in constructing this research.

The production of sports spectacle as a field

Bourdieu's concept of the field provides us with the opportunity to reflect on interactions between the production of sport spectacle and the production of the city, without being restricted to merely describing the functioning of the institutions – especially the IOC and FIFA – that command this field. Here, I refer to the concept of the field in terms of a field of forces, paying special attention to struggles to conserve or transform power relations as the starting point for such exploration.

> In analytic terms, a field may be defined as a network, or a configuration, of objective relations between positions. These positions are objectively defined, in their existence and in the determinations they impose upon their occupants, agents or institutions, by their present and potential situation (*situs*) in the structure of the distribution of species of power (or capital) whose possession commands access to the specific profits that are at stake in the field, as well as by their objective relation to other positions (domination, subordination, homology, etc.).
>
> (Bourdieu & Wacquant 1992, p. 97)

Regarding the production of sport spectacle as constituting a field therefore implies thinking of the social world in relational terms and considering that a given object of research cannot be isolated from a set of objective relations. For Bourdieu and Wacquant (1992), it is precisely from this set of relations that a field takes on its essential properties in their twist on Hegel's famous formula from the notion that "the real is the relational" (ibid., p. 97). Consequently, we must examine the extent to which structural constraints exerted on this field – which is itself dominated by pressures of the economic field – relate to and modify relations within the field in which the city is produced, thereby affecting what is done and produced there.

Bourdieu, in a convergence with Marxist thought, recognizes the existence of objective structures in the social world which can guide and coerce the actions and representations of agents independently of these agents' own consciousness and will. Yet, he also emphasizes the existence of a simultaneous and permanent social genesis of schemata of thought, action, representation, and social structures. Although the field of production of sport spectacle presents itself as the result of, over the historical process of its formation, preexisting economic structures, it cannot have been configured without the objective interference of the actions of individual and collective subjects within it.

Considering the concept of the field also implies considering Bourdieu and Wacquant's (1992) definition of social space, which they see as multidimensional space built on the principles of differentiation or distribution that comprise all active properties within a given universe. Different forms of power or capital that occur in different fields act as principle elements in constructing social space. Each field or subfield corresponds to a prevailing kind of private capital, both as power and as an object. Bourdieu's understanding of capital, therefore, is not limited to economics. Instead, it can be understood as power within and over a given field. This power can take various forms, including economic, cultural, social, and symbolic capital, among others. Like economic capital, other forms of capital can also accumulate, be transmitted, and have the potential to create profit. They can exist objectively in the form of goods, be incorporated into the body, or be secured through legal means. According to Bourdieu, symbolic capital – which can also be understood as prestige, reputation, or fame – is recognized as a legitimate form of different types of capital (Bourdieu 1991).

Within this aforementioned social space, a hierarchy is created through the unequal distribution of capital, and all agents or groups of agents can be defined through the relative positions they occupy. Each of these positions is defined by positions that agents occupy in different fields, based both on the total capital and different types of capital they possess (Bourdieu 1991). In each field, individuals or groups of individuals are committed to modifying or maintaining the positions they occupy by increasing, maintaining, or improving the capital they possess. This, in turn, leads to disputes as individuals aim to expand their shares of the most valued capital in the field or to increase the relative value of the capital they hold. Thus, within the social space, social classes and segments of classes are involved in a constant struggle. At stake in this symbolic struggle is the imposition of a worldview that best conforms to their interests in modifying or maintaining their social positions.

In this sense, I have conducted an analysis of what I call, in a nod to Bourdieu, the "field of production of sport spectacle." As a social space structured through its interaction with other social spaces, the field of production of sport spectacle acts as a forcefield containing both dominant and dominated agents who hold different types and quantities of capital. Within this field, struggles develop at multiple scales in order to alter or preserve individual social standing.

Analysis across multiple scales

The theme of spatial "scales" occupies an increasingly prominent place in contemporary examinations of theory and politics. Although its centrality is not especially new, issues concerning surrounding territorial frameworks have taken on new meaning in recent decades.

Capital, in its incessant movement toward a spatiality that favors accumulation, confers an increasingly complex role to spatial dimension in the reproduction of social life. Given the nature of this complexity, infinite possibilities of scale can be established both in terms of strategies for political action and narratives that seek to explain social phenomena and their rebuttals through spatial relations.[8]

The production of sport spectacle is the result of multiple interactions between individuals and groups acting in different fields and at different scales throughout history. To better understand the social phenomena related to the field of sporting mega-events, I have utilized a cross-scale approach in conducting my research. I have questioned urban policy models dedicated to attracting sporting mega-events, which in turn encourage local political authorities to take on the role of entrepreneurs in order to form a relation with global scales of production.

Scholars who adopt a critical perspective in observing capitalist society agree that cooperation and competition between different forms of capital establish multiple and interlinked scales. Similarly, different forms of domination and oppression are constantly (re)produced or transformed through tensions and power struggles that also operate in different dimensions and across different scales.

As Brandão (2009) writes, every scale-level analysis "enables us to grasp real, concrete dimensions that could not be assimilated from another perspective." The privilege of certain scales, therefore, not only reflects the political and ideological positions of the actors who choose them, but also leads to explanations or results that reinforce the contents of such positions (Swyngedouw 1997). According to Swyngedouw, who has since been echoed by other researchers, scales are not neutral; instead, they express power relations.

> [S]cale is neither an ontologically given and a priori definable geographical territory nor a politically neutral discursive strategy in the construction of narratives. Scale, both in its metaphorical use and material construction, is highly fluid and dynamic, and both processes and effects can easily move from scale to scale and affect different people in different ways, depending on the scale at which the process operates. Similarly, different scalar narratives indicate different causal moments and highlight different power geometries in explaining such events.
>
> (Swyngedouw 1997, p. 140)

As such, I understand scales as arenas of confrontation in which conflicts are established, mediated, and regulated and in which commitments can be sealed; in scales, struggles deepen, thereby leading to reconfigurations of social relations and redistributions of resources and positions. Scales present themselves as products of social relations, but they are more than that: the simple act of defining scales constitutes engaging with an object of contestation that is permanently in question. From each partial outcome of disputes, agents position themselves in different ways, creating new strategies, and (re)establishing correlations between forces. Therefore, at the same time that the production of scales presents itself as a result, it is also a determining factor of social processes. In other words, using Massey's (2012) expression, someone who holds the power to define scales and operate at different scales also has the ability to define "power-geometries."[9]

In carrying out my research, I have been mindful of the impossibility of understanding the phenomena occurring in the cities that host sporting mega-events through restricted, local-level observation. As such, I have sought to utilize a perspective that considers existing articulations of global, national, regional, and city-wide scales, while also recognizing the simultaneity and reciprocity of interactions within and between these different scalar universes.

Rio De Janeiro as an object for local-scale observation

Marcel Mauss (2013), in his "Essay on Seasonal Variations of the Eskimo Societies," demonstrates how certain experiences can be crucial to developing a methodological analysis of particular social processes. In this sense, Rio de Janeiro holds a particular heuristic potential that led me to choose it as the main object for observation on a local scale.

Since the beginning of the 1990s, competing to host sporting mega-events has featured prominently in Rio de Janeiro's urban agenda. It was the main development strategy in the city's First Strategic Plan (Cidade do Rio de Janeiro 1996), which adopted a neoliberal planning model. Thus, before finally winning hosting rights for the 2014 Football World Cup and the 2016 Olympic Summer Games, Rio de Janeiro had already bid to host the 2004 and 2012 Olympics and had already hosted the 2007 Pan American Games. At least three uniquely specific factors of Rio de Janeiro's experience not only make the city an excellent case study but also allow us to enumerate certain regularities that can be applied in other host cities.

Rio's role as host city for three sport mega-events in less than a decade – the 2007 Pan American Games, the 2014 Football World Cup, and 2016 Summer Olympic Games – presents the first specific factor to be studied: namely, the unique variety and scalar scope of different applications and processes of organization. This scope allows us to compare processes that, by adopting as a single city as their stage, involve multiple articulations at entirely distinct scalar levels.

The second of these factors is Rio's persistence in bidding to host mega-events, which has been also central to urban policy strategies in many of Brazil's major cities.[10] Rio de Janeiro's near-constant attempts to host sporting mega-events persisted over the course of more than two decades. As the city constructed this trajectory, it consolidated a planning strategy focused on mega-events as part of a political project for national development. As such, it was able to bring together Brazil's three central spheres of public administration: federal, state, and municipal governments. This allows us to analyze different political and institutional arrangements during different historical moments.

Finally, the third specific factor in Rio de Janeiro's experience derives from the challenge the city faced in executing the 2016 Summer Olympics after the improbable success of its candidature. As a city located in a peripheral country on a peripheral continent, featuring with a barebones initial project, and having previously only made it as far as the final round of the selection of a host city, Rio still managed to surpass other cities with far greater international prestige and with more developed physical and economic structures. This, in turn, affords us an exceptional opportunity to observe cross-scale articulations in the construction of mega-events.

An overview of the contents

This book is divided into two parts consisting of three chapters each. In the first part, I observe sporting mega-events by focusing on processes that occur within the field of production of sport spectacle. Here, interests and disputes are concentrated primarily on the global scale, although I am careful to always consider cross-scale articulations. In the second section, I observe sport spectacle from a viewpoint that privileges understanding its territorialization, thereby focusing on interests and disputes that operate primarily on national, regional, and city-wide scales.[11]

Chapter One investigates the historical conditions of the formation of production of sport spectacle as an autonomous field with its own particular history, disputes, and rules. By establishing a genealogy of this field's formation, I aim to identify central elements within the field that, over the course of history, have been either autonomous or submissive in relation to other fields. Through this genealogy, I seek to understand mechanisms by which the field of production of sport spectacle has exercised control over the field of production of the city.

The second and third chapters explore the present-day functioning of the field. Chapter Two focuses on players operating in the field of production of sporting mega-events using an analogy of the concept of the field and the idea of the game as established by Bourdieu and Wacquant (1992). The chapter identifies predominant agents, groups of agents, and coalitions within the field, as well as their positions and strategies. Chapter Three presents systems of rules and arbitration in sporting mega-events, in addition to mapping out power structures, rules, and established contracts within the current composition of the field. This chapter also explores important transformations in these rules that took place following the organization of the 2016 Olympic Summer Games in Rio de Janeiro. As such, the chapter aims to fulfill two objectives: first, to unveil the system through which sport spectacle subjects the city to the interests of the economic field; and second, to understand how this system metamorphoses to adapt to new contexts.

The book's second part presents the territorial anchoring of this system's operation from a perspective that privileges observing its effects in the political-institutional dimension.

In Chapter Four, I observe various players involved with the use of sporting mega-events as a development strategy for producing the city. Clarence Stone's urban regime theory and Logan and Molotch's studies of the "growth machine" provide the foundation for this approach.

Chapter Five examines the convergence between the field of production of sport spectacle and market-oriented planning practices. Here, I examine disputes over mega-events by focusing on cities that, in their zeal to host these events, submitted multiple candidatures, which subsequently became intertwined with their overall development strategies. This chapter aims to demonstrate how sport spectacle can provide a suitable arena and context for consolidating a coalition of dominant interests.

Finally, Chapter Six consists of mapping out and analyzing political and institutional changes in the cities that have most recently hosted sporting mega-events. Here, the emphasis on Rio de Janeiro illustrates more clearly how the production of sport spectacle functions as a means of producing authoritarian forms of power as well as forms of public administration that enable land to be appropriated for capital accumulation. This chapter examines the relations that Poulantzas (1974) establishes between crisis and exception as well as Giorgio Agamben's thesis of the "state of exception as a contemporary paradigm of government," leading, in turn, to reflections on the concept of "city of exception."

In the book's conclusion, I once more examine the central issues of my research and seek to identify certain regularities in patterns of interactions between the field of production of sport spectacle and the field of production of the city. In addition, I observe certain specificities of such interactions when territorialized in some countries.

Notes

1 Portions of this introduction first appeared in the book *O Poder dos Jogos e os Jogos de Poder: Os interesses em campo na produção da cidade para o espetáculo esportivo* (de Oliveira 2015), published by Editora UFRJ. The English translation is by Raphael Soifer.

2 Boston withdrew in time to be replaced by Los Angeles as the official candidate of the United States Olympic Committee (USOC). Meanwhile, Toronto abandoned the candidature process just hours before being announced as an official candidate. As the result of a public referendum, Hamburg left the contest shortly after its candidature was announced. Finally, Rome and Budapest announced their withdrawals over the course of the candidature process.

3 Applications from Oslo, Stockholm, Lviv, Krakow, and a joint bid from St. Moritz and Munich were all aborted.

4 The concept of the Olympic Movement as collective subject, as well as further considerations regarding its existence, will be discussed in greater detail in Chapter 2. For now, it is sufficient to note that any invocation of the Olympic Movement refers to all entities directly involved in producing the Olympic Games.

5 Examples of authors who defend mega-events as a development strategy include Jordi Borja, Manoel Forn, and Manoel Castells in their recurrent systematizations of strategic planning as a model for urban planning. More specifically, see Borja and Castells (1997), and Castells (1992). For a more critical perspective, see: Burbank, Andranovich and Heying (2001), de Oliveira and Gaffney (2010), Broudehoux (2007, 2012), de Oliveira (2010) and Silvestre and de Oliveira (2012), among many others.

6 The content of the Olympic Charter will be discussed in more detail in Chapter 3. For now, it is worth clarifying that the Olympic Charter is a sort of constitution approved by the International Olympic Committee (IOC), and that it establishes the principles and rules that govern the Olympic Movement.

7 The term "Institutional" is understood here as referring to "institution" as conceptualized by Poulantzas; namely, as "a system of norms or rules which are socially sanctioned" (Poulantzas 1978, p. 115). However, it is also worth emphasizing that Émile Durkheim, beginning with his first analyses of social life, defined an institution as "all the beliefs and modes of behavior instituted by the collectivity" (Durkheim 1982, p. 45).

8 Smith (1993), for example, establishes six scalar levels as references for spatial discussion: the individual body, community, urban, regional, national, and global. Other authors regroup or subdivide these units, thereby establishing new levels of scalar approach.
9 Massey (2012) utilizes the concept of "power-geometries" to discuss multiple relations of domination/subordination and of participation/exclusion through which physical and social nature are transformed.
10 This near-constant pursuit of candidatures to host the Olympic Games is not exclusive to the city of Rio de Janeiro. However, although local politicians supported these candidatures, those primarily responsible were mostly agents linked to the Olympic Movement; as such, these candidatures cannot be considered to constitute an urban policy strategy. See Chapter Five.
11 Considering the fluidity inherent in the determination of scalar divisions, especially in relation to the idea of local, I prefer to use the term "city scale," instead of the more common "local scale."

References

Agamben, G 2005, *State of Exception*, University of Chicago Press, Chicago.
Brandão, C 2009, "Territórios, conflitos e escalas espaciais: anotações críticas em momento de crise estrutural", in *Anais eletrônicos do XIII Encontro Nacional da Anpur*, Anpur, Florianópolis.
Borja, J & Castells, M 1997, *Local and Global: Management of Cities in the Information Age*, Earthscan Publications, London.
Bourdieu, P 1991, *Language and Symbolic Power*, trans. G Raymond & M Adamsom, Polity Press, Cambridge.
Bourdieu, P 1993, "How Can One Be a Sports Fan?" in S During (ed) *The Cultural Studies Reader*, 339–356, Routledge, London and New York.
Bourdieu, P & Wacquant, LJD 1992, *An Invitation to Reflexive Sociology*, The University of Chicago Press, Chicago.
Broudehoux, AM 2007, "Spectacular Beijing: The Conspicuous Construction of an Olympic Metropolis", *Journal of Urban Affairs*, 29.4, pp. 383–399.
Broudehoux, AM 2012, "Civilizing Beijing: Social Beautification, Civility and Citizenship at the 2008 Olympics", in G Hayes & J Karamichas (eds) *Olympic Games, Mega-Events and Civil Societies*, Palgrave Macmillan, London, pp. 46–67.
Burbank, M, Andranovich, G & Heying, C 2001, *Olympic Dreams: The Impact of Mega-Events on Local Politics*, Lynne Rienner Publishers, Boulder.
Castells, M 1992, "The World Has Changed: Can Planning Change?" *Landscape and Urban Planning*, 22.1, pp. 73–78.
Cidade do Rio de Janeiro 1996, *Plano Estratégico da Cidade do Rio de Janeiro – Rio sempre Rio*, Imprensa da Cidade, Rio de Janeiro.
de Oliveira, A 2010, "Mega-Events, Urban Management, and Macroeconomic Policy: 2007 Pan American games in Rio de Janeiro", *Journal of Urban Planning and Development*, 137.2, pp. 184–192.
de Oliveira, NG & Gaffney, CT 2010, "Rio de Janeiro e Barcelona: os limites do paradigma olímpico", *Biblio 3w*, Universidad de Barcelona, XV.895, p. 17, 5 Noviembre.
Durkheim, E 1982, *The Rules of Sociological Method*, trans. WD Hall, The Free Press, New York.
International Olympic Committee (IOC) n.d., *Marketing Report: Rio 2016*, IOC, Louzane.

Massey, D 2012, "Power-Geometry and a Progressive Sense of Place", in J Bird, B Curtis & T Putnam (eds) *Mapping the Futures*, Routledge, Abingdon and New York, pp. 75–85.

Mauss, M 2013, *Seasonal Variations of the Eskimo: A Study in Social Morphology*, Routledge, London and New York.

Poulantzas, N 1974, *Fascism and Dictatorship: The Third International and the Problem of Fascism*, Verso, London.

Poulantzas, N 1978, *Political Power and Social Classes*, trans. T O'Hagan, Verso, London.

Rancière, J 2001, "Ten Theses on Politics", *Theory & Event*, 5.3, pp. 1–16.

Silvestre, G & de Oliveira, NG 2012, "The Revanchist Logic of Mega-Events: Community Displacement in Rio de Janeiro's West End", *Visual Studies*, 27.2, pp. 204–210.

Smith, N 1993, "Homeless/Global: Scaling Places", in J Bird, B Curtis & T Putnam (eds) *Mapping the Futures*, Routledge, Abingdon and New York, pp. 102–135.

Stavrides, S 2008, "Urban Identities: Beyond the Regional and the Global, the Case of Athens", in *Regional Architecture and Identity in the Age of Globalization: Proceedings of 2nd International Conference of CSAAR*, CSAAR, Tunis, pp. 577–588.

Swyngedouw, E 1997, "Neither Global nor Local: 'Glocalization' and the Politics of Scale", in RC Kewin (ed) *Spaces of Globalization: Reasserting the Power of the Local*, The Guilford Press, New York and London, pp. 137–166.

Swyngedouw, E 2010, "Post-Democratic Cities for Whom and for What", in *Regional Studies Association Annual Conference*, Pecs, Hungary, May.

Vainer, C 2017, "Rio de Janeiro's Strategic Plan: Olympic Construction of the Corporate Town", in L Albrechts, A Balducci & J Hillier (eds), *Situated Practices of Strategic Planning*, Routledge, Abingdon and New York.

Žižek, S 1998, "For a Leftist Appropriation of the European Legacy", *Journal of Political Ideologies*, 3.1, pp. 63–78.

Žižek, S 1999a, "Carl Schmitt in the Age of Post-Politics", in C Mouffe (ed) *The Challenge of Carl Schmitt*, Verso, London.

Žižek, S 1999b, *The Ticklish Subject: The Absent Centre of Political Ontology*, Verso, London.

Part 1

Production of sports spectacle on a global scale

1 Laying the field

A genealogy of sport spectacle[1]

Introduction

Strong images, together with rituals and symbolism, are all elements that have given support to sporting events ranging from the most expressive – such as the Football World Cup or the Olympic Games – to schoolyard scavenger hunts. It is difficult to imagine these kinds of event without considering fair play, the forms in which they are celebrated, and the comradery they promote among athletes of different races, cultures, and nations. Magical scenes of the opening and closing ceremonies, moments of surpassing limits while competing for medals, and the emotional tears of spectators watching their country consecrated as champion are all part of this imaginary.

When these occasions take on the character of a mega-event,[2] they can promote the projection and redefinition of the international image of a host country and city. Mega-events – which have always been associated with major urban development projects and with the movement of economic, political, and symbolic capital – have become major objects of desire among governments. Places that host mega-events produce profound regulatory and institutional ruptures and realignments across multiple scales of power.

The idea of amateurism – substantiated by the discourse of disinterest and de-politicization – has come to legitimate the pretense of autonomy of modern sports as a specific field of production and to bestow upon sports the power to constitute their own political and financial structures that are legally autonomous in relation to the rules that govern society in general. In contemporary times, the principles and rules laid out in the International Olympic Committee's (IOC) Olympic Charter (IOC 2019a) and in the statues of *Fédération Internationale de Football Association* (FIFA 2019) – together with a tangle of recommendations, codes, guarantees, contracts, and even specific tribunals – has further consolidated this autonomy.[3] These mega-events hold powers that extrapolate the field of sport spectacle and impose restraints on the legal structures of the countries and cities that host them, as we will see in Chapters 3 and 6.

Researchers who observe the constitution of modern sports as a sort of rupture in relation to their "ancestral" activities (Huizinga 1980; Elias & Dunning 1986a; Bourdieu 1993) identify the development of a more elaborate set of rigid, explicit rules as one of the essential characteristics responsible for the radical differentiation separating modern sporting practices from earlier physical exercises or games.

When a grouping of sports practices is organized around international tournaments and other competitions, the specific rules governing each modality are not sufficient. New rules must be made in order to determine how and in what conditions the system of institutions and agents directly or indirectly connected to these competitions' practices and modes of consumption must function. First, regulations are established for the functioning of groupings intended to assure representation of the interests of athletes in a given modality or grouping of modalities (such as forms of organization, the conditions for membership, deliberative processes, rule-making procedures, etc.). Soon, other rules are added, such as those relating to the functioning of events and associated roles (teachers, coaches, doctors, etc.) or to the necessary conditions for the venues in which these events occur (such as stadium architecture or infrastructure and security demands) as well as other rules that govern the production and commerce of symbols, goods, and services related to these events.

There is a common-sense tendency to consider rules as a given, as existing unto themselves in an ontological sense. However, as Elias (1986b) notes, rules do not have their own existence; even as they dictate behaviors, they are established, (re)produced, or modified as the result of agreements and compromises between agents or groups of agents who act in specific historical conditions. Rules have not always existed; rather, they themselves are products of disputes and represent dominant interests within the institutions that maintain them in a given moment in time. The observance of these rules depends not only on the strength of the institutions that produce them but also on the behavior and efforts of certain groups in maintaining control of their application.

Therefore, understanding current relationships between cities and mega-events must necessarily pass through an understanding of the historical processes of production of rules and conventions that determine the conduct of agents who act in producing sporting spectacles. How and why are particular forms of organization structured in such a way as to make the development of these rules possible? This is one of the questions that this chapter aims to address.

Very rarely has observing rules, their effects, and the conditions that has made their origin and development viable within each historical context been the object of scientific exploration. Among these rarities is the work of Norbert Elias (1986a, 1986b) who conducts systematic studies of the historical development of rules established in different games and disputes involving physical exercise. Elias's studies range from combat games in ancient Greece to tournaments and popular games in the Middle Ages and the forms to which the specific nomenclature of *sport* was attached beginning in the seventeenth and eighteenth centuries. Elias's objective is to identify the moment and the form in which certain pre-existing physical exercises began to take on a radically new meaning, transforming them into *sports* per se, endowed with objectives, functions, rules, and even specific social qualities among their participants.

Bourdieu (1993), in agreement with Elias (1986a, 1986b), also questions scholars who refer to the games of pre-capitalist societies as pre-sporting practices. In considering sporting practices to be something radically new – the appearance of which is contemporary to the constitution of a field of production of "sporting products" – Bourdieu recognizes the importance of studying the social history of sport through a genealogy of sport's appearance as a specific reality. He is interested in identifying the moment in which a specific field of competition was constituted; Bourdieu (ibid.) argues that sports appeared through the constitution of this field and were defined as specific practices without being reduced to simple ritual games or festive amusements.

Considering previous studies by both Elias (1986a, 1986b) and Bourdieu (1993), this chapter will approach the constitution of a specific camp in which "sporting spectacle" is produced through transformations in modern sports competitions. Here, such practices will be considered, in consonance with the aforementioned authors, as ruptures in the practices of pre-existing games. Constructing a genealogy of the field of production of sporting spectacle – through a perspective that relates the construction of autonomy within the field to political, economic, and social aspects of each historical moment – will allow us to understand how structures of power relating to the production of the city in different scales of time and space have been constituted.

How did the relations of modern sports to economic, political, and legal fields develop during the period of time under analysis in this chapter? How did modern sports pass through a discourse of amateurism toward professionalization and, later, spectacularization? How do the formation of the field and the production of the city relate to these different moments? How, and to what extent, did private international institutions relating to this field acquire the power to impose rules that are naturally accepted and obeyed by cities and countries? Might we affirm that this power is linked to the forms in which the field of production of sporting spectacle relates to other fields? What is the intensity of the transformations that have taken place in this field, and what are the elements that accelerate or slow these movements? Finally, when a game transforms into a commodity, can we still consider the activities that take place in this field to be sports?

The timeline in figures 1.1, 1.2, and 1.3 is part of the search for answers to these questions. On the left side of the figures, events are arranged in chronological order; these are events that have taken place within other fields and that relate to the changes within the field under analysis. On the right side are changes in the economic, legal, or political orders that have taken place in rules that govern the functioning of the Olympic Movement, beginning with the first Olympic Charter, which was published in 1908 (*Comité International Olympic* [CIO] 1908), and entitled "Annuaire."[4]

Based on this chronological order, I have identified three periods that maintain a certain specificity in their structures. In the first period (1894–1970), the Olympic Movement concentrated on strengthening its brand and autonomy through a discourse of amateurism; in the second period (1971–1984), Olympic sports

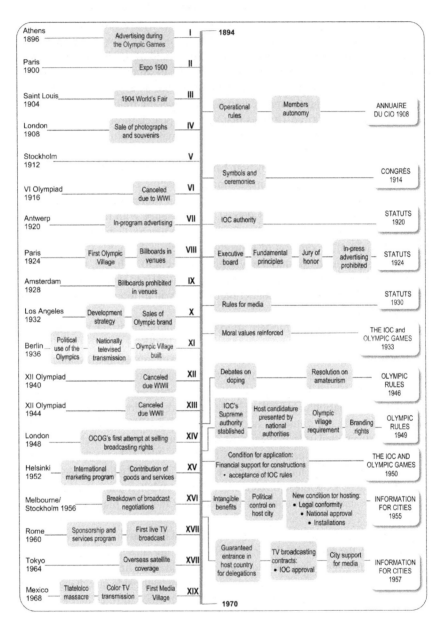

Figure 1.1 Olympic Movement timeline: first period (1894–1970)

began to be professionalized; finally, in the third period (After 1984), the complete spectacularization of sport began to take hold. Before entering into the narrative of this timeline, I will present some introductory considerations that may facilitate the reader's understanding.

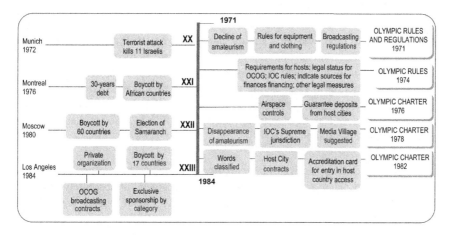

Figure 1.2 Olympic Movement timeline: second period (1971–1984)

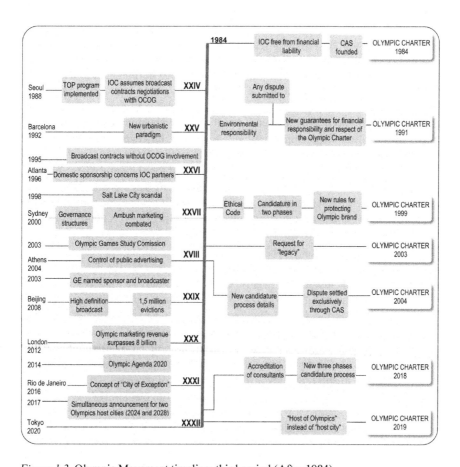

Figure 1.3 Olympic Movement timeline: third period (After 1984)

Prologue: games or sports? concepts in dispute

Aristotle (2009) referred to forms of entertainment as practices chosen entirely on the realization of their own ends. In this same sense, Kant affirmed that a game, as opposed to work, is "an occupation which is agreeable on its own account" (Kant 1987, §43, 171). In the nineteenth century, this concept of "disinterested" games became fundamental in establishing the discourse of so-called "modern sport." Huizinga (1980) seeks to combine the most familiar descriptions of games in the majority of modern European languages, through which he also emphasizes "disinterest" as an essential characteristic:

> play is a voluntary activity or occupation executed within certain fixed limits of time and place, according to rules freely accepted but absolutely binding, having its aim in itself and accompanied by a feeling of tension, joy and the consciousness that it is "different" from "ordinary life."
>
> (Huizinga 1980, p. 28)

Elias (1986b) – who argues that not all sports are games, and that, by the same measure, not all games are sports – establishes a definition for sports as confrontations among organized groups involving physical force. It is worth noting the emphasis that Elias's definition gives both to rules as a form of controlling violence and to his original idea of a function as an end to be accomplished beyond amusement per se.

Many contemporary modalities of sports began in England during the eighteenth and nineteenth centuries. From there, they spread to other countries, especially during the end of the nineteenth century and the beginning of the twentieth. In the official discourse of the Olympic Movement, however, the contemporary Olympic Games are a renaissance of the great festivals of games that took place in ancient Greece between the eighth century BCE and fourth century CE.[5] According to the IOC (1950), the origin of these competitions dates to the early days of ancient Greece, when winners were crowned with olive branches from the sacred temples of Zeus. The games that took place in the sanctuary of Olympia were the most famous of these festivals. In the words of Pierre Frédy, Baron de Coubertin, the IOC's founder and first president:

> In reviving this institution, twenty-five centuries old, we have wished you to become devotes of the *religion of Sport* in the same sense as it was conceived by your famous ancestors. In the present world, where possibilities are great, and yet threatened by so many risks of degeneration, Olympism may be a school of moral nobility and purity, as well as of physical endurance and energy, provided that you always keep your conception of honour and disinterestedness in sport on a level with your physical powers.
>
> (Coubertin, cited in IOC 1933, p. 10)

Elias (1986a) notes the existence of substantial differences between ancient competitions and those that began during the modern era. He questions the existence of an inexplicable "rebirth" of something that existed in antiquity, died in the Middle Ages, and for unknown reasons, was reborn in modern times. He asks whether the representation of modern sports as restoring ancient festivals is not merely an ideological legend intentionally activated in order to strengthen the unity of a movement full of tensions and to enhance its enchantment and prestige.

In point of fact, Baron de Coubtertin's discourse – as well as that of his comrades[6] – in relation to the re(?)birth of the ancient Olympic Games invokes only those aspects considered to be glorious within a contemporary, bourgeois, capitalistic ethos. Lofty values associated with the Olympics in the areas of art, philosophy, and science become adapted perfectly. Meanwhile, the Olympic Truce, intended to have the power to interrupt armed conflict so as to guarantee the safe passage of spectators on their way to the host city, completes the paradigm of the Olympic Games as a symbol of unity among different peoples.[7]

This text will not attempt to judge these values in relation to what might be considered "civilized" or "ethical" conduct in distinct historical moments. However, it is worth emphasizing that certain aspects of the ancient Olympic Games that might be considered "barely ethical" or "uncivilized" according to the moral standards of modern society are completely omitted from references to Olympic antecedents of "honor" and "glory" in the modern practice of sports. For example, ancient Greek society's tolerance for violence was reflected in its sporting practices (Elias 1986a, 1986b) which normally led to the serious injury or death of competitors in the name of delighting spectators and bringing honor and glory to the family and clan to which competitors belonged.

Tournaments and games practiced in the Middle Ages – such as ancestral or folk football – also go unmentioned in the discourse of the honorable origins of modern sport. Due to the tendency of these games to provoke disorder and tumult and to damage private property on narrow medieval streets, authorities tended to prohibit, persecute, and devalue them (Elias & Dunning 1986b).

Moreover, the ethos of "justice" cannot be attributed to an inheritance of the ancient Olympic Games, as is often alleged. As Elias (1986a) mentions, justice was not a primary concern in ancient Greek combat. In these fights, there was no classification system – such as those based on weight or age – capable of producing some sort of equilibrium. From the point of view of the warrior ethos of antiquity, there was also no place to punish a player who assassinated his adversary in competition. Concerns regarding equal opportunities, or "fair play," only came into being with the rise of sports-based gambling. "Fair play" is a paradigm that assures equal conditions to bettors. Equal opportunity is also associated with prolonging and intensifying the pleasure brought about by the tension of challenges in and of themselves. This, in turn, dislocates the previous idea of concentrating all pleasure and excitement in the brief moment of victory.

Although we could present many differences between ancient competitive practices and modern sports, they do possess something in common: their elitist and aristocratic character. As Elias (1986a) demonstrates, participating in this type of ancient championship demanded arduous preparation. A young man with no possessions would never be able to compete unless a wealthy patron or a coach believed in his potential. Similarly, the constitution of modern sports based on amateurism presupposed that athletes would be sufficiently wealthy to be able to set aside the time necessary for training without depending on gains derived from their activities. The laborers, who used to work 12 or 16 hours a day, had no possibility of participating in these competitions.

In fact, amateurism was the principle adopted in the systematic insertion of sporting practices in English "public" schools during the nineteenth century and in the later organization of these practices into championships. As Bourdieu (1993) attests, this contributed to the construction of a moral code based on ideas of virility, courage, character formation, and hierarchy, as well as the will to win based on the chivalrous principles of fair play, voluntary adherence to rules, and the valorization of strictly defined game time. This moral sense – organized and guaranteed by aristocrats[8] – also suited the education of future private businesses leaders (Bourdieu 1993; Rigauer 1981); it thereby integrated the essential foundations of bourgeois ethos (Weber 2013).

In accordance with the principles of fair play, a sought-after victory cannot ever be acquired through vulgar means; instead, it must be based on principles and rules that have been previously determined, recognized, and honored by all participants. Thus, carrying out sporting practices in the context of amateurism made necessary rules and principles that assume socio-cultural equity among participants. Based on these values, the origin of modern sports was founded on the distinction of a determined social class. This distinction was maintained until these sports' professionalization, at which point they became accessible to other classes as well.

Bourdieu frequently utilizes the analogy of a card game to explain his concept of a field. In this research specifically, I will explore the field of production of sporting spectacle as an object of study, meaning that I will adopt the game not only as an analogy, but also as an articulating element of the field. Utilizing Bourdieu's (1991, 1998) concept of the field as a field of disruptive forces implies considering that the dispute that stands out among all those developed within this field is that of the legitimate imposition of the concepts of game and sports. Are sports ludic or functional activities? Are they amateur or professional? Do games belong to the elite or to the masses? Fair play or business? Fun or spectacle?

The outcomes of these disputes are neither static nor definitive, inasmuch as the state of relations of strength among those players who define the structure of the field is in constant flux. Within this perspective, the evolution of the Olympic Movement can be seen from the founding of the IOC – which oversees it – to the constitution of a completely autonomous field that produces sporting spectacle. What we are denominating as a field of production of sporting spectacle can be seen as a social space constituted by a number of other autonomous micro-spaces, i.e., "spaces of objective relations that are the site of a logic and a necessity that are specific and irreducible to those that regulate other fields" (Bourdieu & Wacquant 1992, p. 97).

If determined historical conditions made possible the formation of this specific, autonomous field endowed with its own logic and with a capacity for self-administration and self-regulation, its autonomy is relative. Whether based on historical tradition or on state-sanctioned guarantees (Bourdieu 1993), this autonomy does not separate the field from economic and political events even as it confers upon the field the specificity of possessing its own chronology as well as the capacity to intervene definitively in the autonomy of other fields.

First period (1894–1970): strengthening the Olympic brand and the autonomy consolidated by the discourse of amateurism

The International Olympic Committee (IOC) was founded in Paris in 1894 through the initiative of Baron Pierre de Coubertin, with the goal of organizing the modern era's first Olympic Games. In 1896, in Athens, Greece, the institution brought its goal to fruition. Still without significant potential to mobilize resources, the organization of the Olympic Games at the beginning of the twentieth century was anchored to World's Fairs in Paris (1900) and St. Louis (1904).

For the fourth edition of the modern Olympic Games, in 1908, the IOC published official rules for the event (CIO 1908). The first Olympic Charter had a simple format dealing only with the Games' objectives, the recruitment of members, and administration functions, all of which were exercised by the president of the IOC. This structure continued in the second edition of the document (CIO 1911), which only took the form of a statute in 1920 (CIO 1920).

Over the first half of the twentieth century, the IOC's published rules concentrated primarily on the institution's political and administrative structures, the functioning of the Olympics, and most emphatically, the creation and strengthening of symbolic elements of Olympism.[9] Destined to consolidate the universalist ideals and moral values mentioned earlier, these symbols created the bases that reinforced the Olympics' hoped-for political and legal autonomy and, later, became the most significant exponent of the Olympic brand's value.

Football (known in the US as soccer), which had already attained a mass following far greater than other forms of sports, was first included in the 1900 Olympics but only as a demonstration; medals were not awarded until 1908. *Fédération Internationale de Football Association* (FIFA) was founded in 1904 and, in 1920, football became part of the official program of Olympic sports (IOC 2015; FIFA n.d.a, n.d.b, n.d.c).

In 1924, disputes regarding the legitimate definition of the concept of sports became evident. While the aristocratic majority of the IOC insisted on the idea of amateur sports[10] of a closed and elitist nature, football had already, by the final decades of the nineteenth century, spread throughout the world and mobilized tens of thousands of spectators in stadiums. The spillover of industrial capitalism has been the most cited argument for football's rapid popularization. Companies not only encouraged their employees to participate in competitions but also constructed practice spaces and financed official teams and leagues. Rigauer (1981) and Dunning (1986) highlight the existing interplay between the practice of this model of sporting and the formation of docile, servile workers as the principal motive behind companies' interest. Certain other characteristics of this sporting model also contributed to its adoption, such as discipline, teamwork, the precise measurement of time, the valorization of individual effort, and the possibility of offering mass diversion to an intensely exploited working class.

Thus, the organization of football championships took on commercial features and led to substantial revenues from ticket sales and financers. In addition, it involved specific forms of competence from coaches, administrative bureaucrats, and from the athletes themselves. Facing disagreement with the IOC regarding the size and character of sporting events, FIFA decided to promote its own world championship beginning in 1930. After FIFA's polemic disagreement with the IOC regarding the concept of amateurism and the realization of its own event, football was removed from the 1932 Olympic Games (IOC 2015; FIFA n.d.b, n.d.c).

Football returned to the 1936 Games as an amateur sport. However, from that point forward, FIFA began to construct its own autonomous system of ever-more professional rules for the championships that it organized. Nevertheless, the two entities' paths have overlapped throughout the history of modern sports.

Emphasis on symbolic values and the first steps toward political and legal autonomy

The IOC's first Olympic Charter (CIO 1908) sketched out its desire for political autonomy. The section on member recruitment gave members the primordial function of representing the IOC's interests in their own countries. However, this rule also impeded members from receiving any mandate related to the IOC from their own countries.

In 1920, after World War I forced the cancellation of the 1916 Olympic Games, the IOC was preoccupied with establishing its own chronology. The Olympics were thenceforth scheduled for every four years (CIO 1920). Thus, even if the celebration of the Olympic Games did not occur, the counting of the Olympic calendar would continue normally and neither its order nor the time between Games could be altered due to cancellation.

In the 1924 Olympic Charter (CIO 1924), the fundamental and constitutive principals of the Executive Board appear for the first time. The IOC's first attempts at establishing legal autonomy are clear in the Committee's authorization to take on the role of Jury of Honor to intervene in conflicts of a non-technical order during the realization of events.

Meanwhile, symbolic elements of the Olympic Movement became ever more elaborate and regulated. During the IOC's 1912 Congress, the Olympic symbol, flag, motto, and emblem were all created. During the 1920 Games, the Olympic flag was raised for the first time, and athletes pledged allegiance to it. These symbols appeared in the 1921 Olympic Charter (CIO 1921) alongside a detailed description. This same document also laid out protocols for the Olympic

Ceremony, with carefully prepared and directed rituals for the symbolic valorization of the event. In 1928, the first Olympic Torch was lit. In the Olympic Charters of 1933 and 1946 (IOC 1933, 1946), the organization's focus returned to moral values and the principles of amateurism with emphasis given to eligibility criteria defining the condition of amateur athletes.

The Olympic motto, expressed through three spirited, superlative adjectives – *Citius, Altius, Fortius* (Faster, Higher, Stronger) – indicates a model of behavior that is socially oriented for success, i.e., toward the principles of industrial society. The rings and the flag, meanwhile, allude to the idea of unity among peoples, thereby evoking the ancient Olympics. The Olympic rings were created in 1914, in accordance with Baron de Coubertin's proposals, and appeared for the first time in 1920 on a flag with a white background. Their colors symbolize five continents: Europe (blue); Asia (yellow); Africa (black); Oceania (green); and the Americas (red). In addition, there is no nation in the world that does not feature at least one of these colors in its own flag (IOC 1950, p. 18).

The first Winter Olympic Games were held in Chamonix, France, in 1924. However, the event was only mentioned in the Olympic Charter eight years later (IOC 1932). It is worth highlighting that, at that time, the Winter Games were held in the same year and the same country as the Summer Games.

1932 marked the first time that a city used the Olympics as a development strategy. Devastated by the 1929 economic crisis, Los Angeles harnessed the Olympic project to its plans for recuperating the local economy. In 1936, the Olympic Games in Berlin were used to mark Germany's return to the world stage after the country's isolation following its defeat in World War I. The effort of producing the largest Olympic Games in history – as well as the inauguration of televised broadcasts (IOC 2019b) – translated into what the Nazi dictatorship perceived as an opportunity to showcase Germany's power and to prove the so-called "superiority of the Aryan race." Even as the regime disguised its political violence – temporarily removing anti-Semitic posters or softening its rhetoric against Jews and Roma people in the press – the Nazi government used the image of German athletes to prove the myth of "Aryan racial and aesthetic superiority." Although athletes from various parts of the world urged a boycott of the Berlin Games, the discourse of political neutrality and fair play led most countries to participate; only the Soviet Union and Spain did not.

The political use of the Berlin Olympics, together with Los Angeles' development project, made apparent three important new aspects of the relationship between the production of sporting spectacle and the production of the city. The first was the discovery of the event's potential to mobilize political and economic capital. The second was the IOC's discovery of the possibility of utilizing this potential to seduce local and national leaders to compete to host the events and to use this competition among leaders to the IOC's own benefit. The third and final aspect was the step toward spectacularization. Large-scale installations, significant public reach, and televised transmission all produced a complete reconfiguration of the sporting field and its relation to other fields.

First relations with the economic field: discrete and increasingly regulated commercialization

The discourse of amateurism and fair play as principal objectives for modern sports guaranteed athletes' pleasure, making spectators' pleasure secondary. The emphasis on the discourse of autonomy in relation to any economic or political interests served as an axiom in this thinking. Therefore, neither those responsible for organizing competitions and teams, nor those responsible for training athletes, could be remunerated.

In spite of this discourse of economic disinterest, the first edition of the Olympic Games in 1896 already featured commercial advertising (IOC 2019b). Souvenirs and photographs were sold at the 1912 Olympics; advertisements were introduced in the Games' official printed material in 1920, and advertising billboards at venues were first featured in 1924 (ibid.). The first published rules referred to amateurism as a demand made of competitors, but made no such restrictions on the commercialization of the events themselves. Only after the 1924 Paris Games did the IOC – in direct opposition to FIFA and having identified advertisements within the competitions as a threat to the original discourse of economic disinterest – prohibit advertisements in competition venues and in the official press (CIO 1924). This prohibition served as a fundamental step in the later valorization of the Olympic brand.

Television transmission and a new dynamic in relations between mega-event production and the economic field

The first televised transmission of the 1936 Berlin Games (IOC 2019b) did not go unnoticed. After an interval of two Olympic periods (1940 and 1944) with no Olympic Games owing to World War II, the rules of the 1946 Olympic Charter (IOC 1946) recognized the existence of television. However, it referred only to the restrictive character of televised recordings and broadcasts – in other words, as it had treated the press in general since 1930 (CIO 1930). Registering events was permitted and even desirable, but no interference in their functioning would be tolerated.

The first post-war Olympic Games took place in London in 1948, and showed a greater capacity to attract the interest of political leaders, corporations, and athletes. Television broadcasts allowed a glimpse of new chances for political and economic power. The Cold War further highlighted this potential, as the superpowers of the East and West transferred the rivalry of their geopolitical disputes to competition for medals. The 1948 Games also marked the Olympics' first attempt at selling broadcasting rights. The BBC agreed to pay approximately US$3000, but the Organizing Committee for the Olympic Games (OCOG) ultimately did not accept the payment out of concern for the economic toll that this might take on the company (IOC 2019b).

The first successful contract for Olympic broadcasting rights was for the 1952 Helsinki Games. These Games also marked the first program for the international commercialization of the Olympic brand under the control of the OCOG. In 1956, failed negotiations for the television rights to the Melbourne Games impeded the broadcast of that event in important markets (IOC 2019b).

The decisive moment for television in the Olympic Games came in 1960 when the Rome Games were transmitted live to 18 Europeans countries and to the United States, Canada, and Japan with a delay of only a few hours (ibid.). Shortly before the event, the first Olympic guidelines for television broadcasts were published (IOC 1958). The OCOG still controlled contracts, but these were ultimately subject to the IOC's approval. IOC guidelines also established rules that defined the Olympic brand as property and prohibited its use for commercial ends as already proposed in 1949 (IOC 1949). In 1954, these rules were extended to the property of words (IOC 1954).

At the same time, the 1950 Football World Cup, which took place in Brazil, brought 200,000 spectators to Maracanã, a stadium built in Rio de Janeiro specifically for that event (FIFA 2007). In 1954, the World Cup took place in Switzerland and was televised for the first time. In 1958, the broadcasting rights for the World Cup, which took place in Sweden, were sold to Sveriges, a Swedish state-owned radio and television consortium. Games were broadcast in 11 European countries.

In addition to affecting the visibility and economic power of mega-events, the phenomenon of television elevated the complexity of their political and legal power to another level. Consequently, it also led to redesigned relations between the production of mega-events and the production of cities.

The consolidation of political and legal autonomy in relations with the city

Since the end of the 1940s, with the incremental growth of the complexity and cost of the Olympic Games, Olympic rules have changed, progressively transferring an ever-greater burden of organizational responsibilities to host cities. The IOC's demands have modified with the evolution of contracts for broadcasting rights. In turn, the use of mega-events as a strategy for urban development has created favorable conditions for such demands.

In 1949, the IOC proclaimed supreme authority over the entire Olympic Movement (IOC 1949), thereby centralizing the institution's conquest of autonomy. The same document (ibid.) established that the responsibility of presenting a candidate for host city – previously held by a given country's National Olympic Committee (NOC) – would be transferred to the candidate city itself. In 1950, the guarantee of financial support for constructions (IOC 1950) was added to the demands made of these authorities.

In 1955, the first exclusive document containing information for cities that aimed to host the Olympic Games was published (IOC 1955). The demands it contained soon grew exponentially, especially in relation to installations and infrastructure offered to the print media and to television broadcasters. The publication of this first document made the justification for these pledges explicit: namely, the "incalculable intangible benefits" that the event offered.

> There has in fact been little or no direct profit in most cities where the Games have been held. The intangible benefits, however, are incalculable. First, the pleasure enjoyed by the citizens of the community in acting as host for the greatest of all sport events. Second, the facilities provided for the Games become civic assets, which benefit succeeding generations. Third, during the Games the fortunate city becomes the capital of the world of sports and the centre of attention of all sportsmen of every country.
>
> (IOC 1955, p. 9)

Thus, the attempt to group athletes in shared housing during the 1924 Paris Olympics – consolidated with the construction of an Olympic Village in Los Angeles in 1932 – became one of the demands made of the OCOG responsible for the Games (IOC 1949). Soon after, each OCOG also had to prove its city's capacity to house visitors (IOC 1955) and support the presence of the media (IOC 1957). After the construction of Media Village for the 1968 Mexico City Games, the IOC's demand for media support was transformed into demand for media accommodations (IOC 1974) and, later, into the suggestion of constructing a Media Village (IOC 1978) just like it was made in Mexico.

Similarly, the demand that a city's local leadership present its candidacy (IOC 1949) was followed by the demand that the city pledge to accept the IOC's rules for its candidature (IOC 1950) as well as having its candidature approved by a responsible national authority (IOC 1955). In 1955, prohibitions of political propaganda and of the realization of any other official events in the host city during the Olympic Games (ibid.) gave the IOC the capacity to intervene directly in a host city's political sovereignty. The demand of guaranteed entrance into the host country for all members of Olympic delegations (IOC 1957) extended this capacity for intervention in political sovereignty to a national scale.

If the 1936 Olympic Games in Berlin inaugurated the practices of utilizing mega-events to legitimize hegemonic power, other editions of this type of event also functioned as arenas of resistance. Some of these movements were subject to strong repression and did affect the number of participating delegations. This was the case, for example, of the 1968 protests by thousands of Mexican students against the massive political resources invested in the Games. The government's violent repression of this student movement – leading to the Tlatelolco massacre in which hundreds of protestors were killed – did not provoke a response from the Olympic Movement or from the international community in relation to participation in the event.

It was also at the 1968 Mexico City Games that two African American athletes used the medal podium to protest racial segregation in the United States through the Black Power salute. The Olympic Movement reacted swiftly, stripping the athletes of their medals in the name of political "independence." Yet in other cases, such as Berlin in 1936, the IOC consented to and even stimulated the use of Olympic Movement symbolism with the objective of reaffirming power relations.

Professional or amateur games (?): an issue under debate

Between the end of the 1950s and the end of the 1960s, the idea of professionalization gained traction in the Olympic Movement. Official documents published during this period emphasize the discourse of amateurism and political autonomy suggesting a level of intensification in these debates. A great deal of evidence suggests the necessity of positions affirming the support of amateurism, still dominant at this time.

The 1956 Olympic Charter (IOC 1956) contained a section entitled "General Information," the content of which was dedicated to the historic symbolism of the Olympic Movement, reaffirming its political autonomy and the moral assertion of fair play and amateurism. At the end of this section – which repeats in subsequent Olympic Charters (IOC 1958, 1966, 1967) – six IOC decisions clarify polemical issues regarding the definition of amateurism. Symbolically, the document opens and closes with quotes from Baron de Coubertin.

> First of all, it is necessary to maintain in sport the noble and chivalrous character which distinguished it in the past, so that it shall continue to be part of the education of present day peoples, in the same way that sport served so wonderfully in the times of ancient Greece. The public has a tendency to transform the Olympic athlete into a paid gladiator. These two attitudes are not compatible.
>
> (Coubertin, cited in IOC 1956, p. 99)

Presenting still further evidence of the centrality of this debate, a 1962 document established rules regarding conditions of admission to the Olympic Games (CIO 1962). The text, which was quite restrictive, instituted clear distinctions regarding the social class of participants. Article 26 of the document prohibited the admission of any athletes without the material wealth to guarantee their present and future well-being (ibid.), as well as those who might receive or who have already received payment for their participation in sports. However, a paragraph added at the end of the document only two years later gave the IOC the right to make exceptions to these restrictions (IOC 1964), reiterating the content of the previous text and making the intensity of the dispute even clearer.

The debate regarding concepts of amateur and professional games gained further importance after João Havelango[11] and Juan Samaranch[12] joined the IOC's membership in 1963 and 1966, respectively. Ardent defenders of professionalization, the two new members confronted Avery Brundage, the IOC president who was radically opposed to their position. In any event, while the results of these disputes were still fairly balanced, some of the content of the Olympic Charter's "General Information" remained in documents released at the start of the following decade (IOC 1971a, 1971b, 1973, 1974, 1975).

Second period (1971–1984): professionalization

Like the capitalist system of the time but still under the shield of the welfare state, the Olympic Movement denied emphatically the defining role of the market in its proceedings despite the fact that the market was ever-present in its events. Until 1973, the rules of the Olympic Movement appeared to ignore the existence of proceeds from the sale of publicity rights, although by this time, they already addressed the subject tangentially through restrictions on commercial uses of the Olympic Games.

In the beginning of the 1970s, when the first manifestations of the capitalist crisis that has remained and deepened to the present day began to be felt, the dominant concept of games began to be inverted, and a gradual process of the professionalization of sports began to make itself clear in the institution's rules.

In 1971, certain exceptions were introduced to the code of amateur eligibility in relation to the prohibition on competitors' material gains or compensation (IOC 1971b). However, commercial issues were only dealt with openly in the Olympic Charter of 1973which established the conditions for commodifying the Olympic emblem, the rights to which were conceded to OCOGs[13] (IOC 1973).

The 1974 Olympic Charter referred to a reformulation in the text regarding eligibility to be voted on in the following year (IOC 1974). In 1975, the text enunciating the IOC's objectives was subject to subtle new wording: "encouraging the organization and development of amateur sport and competitions" (IOC 1974, p. 5) was altered to "encouraging the organization and development of amateur sport and sport competition" (IOC 1975, p. 8). Competitions incentivized by the IOC were no longer restricted by amateurism. Still, the criteria for eligibility remained.

In this way, alterations were introduced progressively until, in 1978, the term "amateur," along with any restrictions linked to amateurism, disappeared entirely from the content of the Olympic Charter (IOC 1978). It is worth noting that changes were made to each edition in a gradual and subtle way, so as to be almost imperceptible to less attentive readers. The caution with which this issue was treated reveals the conflicts and disputes that probably occurred around it within the field.

New means of regulating professionalism, protecting the Olympic brand, and reinforcing political and legal autonomy

From their beginnings, modern sporting practices – even if they were sustained by principals of amateurism – configured a specific field that, like all fields, is the object of disputes (Bourdieu 1991). The passage from amateur to professional sports – which cannot be separated from class differences among participants – increased the complexity of these disputes. Since then, they have developed on multiple different scales: between class fissures within dominant classes; between different classes within the field; as well as between the field of sporting and other fields.

With professionalization, regulations for new services linked to sporting practices were born, demanding a specific kind of competence (sports teachers, coaches, doctors, and journalists) and treating athletes as service providers. The 1967 Olympic Charter (IOC 1967) articulated the specific grouping of professionals needed to accompany every team. These regulations, with their new demands, were perfected over time. In 1974 (IOC 1974), a questionnaire dedicated to conditions for logistical support of sponsors and broadcasters was created for cities aiming to host the Olympic Games.

Beginning in 1978, athletes intending to participate in the Olympic Games were required to sign a declaration ceding all rights to their images to the IOC, which could use them for whatever ends it found fit.

> I, the undersigned, declare that I have read the eligibility conditions for the Olympic Games and that I comply with them. I agree to be filmed and photographed during the Games under the conditions and for the purposes authorized by the International Olympic Committee, and to observe the provisions of article 49 of the IOC Rules concerning the press, television and the Olympic film.
>
> (IOC 1978, p. 21)

1978 also marked the consolidation of mechanisms protecting the Olympic brand and controlling broadcast rights. In 1971, the use of brand-names on equipment and clothing began to be restricted (IOC 1971a); in 1978, the control of advertising – previously restricted to the interior of stadiums and other sporting installations – was extended to airspace (IOC 1978). In 1971, the IOC emphasized the advantages of exclusive, rather than free, broadcasting (IOC 1971a).

The 1974 Olympic Charter (IOC 1974) established the IOC's definitive interference in the legal autonomy of host city candidates. Under this Charter, countries were required to obey the rules of the IOC and of International Federations (IFs), conceding legal status to the OCOG and adopting legal measures to guarantee that IOC demands not covered by current legislation would be met. This same Charter also demanded that funding sources for the realization of the Olympic Games be identified during the candidature process.

Since 1976, the candidature process has been tied to written agreement with the "Conditions Laid Down for Candidate Cities" (IOC 1976). The 1978 Olympic Charter went further, demanding that people and institutions involved with the Olympic Movement submit to the ultimate jurisdiction and authority of the IOC (IOC 1978). This Charter also established that the NOC and the chosen host city should be entirely responsible for every aspect of the event's realization, including financially (IOC 1978). During this period, the legal autonomy of the IOC in relation to host cities was consolidated further, and the demand for new legislative changes increased progressively.

Threats to the survival of the Olympic Movement

Despite the discourse of "neutrality" in modern sports, the production of sporting mega-events has always been closely linked to the field of politics. Throughout history, symbolism related to these events has been used to set the scenes for power disputes, whether reaffirming a dominant power[14] or as a staging ground for the contestation of that power (Benedicto 2008). During the 1970s, certain events with an explicitly political character had a definitive influence on the unfolding of subsequent phases.

During the 1972 Munich Games, terrorist attacks culminated in the murder of 11 Israeli athletes (Pound 2006; Payne 2012), revealing the event's vulnerability and establishing the centrality of security issues that still reverberate today. During the organization of the 1976 Games, the choice of spectacular architecture together with the global recession of the 1970s, transformed Montreal's dream of an "Olympic paradigm" into a US$1.5 billion debt (COJO 76 1978) which, combined with other financial obligations, reached almost US$3 billion and took almost 30 years to resolve. In 1972, Denver pulled out of its chosen role as host city for the 1976 Winter Games (LAOOC 1985; Burbank, Andranovich & Heying 2001), when, in a plebiscite, residents voted against the use of public resources for the event. Finally, the 1980 Moscow Games, which 66 countries boycotted in protest of the Soviet invasion of Afghanistan, challenged the supposed political neutrality of the Olympic Movement (Pound 2006; Payne 2012).

The toll that these events took on the IOC's carefully cultivated symbolic values placed the Committee's quest for legal and political autonomy at risk. At the same time, the Committee confronted problems in relation to the economic field. By then, the Olympic Games had reached a level of complexity for which neither the Olympic Movement nor potential host cities were prepared. The IOC's financial reserves faced serious difficulties, with less than US$200,000 available in liquid funds and only US$2 million in reserves (Payne 2012). Low profits from the 1980 Moscow Games were spent almost entirely in paying for the event's organization.

Thus, the Olympic Movement reached the end of the 1970s with its institutional autonomy consolidated while facing a profound political and economic crisis. The task of finding cities willing to host the Games became increasingly difficult, a situation that culminated with only a single candidature to host the 1984 Games.[15] These conditions made it almost impossible to justify the established institutional apparatus.

In fact, the lone candidature of Los Angeles to host the 1984 Olympic Games challenged the strength of the Olympic Movement. With no bargaining power, the IOC was forced to accede to unprecedented conditions. After the city's population voted, by plebiscite, against financing the event with public tax dollars, local authorities refused to take responsibility for the games. Facing the threat of Los Angeles withdrawing its candidature – and a potential cancellation of the Games for lack of a host city – the IOC violated its own Olympic Charter (IOC 1978), absolving local political leaders of any responsibility. The Los Angeles Olympic Organizing Committee (LAOOC), and United States Olympic Committee

(USOC) assumed full responsibility for the organization and costs of the event, which was financed completely through private initiatives (LAOOC 1985; Burbank, Andranovich & Heying 2001). At this moment, it became clear that the Olympic Games would either need to be reinvented or face extinction.

Third period: spectacularization (after 1984)

During the two final decades of the twentieth century, the IOC found a way to reconcile the two apparently antagonistic forms of logic that steer modern Olympic philosophy: namely, non-commercial values and the market. After all, it is the discourse of non-commercial values that has proved most commercially valuable to its "partners." Michael Payne,[16] creator of the IOC's current marketing program, wrote *Olympic Turnaround*, a book in which he presents both the challenges he faced and the strategies he adopted in order to pull the Olympic Movement back from the brink of extinction in the early 1980s and to transform it into the owner of the most valuable brand in the world. Payne writes:

> There is an obvious tension between the idealistic and commercial principles that resonate with modern Olympic philosophy and the need to finance the world's largest athletic and media event. More and more Olympic observers admit that this tension is no longer a conflictual one, but rather a dynamic balance where the identity of the Olympics as embodying a special set of values engages a delicate dance with commercial entities eager to use that identity to sell product.
>
> (Payne 2012, p. 17)

The solution Payne found to this paradox was to promote the idea of possible reconciliation between the market and the moral values of Olympism. He elaborated a revolutionary marketing program based on two strategies: first, the centralized control of exclusive broadcasting rights in every part of the world; and second, the sale of exclusive rights within every product category, so as to associate a given brand with the Olympic brand. Through this program, which marked one of the greatest turnarounds in business history, the most valuable items became precisely those that represent the non-commercial values associated with the Olympics.

Payne knew that the symbolic capital accumulated by the Olympic brand could be highly valuable in marketing products. Honor, integrity, determination, and striving for excellence are all attributes symbolically associated with the Olympic Games and with which companies want to be associated. He emphasized that sponsors would be willing to pay dearly to link their products to the valuable adjectives used to describe these events, such as "dignified," "cosmopolitan," "global," "modern," and "multicultural" (Payne 2012).

Through an equally innovative marketing program, FIFA arrived at a similar position to that of the IOC – albeit in a less institutionalized way – with rules that were less clear, and with less concern for maintaining the values of the brand associated with its property.

It is not merely the Olympic Movement's discourse of a love for sports with no ulterior motives that united FIFA and the IOC. During their commercial turnabout, both institutions were led by authoritarian strongmen. João Havelange, a close friend of the generals who commanded Brazil's military dictatorship,[17] was elected president of FIFA in 1975 and held his post for 23 years. Juan Antonio Samaranch, president of the IOC from 1980 to 2001, was a longtime collaborator of Franco's fascist government in Spain.

We can identify a point of convergence in these two men's lives: namely, the significant presence of Horst Dassler.[18] Dassler, heir to the Adidas company, donated or subsidized sporting materials for each of these federations with the aim of promoting his brand. In this way, he established close ties to directors of the planet's leading sporting events, becoming the most powerful man in the universe of sports from the beginning of the 1970s until his death in 1987. During this period, Dassler influenced the world's most important elections for sports-related positions, including the elections of Havelange and Samaranch to the presidencies of FIFA and the IOC, respectively (Pound 2006; Jennings 2007; Payne 2012). This was part of Dassler's strategy of maintaining executives he confided in within important roles in athletic federations and agencies throughout the world. Thus, Dassler brought Payne to the IOC and Josef Blatter[19] to FIFA. Before Blatter was invited to create a global marketing program for the IOC, he already owned marketing rights to FIFA and to the Davis Cup.

The TOP Program and new strategies for broadcasting contracts

When Samaranch became IOC president in 1980, the Olympic Movement was at the edge of collapse. The aforementioned political and economic crises as well as difficulty in finding cities willing to meet the IOC's demands for hosting the Games placed the continuity of the Olympic Games at risk. According to Payne (2012), when faced with this scenario, Saramanch adopted three main, interdependent strategies: first, recuperating the unity of the Olympic movement, which was then in a state of crisis; second, taking control of the Olympic agenda through diplomatic work with political leaders; and third, establishing the IOC's financial independence through global marketing.

Saramanch, who considered this final task necessary in order to accomplish the first two, was an eloquent defender of the end of amateurism and of the diversification of income sources for the IOC. He enlisted the aid of his friend Horst Dassler, under whose orientation he confronted the challenges of increasing revenues from broadcasting and sponsorship programs. The IOC soon took direct control of contracts for broadcasting rights, for which Dick Pound,[20] one of its vice presidents, became responsible. At first, negotiations took place together with the OCOG[21] responsible for the organization of a given Olympic Games. Beginning in the mid-1990s, however, the IOC adopted a new strategy in which it signed long-term contracts involving more than one event. Whenever possible, these contracts were created before choosing host cities. This strategy completely eliminated any OCOG's role in the negotiation process.

Not only did the IOC bet on the income broadcasting rights to create the solid financial base it desired; it also aimed at creating a consistent strategy for sponsorship on a global scale. In 1982, International Sport and Leisure (ISL) – Dassler's business – presented The Olympic Partners (TOP)[22] with an idea for a single global sponsorship program. The program established exclusive sponsorship categories for goods and services, involving the entire Olympic Movement without restricting itself exclusively to the event.[23] Through ISL, negotiation and distribution of profits were centralized in the IOC, in a departure from the earlier practice of direct negotiations with OCOGs and NOCs. The financial success of the marketing strategy utilized by the Los Angeles OCOG[24] for the 1984 Olympics served as inspiration.

Financial challenges also played a central role in the strategies adopted by FIFA. The promise of increasing the number of countries participating in world championships had been fundamental for Havelange to secure the support of National Federation directors for his 1974 election to the FIFA presidency. This argument allowed Havelange to unseat Stanley Ross (Jenning 2007), FIFA's president from 1961 to 1974, whose policies focused on Europe and ignored pressure from African football organizations for a place in these championships. Havelange kept his promises, doubling the number of participating countries during his time as FIFA president: in 1974, 16 countries competed, a number that expanded to 32 in 1998. Havelange needed money to accomplish this expansion; he adopted the strategy of transforming football into one of the most world's most magnificent commodities, in direct confrontation with Ross's earlier posture. To this end, Havelange also depended on Horst Dassler's help. Dassler became responsible for negotiating with broadcasters and sponsors – now known as "partners" – to commercialize FIFA, even before TOP was adopted to valorize the Olympic brand. Meanwhile, an increased number of teams expanded the World Cup's audience to new countries, thereby resulting in a greater reach for sponsors, greater dispute among broadcasters for the spectacle, and as a result, more money.

Instruments of political control as forms of consolidating economic pacts

With the implementation of its new marketing program and new demands for candidate cities, the IOC began to ask for a series of new guarantees, especially in relation to protection of the Olympic brand. The 1982 Olympic Charter (IOC 1982) demanded that a Host City Contract be signed by every host city's mayor, and that entrance visas to host countries be made available to everyone holding an Olympic identity card. In 1984, the creation of the Liaison Commission (IOC 1984) served as a blueprint for the future IOC Evaluation Commission (IOC 1993), which retained the power to authorize or veto alterations to the Olympic project. In other words, the Commission held decisive power over any interventions in the urban space linked to the Olympics.

In 1985 (IOC 1985), the selection of host cities was divided into two separate phases: first, each interested NOC selected a single candidate city for its country

(IOC 1985), after which the IOC would choose the winning bid. In 1991, as a result of the discourse of sustainability, the Olympic Charter made its first mention of environmental responsibility (IOC 1991), further raising the costs to host cities.[25] In 1992, the urban restructuring of Barcelona created a new development paradigm, thereby increasing disputes for the Games and elevating the mobilization of economic capital related to the Olympic project.

Two political events in the 1990s had profound effects on the production of sporting spectacle. In 1996, the IOC's partners in TOP, as well as the press, accused Atlanta of promoting an "excessively commercial" event owing to sales of advertising space on public streets to raise funds for the city's Olympic Games. Negative reports in the international media of chaos in the city's transportation system during the event exacerbated the situation. In 1998, denunciations of corruption in Salt Lake City's selection to host the 2002 Winter Olympics led to an internal IOC investigation, culminating in the expulsion of ten of the committee's members (Burbank, Andranovich & Heying 2001; Pound 2006; Payne 2012). These episodes caused significant damage to the Olympic brand, which became evident through both political and economic losses.

To recuperate its lost symbolic capital, the IOC published two Olympic Charters in 1999 (IOC 1999a, 1999b) and another in 2000 (IOC 2000), introducing significant changes within the Olympic Movement and in relation to host cities. The selection process was modified to three different stages. The first consisted of selection on a national scale, as established in 1985. However, the IOC introduced a new phase in the process: the Executive Board would now select cities that it deemed able to compete for hosting duties before the final selection during the IOC's conference.

In addition, the IOC began to demand further pledges from host city candidates during the selection process itself. The Anti-Doping Code was created as well as a commission to establish related measures and sanctions and to propose a Code of Ethics. Rules governing broadcasting rights and the exclusivity of the Olympic brand became even more strict.

The events of Atlanta also added to preoccupations concerning the IOC's agenda and priorities, such as the coordination of tasks taken on by different levels of government, the threats of increasingly banal attitudes to the use of Olympic property, and so-called "ambush marketing," defined as any unfitting use of the brand. The potential of "ambush marketing" to worsen relations with "partners" justified the priority given to it in the Technical Manual on Brand Protection.

> Official Olympic marketing partners provide substantial resources to the entire Olympic Family, while at the same time promoting the ideals of Olympism. Consequently, they, and no other commercial entities, should benefit from their Olympic involvement. Ambush marketing occurs when an unauthorized commercial entity implies an association with the Olympic Movement without a marketing agreement with an appropriate Olympic party.
>
> (IOC n.d., p. 13)

Some cities began to implement these changes even before the IOC converted its preoccupations into formal pledges required of candidates.[26] Sydney passed laws protecting the Olympic brand and combating "ambush marketing," and establishing a governance structure created specifically to facilitate communications between different levels of government regarding the Olympics.[27] Meanwhile, Athens established rigorous control of advertising in public spaces during the 2004 Games.

The lack of a governing structure during the organization of the 2008 Beijing Games led to negative comments from the IOC in its final report on the event (IOC 2010). For the 2012 Games, the legal status of such a governing structure became one of the pledges required of candidate cities along with other legislative measures aimed at preventing ambush marketing (IOC 2004). During its candidature, Rio de Janeiro offered – in addition to strict measures to protect the Olympic brand – a governance proposal similar to those of London and Sydney but with greater powers. This proposal was denominated the Olympic Public Authority (*Autoridade Pública Olímpica* – APO). However, these powers were undone during the organization of the 2016 Games as a result of disputes between different levels of government.[28]

Within its relatively well-institutionalized legal framework, the IOC still lacked a tribunal that would establish it as occupying an autonomous political and legal field. To this end, it created the Court of Arbitration for Sport (CAS) at the beginning of the 1980s. This development will be discussed further in Chapter 3.

In 2001, concerned with the increased scale and scope of the Olympic Games, the IOC created a commission to study recommendations for managing their size, complexity, and cost. Among the 117 recommendations published in the resulting report (Pound 2003) is the idea of separating the event's operational costs (taken from the OCOG's budget) from those invested in installations and infrastructure (through a non-OCOG budget) intended to remain as a "legacy" for the host country and city (ibid.). Thus, the 2003 Olympic Charter (IOC 2003) contained a new requirement for candidate cities: a pledge to leave a "legacy," further examined in Chapter 3.

Unlike the IOC, FIFA only published specific regulations concerning the choice of a host country for the Football World Cup in its 2013 Statute which established FIFA's Congress as the institutional space in which this selection would occur (FIFA 2013). Until then, there were no clear rules regarding this selection, which was made by the institution's Executive Board. Although FIFA had long acted as aggressively as possible to achieve financial independence, the organization had always trailed the IOC in institutionalizing its legal and political autonomy. Even without significant regulations, however, FIFA followed the IOC's path in establishing similar demands for countries hosting the World Cup.

Thus, the Olympic movement entered the second decade of the twenty-first century with a perfectly elaborated institutional structure that gave it the capacity to impose constraints on the political and legal order of host countries and cities. As part of this movement, FIFA felt comfortable in taking advantage of its conquests and exercising the same autonomy, although it did not exert itself in creating a structure to guarantee it.

Change or be changed

Everything seemed almost perfect when the specter of crisis returned to threaten sporting spectacle during preparations for the 2016 Rio de Janeiro Olympics. The cooling in the dispute to host the 2022 Winter Games was symptomatic of the problem: of seven potential candidates, only two cities – Almaty and Beijing – made it to the final round. Other cities' arguments for dropping out were inevitably linked to the lack of political support to take on the high economic, political, and social costs related to organizing the Olympics.

Forced evictions have occupied a central position in discussions of the social costs of sporting mega-events, and a significant body of literature has been produced on that theme. Among the most important contributions is the research carried out by the Centre on Housing Rights and Evictions (COHRE) since the 1998 Olympics. The 1.5 million people removed from their homes in Beijing represents the most emblematic case discussed in the Centre's report (COHRE 2007). Denunciations of the persecution of certain ethnic and racial groups as well as the expulsion of homeless populations are also frequent.

The high economic and political costs related to the organization of these events have also been constant targets for criticism. The large volume of public resources dedicated to underutilized and expensive construction projects is undoubtedly the primary object of such condemnation. Other factors, such as limits imposed on the ordering of urban space and the scale of priorities of public investments as well as real estate speculation, provide other motives for questioning. Even cities like Sydney, London, and Barcelona, which have come to set a standard for the Olympic Games, have not managed to escape this criticism.[29] Studies of the 2008 Olympic Games in Beijing add elements of tightened repression, behavioral control, and the use of the event to legitimize power to the discussion (Brady 2009; Broudehoux 2007, 2012).

Certain peculiarities of the Brazilian case, especially in the experience of Rio de Janeiro, confer particular visibility to these criticisms. First, resistance to the impact of mega-events in the country, especially in relation to evictions, stands out. Second, the idea of a "city of exception" produced by neoliberal planning models – as articulated by local academics – reaches a radical peak in sporting mega-events.[30]

In fact, those affected by the 250,000 evictions (ANCOP 2013) and other conflicts produced by sporting mega-events in Brazil were not silenced. The direct targets of these evictions – who organized through the National Popular Committee of the World Cup and Olympics (*Articulação Nacional dos Comitês Populares da Copa* – ANCOP) and who were supported by academics, judges, lawyers, and activists – resisted by documenting these human rights violations in cities throughout Brazil and denouncing them to the world (ANCOP n.d.; Comitê Popular Rio da Copa e das Olimpíadas n.d.). They also made denunciations to the IOC, the Inter-American Commission on Human Rights of the Organization of American States (IAHRS – OAS) and the twenty-second session of the United Nations' Human Rights Council (HRC – UN).

Although Brazil's mainstream media practically ignored them, these denunciations served as objects for academic work both within (Sánchez et al. eds 2014; Jenning et al. 2014; de Oliveira 2016; Vainer et al. eds 2017) and outside of Brazil (Silvestre & Oliveira 2012; Horne & Gruneau eds 2016), in addition to being covered by media organizations from throughout the world.[31] The case of Vila Autódromo – a community founded more than 30 years before on an area of land coveted by real estate developers next to the Olympic Park in Rio's upscale Barra da Tijuca neighborhood – was symbolic. Although Vila Autódromo's residents retained the legal right to use the community's land for housing, they suffered threats of eviction beginning with the 2007 Pan-American Games. While the original projections for the Olympic Park – which won a competition organized by the Brazilian Architect's Institute (IAB) – envisioned the community's permanence, Rio's mayor took advantage of a number of different pretexts to call for Vila Autódromo's removal. Beyond any of his excuses, however, a very solid reason made itself clear: negotiation with a private consortium concerning a territory of 1.18 million square meters (roughly 127 million square feet) inside of the Park for the construction of luxury condominiums after the Games. Future residents of these condos would find Vila Autódromo to be a community of unwelcome neighbors.

As an alternative to eviction, the Vila Autódromo Residents Association created a Peoples' Plan for Vila Autódromo with the assistance of two universities. The proposal guaranteed adequate living conditions and urbanization for a lower cost than would be necessary for removal and resettlement. The plan won the Urban Age Award, conferred by a partnership between Deutsche Bank and the London School of Economics, attracting further visibility to the struggle of Vila Autódromo's residents. Yet, Rio's mayor ignored the work's recognition and continued to build pressure toward the community's eviction. Of the nearly 500 families who lived in Vila Autódromo, only 20 remain today, but they have continued their resistance and still live on their land. Vila Autódromo's insistence on survival became a worldwide symbol of resistance in the face of removal.

Resistance movements opposed to mega-events have also materialized in other countries, including the Bread, Not Circus Coalition in Toronto; the World-Class Cities for All campaign in South Africa; and the No Games movement in Chicago. The exaggeration and lack of social control in Brazil, however, conferred another level of visibility to conflicts in that country.

In their attempts to overcome the contradictions seen in host cities and guarantee the interests they represent as organizations, FIFA and the IOC have aimed to reinvent themselves. In May 2014, the IOC announced the establishment of 14 working groups to set a "strategic plan for the future of the Olympic Movement," which it calls the "Olympic Agenda 2020" (IOC 2014). Organizational costs, sustainability, and the choice of host cities were all central themes in these groups' final reports, which included 40 recommendations and were approved in an Extraordinary Session of the IOC held in Monaco in December 2014.

Based on this document, the IOC adopted new strategies for areas including the candidature process for potential host cities, budget organization, and the role and conduct of consultants (IOC 2018). The candidature process, which currently consists of two eliminatory phases before the final IOC decision, concentrates greater decision-making power in the Executive Board and demands greater control of the host city's political context.[32] The emphasis on discourses of legacy, sustainability, and governance are associated with harnessing the Olympic Project to a given city's necessities and development projects. Budgets undergo a new organizational process, leaving aside infrastructural costs. The IOC also makes new demands of consultants, who must now be credentialed by the committee itself.

Even after these strategies were introduced in Agenda 2020, lack of interest in hosting the Olympics became only more evident when five cities abandoned their bid to host the 2024 Games. The simultaneous announcement of Paris and Los Angeles as host cities for the 2024 and 2028 Olympic Games in September of 2017 was a strategy that allowed the IOC time to construct a more favorable scenario, but its success is not guaranteed.

Less than one month after this simultaneous announcement, a new corruption scandal – this time involving the choice of Rio de Janeiro as the host city for the 2016 Olympics – further tarnished the IOC's image. An investigation by the French justice system and a Brazilian Federal Police operation called *Unfair Play* resulted in the preventative arrest of Carlos Nuzman – then-president of the Brazilian Olympic Committee (BOC) – for 15 days. During his imprisonment, Nuzman resigned from his post. In September 2019, Sérgio Cabral, the former governor of Rio de Janeiro state who was already imprisoned for other crimes, admitted to buying nine IOC votes for US$2 million to guarantee Rio de Janeiro's selection as a host city (Panja 2019). These events made the task of revalorizing the Olympic brand even more arduous.

In 2019, the Olympic Charter underwent further alterations in an attempt to increase interest in hosting the Olympic Games. The most significant of these alterations was the substitution of the concept of "host city" for "host of the Games," opening the possibility of the candidature of "several cities, or other entities, such as regions, states or countries, as host of the Olympic Games" (IOC 2019a, p. 69). In addition, the Charter did away with the demand for a seven-year period between the announcement of a host city and the realization of the Games.

In 2020, an unprecedented situation once again shook up the Olympic Movement. As the coronavirus (COVID-19) pandemic took hold of the world, paralyzing economic and social activities everywhere, the IOC and the Tokyo 2020 Organizing Committee surrendered to the inevitable. On March 23, they announced that the Tokyo Olympics – originally scheduled to occur between July 24 and August 9, 2020 – would be postponed. Because the four-year Olympic calendar is autonomous, regardless of whether an event is executed or not, the Olympics planned for 2021 will still be called the Tokyo 2020 Olympic Games.

The Olympic Games have been cancelled three times – in 1916, 1940, and 1944 – due to the two World Wars, but they have never before been postponed. The possibility of postponing the event proved to be polemic, and the IOC's delay in addressing the issue made it the target of harsh criticism.[33] On the one hand, the event's organizers were concerned with administering the billion-dollar contracts (with sponsors, broadcasters, and local entrepreneurs) involved in hosting the Games. On the other hand, athletes worried about the lack of adequate training conditions as well as the risks of contracting COVID-19. In addition, social distancing measures and the cancellation of numerous international air travel routes made it impossible to carry out certain classifying stages for the competitions. Before the games were postponed, Canada and Australia's NOCs announced a potential boycott of the games, which directly challenged the IOC's authority and threatened its protagonism within the Olympic Movement. In an attempt to recuperate some of the symbolic capital it had lost, the IOC used the rhetoric of the Olympic Games as a symbol of hope for overcoming the coronavirus.

> The leaders agreed that the Olympic Games in Tokyo could stand as a beacon of hope to the world during these troubled times and that the Olympic flame could become the light at the end of the tunnel in which the world finds itself at present.
>
> (Thomas Bach, apud, Goh & Kano 2020)

To a certain extent, this attempt led to a degree of success inasmuch as major media outlets in certain countries, including Brazil, created marketing campaigns representing the postponement of the Olympic Games as a good example to be followed by political leaders and populations hesitant to adopt necessary social-distancing measures.

FIFA also introduced certain important changes in its 2013 and 2016 Statutes (FIFA 2013, 2016). The most significant alteration in 2013 was the definition of a new candidature process for hosting the World Cup, quite similar to the Olympic Games' process before Agenda 2020. The 2013 Statute also included a greater emphasis on a discourse of ethics, the possibility of the FIFA Congress firing the organization's president and other members of the Executive Board, and small alterations in the presidential electoral process, although the presidency was still not subject to term limits. The 2016 Statute (FIFA 2016) limited the maximum number of presidential terms to three.

More than two decades after the IOC's introduction of significant institutional changes during the 1990s, FIFA tried to follow suit. However, this initiative was not enough to contain the storm of corruption denunciations that the organization had suffered for years and that had made it subject to investigation in a number of different jurisdictions, including Swiss courts, Brazil's Congress, the US Department of Justice, and by FIFA itself (Canton of Zug Prosecutor's Office 2010; Brasil 2001; Rebelo and Torres 2001). This situation grew more dire in 2015, when 40 people – including organizational and business leaders – were indicted: Jérôme Valcke was removed as the organization's secretary-general and a number of FIFA executives were imprisoned in the United States under accusations of corrupt marketing contracts. Joseph Blatter's resignation – shortly after his reelection to FIFA's presidency – and the subsequent suspension of his FIFA membership marked the culmination of these troubles. Since then, the number of FIFA's sponsors has decreased. While the 2014 World Cup in Brazil had eight official sponsors, the 2018 edition in Russia had only five. Although it maintained ties with six official partners, the 2018 World Cup lost important ties such as those with Sony, an official FIFA partner since 2010, and the Emirates Group, a partner since 2006.

Partial considerations

Observing this timeline of the Olympic Movement allows us to identify certain patterns and regularities. The institution of rules does indeed contribute to the construction of legal and political autonomy in the field of sporting-spectacle production. These processes, however, did not occur instantaneously. They took place slowly and gradually, at times almost imperceptibly.

Two factors have been decisive in slowing these processes. First, each proposed change requires a certain amount of time to be elaborated, approved, incorporated into the candidature process, and eventually, to materialize in a city during the organization of a given event, which generally takes more than a decade. Second, any change requires delicacy in articulating disputes among different interests, both within the sporting field and in its relations with other fields, especially those relating to economics and the production of the city.

Two other factors, however, have functioned as catalysts for a more rapid acceleration of the field: innovation and crisis. Cycles of innovation can be driven by two special situations. The first innovative cycle occurs during the candidature process. The "necessity" of overcoming opponents always challenges cities to offer something more. A new innovative impulse occurs during the organization of a given event. In this case, innovation can be motivated by the desire to please the IOC and to surpass the success of earlier host cities, as Los Angeles did by constructing the first Olympic Village. The desire to reconcile the interests of different locally active groups can also motivate innovation, as is the case in urban restructuring projects in Rio de Janeiro or in Barcelona's major urban design projects. The legislative apparatus against "ambush marketing" for the Sydney 2000 Olympic Games or the spectacular architecture of the 1976 Montreal Games followed by Athens (2004) and Beijing (2008) were all examples of innovation.

When innovation acquires the status of a successful "model," it becomes incorporated voluntarily – through the help of consultancy firms – in the form of pledges made in candidate cities' files. Next, this innovation is introduced through the IOC's regulatory apparatus, first as a suggestion and later as a demand. In this way, it is guaranteed to be reproduced by subsequent host cities and countries, whether as a legal instrument or as a form of concrete interventions in the space of the Olympics. This innovative cycle can cross over various editions of the

Olympics until reaching its full conclusion; in other words, until it loses its innovative character and becomes an Olympic pattern, thereby propelling the "necessity" of further innovations.

As previously identified by Poulantzas (1974) and instrumentalized by thinkers who defend consensual neoliberal planning models, crises have always offered an opportunity for the introduction of authoritarian measures inasmuch as they demand rapid and agile responses. In moments of crisis, there is no space for political debate. In this sense, as Payne (2012) affirms – citing Samaranch – crises, like those experienced by the Olympic Movement at the beginning of the 1980s or after the 1996 Atlanta Games and the scandal of the Salt Lake City Games, made it possible for the IOC to accelerate changes that, under normal circumstances, would have taken more than a decade to implement.

Nevertheless, the main finding that we can extract from this genealogy is that, in spite of the discourse of disinterest, the field of economics has always interacted in a marked way with the field of production of sporting spectacle, even when the latter was not yet constituted as an autonomous field. This interaction occurred in a more subtle way – at times even presented as undesirable – until the end of the 1960s, a period in which hegemonic thinking within the economic field tolerated limits on the action of the market.

It can be said that, in its early moments, the relationship between capitalist accumulation served more as mutual ideological support – of modern sports as a support mechanism for bourgeois moral and social distinction, and vice versa – than through the production and commercialization of commodities. Through the crisis of capitalism that created bases for neoliberal globalization and transformed spectacle itself into a star of commodification (Debord 2002), this relation began to occur in a more intimate and explicit way. With the consolidation of the neoliberal project, it became aggressive, and the market began to dictate the rules of the game openly. Television, primarily responsible for this spectacularization, took on a decisive role in constituting an autonomous field for the production of sporting spectacle and, therefore, a decisive role in configuring the present-day relationship that this spectacle creates with cities.

Notes

1 Portions of this chapter first appeared in the book *O Poder dos Jogos e os Jogos de Poder: Os interesses em campo na produção da cidade para o espetáculo esportivo* (de Oliveira 2015), published by Editora UFRJ. The English translation is by Raphael Soifer.
2 Most definitions for mega-events contain certain common characteristics: a limited temporal duration; major scale of outreach; the capacity to mobilize people and finances throughout the world; global media space; and the capacity to have an impact on a host city. Major fairs, festivals, and expositions as well as major sporting events are classic examples.
3 See Chapter 3.
4 Originally published in French and/or English, the Olympic Charter is the document that establishes the rules of the Olympic movement's functioning. Historically, the Olympic Charter has taken on various forms and nomenclatures, including Annuaire,

Règles Olympiques, Olympic Rules and Regulamentations, or Statuts. The name "Olympic Charter" was only formally adopted in 1978.

5 In 394 ACE, the Roman emperor Theodosius banned the Olympic Games for religious reasons. See IOC (1950).

6 During the 1890s, when modern sport was already very widespread throughout Europe and other parts of the world, a group of European aristocrats led by Baron de Coubertin began to come together around the idea of a revival of the Ancient Olympic Games (IOC 1933, 1950).

7 Since 1993, the General Assembly of the United Nations has approved a similar resolution for each edition of the Olympic Games. In June 2000, the IOC established the International Olympic Truce Foundation (IOTF) which, among other objectives, promotes the ancient Greek tradition of the Olympic Truce.

8 During the first decades of its existence, the IOC was composed mostly of members of the nobility, military leaders, or heads of state (CIO 1908).

9 According to the Olympic Charter (IOC 2019a), Olympic values are responsible for the unification of members of the Olympic Movement. The principles of moral formation and union among different peoples through sporting practices – which the charter cites as an inheritance from ancient Greece – have been synthesized in the modern conception of "Olympism," which represents itself as a life philosophy serving the harmonious development of humanity.

10 Dunning (1986) suggests that the persistence of the principles of amateurism represent thereaction of elites to the threat of the "lower classes" enjoying the distinction conferred by practicing sports. The isolation of sports in restricted social circles also reveals these elites' fear of being defeated by professionals who play for glory and recognition as well as for fun. Unlike Huizinga (1980), Dunning does not believe that professionalism is responsible for the loss of ludic character; instead, he sees rules imposed on amateur sporting practices as what made them extremely serious.

11 The son of a Belgian who grew rich in Brazil through arms dealing, Jean-Marie Faustin Goedefroid de Havelange presided over the Brazilian Confederation of Sports (CBD) for 17 years (1958–1974), and was president of FIFA for another 24 (1974–1998). Dedicated to various forms of sports, Havelange competed in swimming in the Berlin Olympics 1936, in water polo in Helsinki 1952, and was a member of the Brazilian delegation in Melbourne 1956. In 1963, he became a member of the IOC, and when he withdrew from the presidency of FIFA, he was elected Honorary President. His life as a sporting events director was marked by his commercial vision and discipline. After more than a half century leading sporting institutions, Havelange became one of the most influential names in the world of sports, and perhaps the only person to circulate in both Olympic sports and in football with the same resourcefulness. In 2011, Havelange became the subject of an IOC investigation due to allegations of corruption in selling World Cup marketing rights to the ISL. Just before the results of the investigation were published, Havelange resigned from the IOC due to supposed health problems. According to the IOC's rules, his resignation led the investigation to be discontinued and impeded the results from being published. In 2013, Havelange resigned as Honorary President of FIFA and, in 2015, became the target of a new corruption investigation, this time by the FBI. He died in 2016 when he was 100 years old. See Pereira and Vieira (2011).

12 During Francisco Franco's dictatorship in Spain, Don Juan Antonio Samaranch Torelló (1920–2001) held various public roles, including as Delegate for Physical Education and Sports in Spain's parliament in 1967. In 1973, he was named to the presidency of the regional council (*Diputación*) of Barcelona, from which he resigned in 1977 when he was nominated to be Spanish ambassador to the Soviet Union and Mongolia. In addition to participating in the Spanish Olympic Committee as a member and president, he was elected to the IOC in 1966, acting as chief of protocol for two

terms (1968–1975 and 1979–1980), member of the Executive Council (1970–1978, 1979–1980), and Vice President (1974–1978). In 1980, he was elected to succeed Lord Killian as IOC President, a role he held until July 2001 when he was succeeded by Jacques Rogge. From that point on, he held the role of Honorary President for Life until his death in 2001. The IOC's Olympic Studies Centre published a biography of Samaranch in its "Historical Archives" series. www.olympic.org/Assets/OSC%20Sec tion/pdf/LRes_21E.pdf.

13 Interscalar disputes regarding the commercial exploitation of the Olympic brand will be analyzed further in Chapter 2.

14 In addition to the geopolitical disputes of the Cold War, such events have been used more recently for ends including: the legitimization of authoritarian regimes, such as those in South Korea (Seoul 1988 and Pyeongchang 2018) and China (Beijing 2008); the consolidation of the dominance of rich countries such as Japan (2002 World Cup) and Germany (2006 World Cup); or the visibility of emerging nations, such as China (Beijing 2008), South Africa (2010 World Cup), and Brazil (2014 World Cup and 2016 Rio de Janeiro Olympic Games).

15 Four cities competed to host the 1972 Olympic Games; for the 1976 edition, the number fell to three. Only two cities submitted candidatures for the 1980 Games, and Los Angeles was the only host city candidate for the 1984 Games.

16 Michael Payne, an Englishman considered to be one of the world's foremost specialists in marketing, was born in 1958 and first appeared in Olympic sports as a skier during the 1970s. Although not very successful as an athlete, he became interested in marketing. After beginning his work with the West Nally company, Payne followed Horst Dassler to the International Sport and Leisure (ISL) agency in 1982. It was through Dassler that he joined the IOC in 1983 as director of the Olympic Project. The agency invited Payne to work on creating a marketing strategy for the Olympics, and he was responsible for creating the marketing project that revolutionized the Games. Since then, he has also been a steadfast defender of solidifying the relationship between the worlds of business, media, and sports. In 1988, Payne became the IOC's first marketing director. Until 2002, he remained with the Committee and was responsible for its advertising contracts (Payne 2012). Since then, he has worked as a marketing consultant and had a standout role in preparing Rio de Janeiro's candidature to host the 2016 Olympic Games.

17 Brazil's military dictatorship used the symbolic appeal of the 1970 World Cup to legitimate its violent actions as it persecuted, tortured, and assassinated thousands of people who dared to defy its hegemony.

18 Horst Dassler (1936–1987) was the son of Adolf Dassler, one of the founders of Adidas, which Horst later inherited from his father. The network of influence he developed at Adidas gave him power comparable to the principle directors of sporting bodies and allowed him to influence the results of candidature for positions at all levels of the Olympic Movement. Beginning in the 1970s, Dassler joined Patrick Nally at the West Nally publicity agency, which at that time was already responsible for administering many sports sponsors and which soon controlled sports marketing throughout the world. In 1980, when Samaranch was elected president of the IOC, he invited Dassler to create a marketing program for the committee. In 1982, Dassler left West Nally and, together with André Le Guelfi, created the ISL, a new agency, bringing with him almost all of Nally's former clients. After Dassler's death in 1987, his heirs were unable to sustain the company's dominance, and the IOC parted ways with the ISL in 1995. In 2001, the ISL filed for bankruptcy. Along with FIFA and some of its most prominent members, the ISL was involved in a corruption scandal investigated by different groups in different parts of the world, including the FBI, Brazil's Congress, the IOC, and FIFA itself. For further details on connections between Horst, Dassler, and the world of sports, see Payne (2012) and Jennings (2007).

19 Joseph Blatter was born in 1936 in Switzerland where he played football in amateur leagues from 1948 to 1971. In 1964, Blatter became General Secretary for the Swiss Ice Hockey federation. He participated in the 1972 and 1976 Olympic Games as director of Sports Chronometry and Public Relations for the Longines Corporation. It was during this time that he met Dassler, who recruited him as a director for FIFA. In 1975, João Havelange hired Blatter as FIFA's director of Technical Development Programs. During the first six months of his contract, Dassler personally trained Blatter at Adidas headquarters. In 1981, at Dassler's insistence, Blatter was nominated to serve as FIFA's Secretary General. In 1990, he was promoted to CEO. In 1998, Blatter was elected to succeed João Havelange as President of FIFA, a role to which he was reelected in 2002, 2006, and 2010. During the 2002 elections, Blatter was accused of using FIFA money to buy votes; he recognized his errors and reviewed official procedures, but was reelected nonetheless. On June 4, 2015, four days after his final reelection, Blatter ceded to the corruption scandals consuming FIFA and resigned. In December 2015, FIFA suspended him for eight years. After Blatter appealed the decision, his suspension was reduced to six years. Although the Appeals Committee upheld the accusations of breaking FIFA's Code of Ethics, it considered proof of crimes of corruption and bribery against Blatter to be insufficient. During the time he served as President of FIFA, a biography of Joseph Blatter was available on the organization's official website: www.fifa.com/aboutfifa/organisation/president/aboutpresident.html. After his resignation, it was removed.

20 Richard William Duncan Pound was born in Canada in 1942 and received a B.C.L. at McGill University in 1964. Beginning in 1999, he served as the university's chancellor. He began his athletic career as a swimmer and was a finalist at the 1960 Rome Olympic Games. Pound was elected president of the Canadian Olympic Association in 1977 and joined the IOC in 1978. During Samaranch's presidency, Pound served as the IOC's vice president from 1978–1982 and again from 1996–2000. In addition, he coordinated many of the IOC's most important commissions, including the Anti-Doping Agency (1999–2007). Pound had a fundamental role in the IOC's financial recuperation as head of the Commission for New Financing Sources (later renamed the Marketing Commission), and of the Broadcasting Rights Commission (1983–2001). Pound also led the Coordination Commission for the 1996 Centennial Olympic Games in Atlanta, as well as the Organizing Committees for the 1988 Calgary Winter Games and the 2010 Vancouver Winter Games. He coordinated the commission responsible for investigating corruption scandals in the selection of Salt Lake City as host of the 2002 Winter Games. Between 2001 and 2003, he distinguished himself as coordinator of the Olympic Games Studies Commission (Pound 2003). Pound ran for president of the IOC to succeed Samaranch, but lost to Jacques Rogge, who had Samaranch's support. See Pound (2006), Payne (2012), and Rogge (2004).

21 Note that, up to this point, each OCOG held exclusive control over these contracts with the IOC responsible only for approving them.

22 Originally, TOP stood for The Olympic Programme, but the name later changed to The Olympic Partners (Payne 2012).

23 See Chapter 2.

24 The 1984 Los Angeles Olympics were organized by business leaders who took responsibility for the city's candidature, as well as for the event's organization and execution. This entrepreneurial attitude on a local scale appeared as a response to cuts in federal resources for urban development projects. Through an innovative marketing program, the 1984 Games resulted in US$225 million in profits, setting the standard for a "Capitalist Olympics." In addition to helping recuperate the political strength of the Olympic Games, this marketing program served as inspiration for the IOC's business revolution. See LAOOC (1985). Pound (2006) and Payne (2012).

25 For the 2008 Olympic Games, US$17 billion were invested in the environment (IOC 2010, p. 39).
26 "The Manual for Cities Bidding for the 2000 Olympic Games" (IOC 1992) included a description of measures already in force in a given country that could be used to protect the Olympic brand or to combat ambush marketing. However, the text did not demand specific legislative changes to this end.
27 See Chapter Six.
28 See Chapter Six.
29 For the case of Barcelona see, among others, Capel (2005); for Sydney, see Gold and Gold (2008); for London, see Raco and Tunney (2010).
30 The concept of a city of exception was presented in 2012 in the doctoral dissertation through which this book originated. The concept is developed further in Chapter 6.
31 See, for example, Romero (2012), Watts (2015) and Harvey (2012).
32 See Chapter 3.
33 See, for example, Cohen (2020), Goh and Kano (2020), Panja 2020 and Talmazan (2020).

References

Aristotle 2009, *Nicomachean Ethics*, trans. WD Ross, rev. L Brown, Oxford University Press, New York.
Articulação Nacional da Copa (ANCOP) 2013, *World Cup 2014: Who Wins the Match?* viewed 18 June 2018, <www.youtube.com/watch?feature=player_embedded&v=aAX0 zSfrJK4#at=62>
Articulação Nacional dos Comitês Populares da Copa (ANCOP) n.d., *Megaeventos e violações de direitos humanos no Brasil: Dossiê da Articulação Nacional dos Comitês Populares da Copa*, viewed 5 January 2019, <https://apublica.org/wp-content/uploads/2012/01/DossieViolacoesCopa.pdf>
Benedicto, DBM 2008, "Desafiando o coro dos contentes: vozes dissonantes no processo de implementação dos Jogos Pan-Americanos, Rio 2007", master thesis, Universidade Federal do Rio de Janeiro.
Bourdieu, P 1991, *Language and Symbolic Power*, trans. G Raymond & M Adamsom, Polity Press, Cambridge.
Bourdieu, P 1993, "How Can One Be a Sports Fan?" in S During (ed) *The Cultural Studies Reader*, Routledge, London and New York, pp. 339–356.
Bourdieu, P 1998, *On Television*, trans. PP Ferguson, The New Press, New York.
Bourdieu, P & Wacquant, LJD 1992, *An Invitation to Reflexive Sociology*, The University of Chicago Press, Chicago.
Brady, AM 2009, "The Beijing Olympics as a Campaign of Mass Distraction", in *The China Quarterly*, vol. 197, March, special section on the Beijing 2008 Olympics, Cambridge University Press, Cambridge, pp. 1–24.
Broudehoux, AM 2007, "Spectacular Beijing: The Conspicuous Construction of an Olympic Metropolis", *Journal of Urban Affairs*, 29.4, pp. 383–399.
Broudehoux, AM 2012, "Civilizing Beijing: Social Beautification, Civility and Citizenship at the 2008 Olympics", in G Hayes & J Karamichas (eds) *Olympic Games, Mega-Events and Civil Societies*, Palgrave Macmillan, London, pp. 46–67.
Burbank, M, Andranovich, G & Heying, C 2001, *Olympic Dreams: The Impact of Mega-Events on Local Politics*, Lynne Rienner Publishers, Boulder.
Canton of Zug, Prosecutor's Office 2010, *Translation of the Order on the Dismissal of the Criminal Proceedings of May 11, 2010, in the Investigation Against Fédération*

Internationale de Football Association (FIFA), viewed 10 October 2018, <http://pt.fifa. com/mm/document/affederation/footballgovernance/01/66/28/60/orderonthedismissa-lofthecriminalproceedings.pdf>

Capel, H 2005, *El modelo Barcelona: un examen crítico*, Ediciones del Serbal, Barcelona.

Centre on Housing Rights and Evictions (COHRE) 2007, *Fair Play for Housing Rights: Mega-Events, Olympic Games and Housing Rights*, COHRE, Geneva, viewed 27 October 2019, <www.ruig-gian.org/ressources/Report%20Fair%20Play%20FINAL%20FINAL% 20070531.pdf>

Cohen, K 2020, "Tokyo 2020 Olympics Officially Postponed Until 2021", *ESPN*, 24 March, viewed 25 March 2020, <www.espn.com/olympics/story/_/id/28946033/tokyo-olympics-officially-postponed-2021>

Comité International Olimpique (CIO) 1908, *Annuaire*, CIO, Lausanne.

Comité International Olimpique (CIO) 1911, *Annuaire*, IOC, Lausanne.

Comité International Olympic (CIO) 1920, *Statuts*, IOC, Lausanne.

Comité International Olympic (CIO) 1921, *Statuts: Reglements et protocole de la célébra-tion des Olympiades Modernes et des Jeux Olympiques Quadriennaux*, IOC, Lausanne.

Comité International Olympic (CIO) 1924, *Statuts du Comité International Olympique, Reglements et Protocole de la Célébration des Olympiades Modernes et des Jeux Olym-piques Quadriennaux, Regles Generales Techniques Applicables a la Célébration de la VIIIᵉ Olympiade*, IOC, Lausanne.

Comité International Olympic (CIO) 1930, *Charte des Jeux Olympiques, Statuts du Con-seil International Olympique, Reglements et Protocole de la Celebration des Olympi-ades Modernes et des Jeux Olympiques Quadriennaux, Regles Generales Techniques Applicables a la Célébration des Jeux Olympiques, Reglement des Congres Olympiques*, IOC, Lausanne.

Comité International Olympic (CIO) 1962, *Règles du Comité International Olympique sur les Conditions d'admission aux Jeux Olympiques*, IOC, Lausanne.

Comité Organisateur des Jeux Olympiques (COJO 76) 1978, *Games of the XXI Olympiad Montréal 1976: Official Report*, vol. 1, COJO 76, Ottawa.

Comitê Popular Rio da Copa e das Olimpíadas n.d., *Megaeventos e Violações dos Direitos Humanos no Rio de Janeiro: Dossiê do Comitê Popular da Copa e Olimpíadas do Rio de Janeiro*, viewed 05 January 2020, <https://comitepopulario.files.wordpress.com/2012/04/ dossic3aa-megaeventos-e-violac3a7c3b5es-dos-direitos-humanos-no-rio-de-janeiro.pdf>

Congresso Nacional do Brasil 2001, *Senado Federal, Relatório final da comissão parla-mentar de inquérito destinada a investigar fatos envolvendo as associações brasileiras de futebol*, 4 v Brasília, DF, viewed 10 November 2018, <https://www2.senado.leg.br/ bdsf/item/id/82013>

Debord, G 2002, *Society of the Spectacle*, Black & Red, Detroit.

de Oliveira, NG 2016, "Les méga-événements au Brésil et la réinvention du spectacle sportif", *Problèmes d'Amérique Latine*, 103, pp. 17–36, April.

Dunning, E 1986, "The Dynamics of Modern Sport: Notes on Achievement-Striving and the Social Significance of Sport", in N Elias & E Dunning (eds) *Quest for Excitement*: *Sport and Leisure in the Civilizing Process*, Basil Blackwell, Oxford, pp. 203–221.

Elias, N 1986a, "The Genesis of Sport as a Sociological Problem", in N Elias & E Dunning (eds) *Quest for Excitement*: *Sport and Leisure in the Civilizing Process*, Basil Blackwell, Oxford, pp. 179–190.

Elias, N 1986b, "An Essay on Sport and Violence", in N Elias & E Dunning (eds) *Quest for Excitement*: *Sport and Leisure in the Civilizing Process*, Basil Blackwell, Oxford, pp. 179–190.

Elias, N & Dunning, E (eds) 1986a, *Quest for Excitement: Sport and Leisure in the Civilizing Process*, Basil Blackwell, Oxford.

Elias, N & Dunning, E 1986b, "Folk Football in Medieval and Early Modern Britain", in N Elias & E Dunning (eds) *Quest for Excitement: Sport and Leisure in the Civilizing Process*, Basil Blackwell, Oxford, pp. 179–190.

Fédération Internationale de Football Association (FIFA) 2007, *1950 World Cup: Uruguay Triumph Brings Heartbreak for Brazil*, viewed 10 April 2019, <www.fifa.com/worldcup/news/uruguay-triumph-brings-heartbreak-for-brazil-502075>

Fédération Internationale de Football Association (FIFA) 2013, *FIFA Statutes: July 2013 Edition*, FIFA, Zurich.

Fédération Internationale de Football Association (FIFA) 2016, *FIFA Statutes: April 2016 Edition*, FIFA, Zurich.

Fédération Internationale de Football Association (FIFA) 2019, *FIFA Statutes: June 2019 Edition*, FIFA, Zurich.

Fédération Internationale de Football Association (FIFA) n.d.a, *History of FIFA: Foundation*, viewed 10 January 2019, <www.fifa.com/about-fifa/who-we-are/history/index.html>

Fédération Internationale de Football Association (FIFA) n.d.b, *Olympic Football Tourament (Men)*, viewed 10 January 2019, <www.fifa.com/mm/document/fifafacts/mencom poly/51/98/60/ip-208_01e_oly_men.pdf>

Fédération Internationale de Football Association (FIFA) n.d.c, *Olympic Football Tournament Final*, viewed 10 January 2019, <https://resources.fifa.com/tournaments/archive/mensolympic/index.html>

Goh, Z & Kano, S 2020, "Tokyo 2020 Olympic and Paralympic Games Postponed to 2021", *Olympic Channel*, 24 March, viewed 25 March 2020, <www.olympicchannel.com/en/stories/news/detail/tokyo-olympic-games-postponed-ioc/>

Gold, JR & Gold, MM 2008, "Olympic Cities: Regeneration, City Rebranding and Changing Urban Agendas", *Geography Compass*, 2.1, pp. 300–318.

Harvey, O 2012, "Riover and Out: Families' Agony as 30,000 Are Evicted from Their Homes in £11bn Slum Facelift", *The Sun*, 26 August.

Horne, J & Gruneau, R (eds) 2016, *Mega-Events and Globalization Capital and Spectacle in a Changing World Order*, Routledge, Abingdon and New York.

Huizinga, Johan 1980, *Homo Ludens: A Study of the Play Element in Culture*, Routledge & Kegan Paul, Boston London and Henley.

International Olympic Committee (IOC) 1932, *Olympic Rules*, IOC, Lausanne.

International Olympic Committee (IOC) 1933, *The International Olympic Committee and the Modern Olympic Games*, IOC, Lausanne.

International Olympic Committee (IOC) 1946, *Olympic Rules*, IOC, Lausanne.

International Olympic Committee (IOC) 1949, *Olympic Rules*, IOC, Lausanne.

International Olympic Committee (IOC) 1950, *The International Olympic Committee and the Modern Olympic Games*, IOC, Lausanne.

International Olympic Committee (IOC) 1954, *Olympic Rule Nr. 25*, IOC, Lausanne.

International Olympic Committee (IOC) 1955, *Information for Cities Which Desire to Stage the Olympic Games*, IOC, Lausanne.

International Olympic Committee (IOC) 1956, *The Olympic Games: Fundamental Principles, Rules and Regulations General Information*, IOC, Lausanne.

International Olympic Committee (IOC) 1957, *Information for Cities Which Desire to Stage the Olympic Games*, IOC, Lausanne.

International Olympic Committee (IOC) 1958, *The Olympic Games: Fundamental Principles Rules and Regulations General Information*, IOC, Lausanne.

International Olympic Committee (IOC) 1964, *Eligibility Rules of the International Olympic Committee*, IOC, Lausanne.

International Olympic Committee (IOC) 1966, *The Olympic Games: Fundamental Principles Rules and Regulations General Information*, IOC, Lausanne.

International Olympic Committee (IOC) 1967, *The Olympic Games: Rules and Regulations, Eligibility Code, General Information, Information for Cities Which Desire to Stage the Olympic Games, Bibliography*, IOC, Lausanne.

International Olympic Committee (IOC) 1971a, *The Olympic Games: Rules and Regulations, Eligibility Code*, IOC, Lausanne.

International Olympic Committee (IOC) 1971b, *Olympic Rules and Regulations: Provisional Edition*, IOC, Lausanne.

International Olympic Committee (IOC) 1973, *Olympic Rules and Regulations*, IOC, Lausanne.

International Olympic Committee (IOC) 1974, *Olympic Rules and Regulations*, IOC, Lausanne.

International Olympic Committee (IOC) 1975, *Olympic Rules Bye-Laws and Instructions: Provisional Edition*, IOC, Lausanne.

International Olympic Committee (IOC) 1976, *Olympic Rules Bye-Laws and Instructions*, IOC, Lausanne.

International Olympic Committee (IOC) 1978, *Olympic Charter: Provisional Edition*, IOC, Lausanne.

International Olympic Committee (IOC) 1982, *Olympic Charter*, IOC, Lausanne.

International Olympic Committee (IOC) 1984, *Olympic Charter*, IOC, Lausanne.

International Olympic Committee (IOC) 1985, *Olympic Charter*, IOC, Lausanne.

International Olympic Committee (IOC) 1991, *Olympic Charter: In Force as from16th June 1991*, IOC, Lausanne.

International Olympic Committee (IOC) 1992, *Manual for Cities Bidding for the Olympic Games*, IOC, Lausanne.

International Olympic Committee (IOC) 1993, *Olympic Charter: In Force as from 24th September 1993*, IOC, Lausanne.

International Olympic Committee (IOC) 1999a, *Olympic Charter: In Force as from 17th June 1999*, IOC, Lausanne.

International Olympic Committee (IOC) 1999b, *Olympic Charter: In Force as from 12th December 1999*, IOC, Lausanne.

International Olympic Committee (IOC) 2000, *Olympic Charter: In Force as from 11th September 2000*, IOC, Lausanne.

International Olympic Committee (IOC) 2003, *Olympic Charter: In Force as from 4 July 2003*, IOC, Lausanne.

International Olympic Committee (IOC) 2004, *2012 Candidature Procedure and Questionnaire: Games of the XXX Olympiad in 2012*, IOC, Lausanne.

International Olympic Committee (IOC) 2010, *Final Report of the IOC Coordination Commission: Games of the XXIX Olympiad, Beijing 2008*, IOC, Lausanne.

International Olympic Committee (IOC) 2014, *Olympic Agenda 2020: The Strategic Roadmap for the Future of the Olympic Movement*, IOC, Lausanne.

International Olympic Committee (IOC) 2015, *Football: History of Football at the Olympic Games*, viewed 10 March 2018, <https://stillmed.olympic.org/AssetsDocs/OSC%20 Section/pdf/QR_sports_summer/Sports_Olympiques_football_eng.pdf>

International Olympic Committee (IOC) 2018, *Olympic Charter: In Force as from 9 October 2018*, IOC, Lausanne.

International Olympic Committee (IOC) 2019a, *Olympic Charter: In Force as from 26 June 2019*, IOC, Lausanne.

International Olympic Committee (IOC) 2019b, *Olympic Marketing: Fact File 2019 Edition*, IOC, Lausanne.

International Olympic Committee (IOC) n.d., *Brand Protection: Technical Manual on Brand Protection*, IOC, viewed 15 September 2019, <www.gamesmonitor.org.uk/files/Technical_Manual_on_Brand_Protection.pdf>

Jenning, A 2007, *Foul!: The Secret World of Fifa*, HarperCollins, New York.

Jenning, A, Lassance, A, Vainer, C, Maricato, E, Ferreira, JSW, Lopes, JSL, Souto Maior, JL, MTST, Fernandes, L, Oliveira, NG & Rolnik, R 2014, *Brasil em Jogo: o que fica da Copa do Mundo e das Olimpíadas?* Boitempo, Rio de Janeiro.

Kant, I 1987, *Critique of Judgement*, trans. SP Werner, Hackett Publishing, Cambridge.

Los Angeles Olympic Organizing Committee (LAOOC) 1985, *Official Report of the Games of the XXIIIrd Olympiad Los Angeles, 1984*, vol. 1, LAOOC, Los Angeles.

Panja, T 2019, "Former Rio Governor Describes Extensive Bribery in Bid for 2016 Olympics", *New York Times*, 5 July, viewed 7 July 2019, <www.nytimes.com/2019/07/05/sports/2016-olympics-rio-bribery.html>

Panja, T 2020, "Tokyo Olympics Organizers Considering July 2021 for Opening Ceremony", *The New York Times*, 28 March, viewed 31 March 2020, <www.nytimes.com/2020/03/28/sports/olympics/coronavirus-olympics-postponed-2021.html?auth=login-facebook>

Payne, M 2012, *Olympic Turnarounds: How the Olympic Games Stepped Back from the Brink of Extinction to Become the World Best Known Brand*, Infinite Ideas Limited, Oxford.

Pereira, JM & Vieira, SM 2011, *João Havelange: O dirigente esportivo do século XX*, COB/Casa da Palavra, Rio de Janeiro.

Poulantzas, N 1974, *Fascism and Dictatorship: The Third International and the Problem of Fascism*, Verso, London.

Pound, RW 2003, *Olympic Games Study Commission: Report to the 115th IOC Session*, IOC, Prague.

Pound, RW 2006, *Inside the Olympics: A Behind-the-Scenes Look at the Politics, the Scandals, and the Glory of the Games*, John Wiley & Sons, Toronto.

Raco, M & Tunney, E 2010, "Visibilities and Invisibilities in Urban Development: Small Business Communities and the London Olympics 2012", *Urban Studies*, 47, pp. 2069–2091, September.

Rebelo, A & Torres, S 2001, *CBF-Nike*, Casa Amarela, São Paulo.

Rigauer, B 1981, *Sport and Work*, Columbia University Press, New York.

Rogge, J 2004, *The Olympic Games: Athens to Athens 1896–2000*, Orion Publishing Co, London.

Romero, S 2012, "Slum Dwellers Are Defying Brazil's Design for Olympics", *New York Times*, 4 March, viewed 1 December 2018, <www.nytimes.com/2012/03/05/world/americas/brazil-faces-obstacles-in-preparations-for-rio-olympics.html?mtrref=www.google.com&gwh=E60C1BBF8A899C1F987C8952C45C9B36&gwt=pay&assetType=REGIWALL>

Sánchez, F, Bienenstein, G, Oliveira, FL & Novais, P (eds) 2014, *A Copa do Mundo e as Cidades: Políticas, Projetos e Resistências*, Universidade Federal Fluminense, Rio de Janeiro.

Silvestre, G & Oliveira, NG 2012, "The Revanchist Logic of Mega-Events: Community Displacement in Rio de Janeiro's West End", *Visual Studies*, 27.2, pp. 204–210.

Talmazan, Y 2020, "New Dates Announced for Tokyo 2020 Olympics Postponed Over Coronavirus Concerns", *NBC News*, 30 March, viewed 31 March 2020, <www.nbc news.com/news/world/new-dates-announced-tokyo-2020-olympics-postponed-over-coronavirus-concerns-n1171871>

Vainer, C, Broudehoux, AM, Sánchez, F & Oliveira, FL (eds) 2017, *Mega-Events and the City: Critical Perspectives*, Letra Capital, Rio de Janeiro.

Watts, J 2015, "Rio 2016: The Olympics Has Destroyed My Home", *The Guardian*, 19 July 2020, viewed 1 December 2018, <www.theguardian.com/world/2015/jul/19/2016-olympics-rio-de-janeiro-brazil-destruction>

Weber, M 2013, *The Protestant Ethic and the Spirit of Capitalism*, Routledge, New York.

2 The players and their strategies[1]

Introduction

Generally speaking, a researcher tends to construct his or her object of study by imposing certain limits on the universe to be researched. However, as Dezalay and Garth (1996) note, Bourdieu's concept of the field is sufficiently open and systemic so as to facilitate the exploration of autonomous spaces in objective relationships. Therefore, the field does not establish easily identifiable limits. If an agent or institution is part of a field to such an extent that it feels or produces effects from or within this field (Bourdieu & Wacquant 1992), determining the limits of the field itself is already one of many questions permanently at play. As such, this determination cannot be resolved *a priori* through a simple act of the researcher's imposition; instead, it can only be treated as part of the research object. Without neglecting these difficulties in defining the limits of a field, this Chapter focuses on players operating in the field of the production of sporting mega-events. It aims to identify predominant agents, groups of agents, and coalitions within the field as well as their positions and strategies.

In the field of production of sport spectacle, new individuals and institutions may be incorporated or cast out at any given moment according to the relevance of their roles in disputes either within the field itself or in its relation to other fields. Based on this presupposition, I should clarify two aspects of my research strategy. First, identifying agents involved in the field of production of sport spectacle – in other words, establishing the field's boundaries – was a question that remained open throughout my investigation. Second, the agents identified in this chapter as fundamental to the functioning of the field under review are relevant only in the field's present configuration. Dominant agents from earlier stages were examined in Chapter One.

Bourdieu (1998) presents a program for the analysis of the Olympic Games as "televised spectacle." He suggests investigating the agents and institutions that compete to produce and commercialize images and discourses surrounding this type of event. Considering points of approximation between Bourdieu's explorations (1998) and the approach I have adopted in my research, I have incorporated some of his suggestions into my own investigation. However, it is worth clarifying that the sport spectacle under examination here comprises not only the

Olympic Games but also the FIFA Football World Cup. Together, these constitute the largest contemporary expressions of mega-events. Similarly, my investigation is not restricted to the images and discourses involved in the production of these events; it also involves the production of the events *per se*, especially in relation to the production of the city. This consideration of aspects that differentiate these two objects – as well as the changes that occur in the production of sport spectacle during the time that separates this study from that of Bourdieu. As such, I have cast out certain agents and institutions that he suggests and incorporated others that he leaves unmentioned.

In order to facilitate a greater understanding of objective relationships between these agents, I have distributed them into three distinct universes according to the specific types of capital that they hold:[2] symbolic capital (event-producing institutions); economic capital (individuals involved in commercialization); and cultural capital (those who legitimate strategies). Only an in-depth consideration of these three universes will allow us to determine how each one of them is constituted and who ought to be considered as belonging – or not – to each field.

Symbolic capital

Although I recognize the dominant role played by individual and collective subjects who produce sport spectacle, it is important to perceive clearly the distinction that exists between them and the social space in which they act, are created or transformed, and become obsolete or even reinvented (Dezalay & Garth 1996). From this point of view, the use of the concept of the field seems very adequate – as I endeavor to demonstrate next – inasmuch as it allows us to understand the very existence of these subjects as products of previous symbolic struggles and, therefore, as expressions of relations between forces that exist in any given moment.

Global promoters: the IOC and FIFA as dominant groups

As Bourdieu (1991) affirms, all enunciations that have a collective as their subject presuppose the resolution of the problem of the existence of the group in question. Although the Olympic Movement might be considered a social space functioning within its own logic and obeying specific rules and hierarchies, it cannot formally be considered an institution. Within the rules that conduct the production of the Olympic Games, the expression *Olympic Movement* first appears in the 1946 Olympic Charter, under the topic "Resolutions Regarding the Amateur Status." (IOC 1946) However, the expression did not appear in the IOC's fundamental principles until the 1949 Olympic Rules (IOC 1949), in which it was utilized to enunciate a collective subject charged with leadership and given both established rules to follow as well as benefits.

> 3. The direction of the Olympic movement and the regulation of the Olympic Summer and the Winter Games throughout the world is vested in the

International Olympic Committee whose constitution and powers are defined in these Rules . . . 8. All profits and funds derived from the holding of the Olympic Games . . . are paid to the National Olympic Committee of the country holding the Games and are necessarily applied for the promotion of the Olympic movement or the development of amateur sport.

(IOC 1949, pp. 5–6)

Under the supreme authority of the International Olympic Committee (IOC), the Olympic Movement currently unites all institutions and individuals involved in promoting Olympic sport spectacle. The basic condition for participating in this movement is an acceptance of the rules and conditions established in the Olympic Charter. When the IOC takes on the role of spokesperson for the Olympic Movement, it inserts itself as a subject via the simple fact of enunciation, i.e., "through that magical operation which is inherent in any act of naming" (Bourdieu 1991, p. 250).

The Olympic Movement, constituted primarily by the IOC, International Federations (IFs), and National Olympic Committees (NOCs) also includes Organizing Committees for the Olympic Games (OCOGs), national associations and clubs, and individuals belonging to IFs and NOCs, especially athletes, referees, coaches, trainers, and other sporting officials (IOC 2019a). Other institutions recognized by the IOC[3] – such as associations of NOCs or IFs organized on a continental or global scale – are also included in the Olympic Movement. However, because the Olympic Movement does not exist as an institutional or legal body in its own right, and inasmuch as it is completely controlled by the IOC, it is often confused with the IOC itself. Normally, the IOC invokes the Olympic Movement when it aims to give greater magnitude to its actions.

In its role as Supreme Authority and leader of the Olympic Movement, the IOC has the mission of promoting Olympism around the world (IOC 2019a). The institution – founded in Paris in 1894 and based in Laussane, Switzerland – is recognized by the Swiss Federal Council as a legal entity, specifically as a non-profit, non-governmental organization of unlimited duration. It is organized, in descending hierarchical order, around the following three bodies:

a) the Session, which consists of all IOC members and is charged with approving or altering the Olympic Charter; choosing new members; electing the president, vice presidents, and other members of the Executive Committee; and selecting cities to host the Winter and Summer Olympic Games;

b) the Executive Board, composed of the president, four vice presidents, and ten additional members[4] is responsible for administering and managing IOC business and making decisions regarding complementary institutional regulations, such as codes of conduct and manuals. The Executive Board also establishes and supervises candidature procedures and is responsible for selecting – over the course of two eliminatory rounds – the cities that will compete to host the Olympic Games;

c) the President,[5] who represents the IOC and presides over all of its activities with the authority to make *ad referendum* decisions whenever he or she judges necessary.

In addition to these structures, both the Executive Board and the President can create certain ad hoc committees – both temporary and permanent – for specific affairs. The IOC Congress, which brings together representatives from throughout the Olympic Movement, serves only a consultative function.

As mentioned in Chapter One, the Olympic Movement's finances derive primarily from revenues from the sale of broadcast rights as well as from resources obtained through patronage programs, especially The Olympic Partners program (TOP). The IOC controls contracts in every country in which it sells exclusive broadcasting rights, which it does in blocks involving more than one event. Organizations who purchase these rights can then resell them to one or more broadcasters as they see fit. TOP, meanwhile, consists of a globally scaled sponsorship program that commercializes the rights to the Olympic brand, maintaining exclusivity within each category of products and services. It is worth emphasizing that IOC does not sell advertising space; instead, its only product is the symbolism of the Olympic brand, the commercialization of which involves all of the Olympic movement for the duration of the contract, not only during the Games.

In addition to TOP and broadcasting rights, Olympic marketing revenues also involve ticket sales, licensing the use of the Olympic brand for products and souvenirs, and domestic sponsorship rights, which are usually the responsibility of the host OCOG.

Table 2.1 shows the evolution of IOC revenue sources over the last five quadrennials. In the period between 2009 and 2012, these revenue sources reached a combined total of US$8 billion. In spite of the IOC's tendency to grow since adopting its current marketing program in the 1980s, its total revenue suffered a slight decline during the 2013–2016 quadrennial, when it fell to US$7.8 billion.

Table 2.1 IOC revenues in the past six quadrennials (in millions of US$)

Source	1993–1996	1997–2000	2001–2004	2005–2008	2009–2012	2013–2016
Broadcast	1,251	1,845	2,232	2,570	3,850	4,157
TOP Programme	279	579	663	866	950	1,003
OCOG Domestic Sponsorship	534	655	796	1,555	1,838	2,037
OCOG Ticketing	451	625	411	274	1,238	527
OCOG Licensing	115	66	87	185	170	74
Total	**2,630**	**3,770**	**4,189**	**5,450**	**8,046**	**7,798**

Source: IOC (2019b).

The predominance of broadcasting rights in Olympic marketing revenues is notable, as they have always accounted for almost half of the IOC's total proceeds. Domestic sponsorship initiatives are second most important, but they steer revenue to OCOGs rather than the IOC. The second-most important revenue source for the IOC has been TOP. In the 1993–1996 quadrennial, TOP contributed US$279 million to the IOC, accounting for 10.7% of its total revenue. However, TOP has grown in importance, supplying nearly 25% of the IOC's revenue over the last four quadrennials. The one major exception came during the 2012 London Games when thicketing revenue reached approximately US$1.24 billion, surpassing TOP's revenue sources. However, this revenue also went to London's OCOG.

The Fédération Internationale de Football Association (FIFA), founded in Paris in 1904, is the organization responsible for organizing and producing the most prominent international football tournaments, including the Football World Cup. Like the IOC, FIFA holds the status of legal entity: it is formed as an private, international, not-for-profit organization recognized by the Commercial Register under the Swiss Civil Code (FIFA 2019a). Although it conducts itself as an autonomous social space, it is associated with the Olympic movement, and – through the International Federation (IF) – it obeys the supreme authority of the IOC. FIFA's Statutes determine the organization's operations, as well as the operations of the tournaments it administers. According to these statues (ibid.), FIFA is organized mainly around five central powers:

a)   the Congress – the supreme legislative body that brings together representatives from all affiliated associations.[6] FIFA's Congress is responsible for electing the organization's president, approving and altering statutes and regulations, approving budgets and costs, and selecting the host country for the Football World Cup;

b)   the Council – FIFA's strategic and supervisory body, consisting of the president, eight vice president, and 28 members elected by the Continental Confederations.[7] FIFA's Council is responsible for matters beyond the purview of its Congress, including establishing regulatory norms in accordance with the Statutes governing FIFA's internal functioning, and choosing locations and dates for all FIFA Championships other than the World Cup;

c)   the President – FIFA's legal representative, responsible for implementing collective decisions, recommending the hiring or firing of the General Secretary to the Council, supervising the secretariat's work, and coordinating relations between FIFA and its associates;

d)   the general secretariat – FIFA's executive organ, directed by the Secretary General[8] and supervised by the Council, responsible for controlling the institution's costs and correspondences;

e)   the Bureau of the Council – consisting of FIFA's president and the six federation presidents, responsible for exercising the Council's functions when the Council is not in session.

In addition to these groups, FIFA also has its own judicial bodies (Disciplinary, Ethics, and Appeal Committees), as well as Audit and Compliance Committees, and nine other standing committees that support and assist the Council in specific areas. Like the IOC, FIFA can also construct ad hoc committees – either permanent or temporary – whose functions are established in the organization's statutes or through special rules. The Council is responsible for creating these committees.

FIFA has few clearly established rules; this, consequently, centralizes decision-making power in the president and the Council. The organization operates under the control of a select, drawn from its six Continental Confederations, who is responsible for nominating 36 of the Council's 37 members and, together with FIFA's president, forms the Bureau of the Council.

Although FIFA has adopted practices that, in many aspects, were different than the IOC's, by the 2010 Football World Cup in South Africa, the organization's finances were equally solid. Franco Carraro, Coordinator of the Internal Audit Committee, wrote in FIFA's 2010 Financial Report:

> With the four-year 2007–2010 period having now drawn to a close, the Internal Audit Committee regards FIFA's financial situation as very solid and pleasing. . . . In the space of just eight years, FIFA has been able to raise its reserves from negative figures to more than USD 1.2 billion.
>
> (Carraro, cited in FIFA 2011, p. 11)

Unlike the IOC, and defying many expectations, FIFA's profits continued to grow in the final cycle considered here (Table 2.2), reaching US$6.4 billion in the 2015–2018 quadrennial. FIFA's 2015 scandal (cf. Chapter One) did not diminish the institution's financial health. Alejando Domínguez, chair of the Finance Committee, highlighted this in a speech he gave while presenting the 2018 Financial Report: "Back in 2015, at the beginning of the cycle, few could have foreseen FIFA's resurgence and, indeed, some believed that our organisation was teetering on the brink" (FIFA 2019c, p. 9). Like the IOC, FIFA's main revenues come from broadcasting rights which represent close to half of the institution's proceeds, followed by marketing rights which account for a quarter of total revenues.

Table 2.2 FIFA's revenue in the last three cycles (in millions of US$)

Source	2009–2010	2011–2014	2015–2018
Television broadcasting rights	2,448	2,484	3,127
Marketing rights	1,097	1,629	1,660
Licensing rights	108	177	600
Hospitality/accommodation rights and ticket sales	120	185	712
Other revenues	135	1143	322
Total	**4,189**	**5,718**	**6,421**

Source: FIFA (2011, 2015, 2019c).

Despite similarities in their marketing programs, as well as in their financial results, FIFA and the IOC's strategies differ in certain aspects. FIFA's marketing relies primarily on symbolism relating to passion for football, whereas the IOC appeals to the ethical and moral values associated with the Olympic movement. Unlike FIFA, the IOC does not sell advertising space. The products that the IOC sells to its partners – with exclusivity guaranteed based on territory or product – is the symbolic association between that product and the non-commercial values of Olympism.

Whereas FIFA sells advertising space in stadiums and on television screens during the exhibition of football games, the IOC discovered that rejecting this type of commercialization constituted the Olympic brand's main aggregated value. This explains the importance that the IOC attributes to ensuring that no type of advertising – or any other manifestation other than the games – is presented on screens or inside venues during Olympic events. Michael Payne's introduction to the *Technical Manual on Brand Protection* makes this strategy clear.

> The *Olympic Charter* states that all Olympic events must take place in an environment that is free of commercial, political, religious, and ethnic influence, as well as any kind of publicity. The Olympic Movement's mandate on clean venues is necessary because clean venues: (a) preserve the integrity and image of the Olympic Games, (b) maintain an environment that is focused on sport competition, (c) ensure that the Olympic Games spectacle remains true to the philosophy of Olympism and to the Olympic spirit, (e) ensure that the core presentation of the Games is not tarnished by ancillary messages of any kind, (f) enhance the value of Olympic association, (g) help to protect the exclusive marketing rights of official Olympic partners.
>
> (Payne, cited in IOC n.d.a, p. 6)

In the case of scandals and denunciations of corruption, the IOC aims to identify a few guilty parties and establish punishment or expulsions quickly. FIFA, on the other hand, takes shelter in the aegis of anonymity guaranteed by Swiss legislation to allow those responsible to go unpunished until the situation becomes unsustainable (cf. Chapter One). This situation appears clearly in the case of the ISL: the IOC broke the exclusive marketing rights contract that it had maintained with the company since 1995 and has controlled closely every contract signed since then. FIFA, on the other hand, continued to centralize the sale of marketing rights to the ISL until the company went bankrupt in 2001. The resulting scandal reverberated throughout FIFA and affected some of the institution's principal figures.

Local promoters: NOCs, OCOGs, and national associations

As written in the 2019 Olympic Charter (IOC 2019a), National Olympic Committees (NOCs) retain the exclusive authority to represent their countries in the Olympic games and in other regional, continental, or global competitions sponsored by the IOC. NOCs, which have the mission of developing, promoting, and protecting the Olympic Movement in their respective countries, are responsible for selecting, organizing, and leading their countries' delegations in Olympic competitions and for providing them with equipment, transportation, and accommodations.

National Committees were first recognized under the IOC's 1920 statues, which established that "it is considered as a recognized National Committee, any Olympic Committee which is constituted by the member (s) of the International committee for the country in question or in agreement with them" (CIO 1920, p. 9). It was only in 1921, however, that the IOC delegated the responsibility of organizing the Olympic Games to the National Olympic Committee (NOC) of the country in which the host city was located. In this same text, another collective – the Organizing Committee of the Olympic Games (OCOG) – came into existence. Every NOC became responsible for creating an OCOG, sharing the mandate for organizing the Games with that OCOG, and dissolving it at the end of the event (CIO 1921, p. 8).

In assuming the duty of organizing the Olympics in conjunction with each other, the OCOG and NOC of the host country also took on the responsibility of providing the material conditions necessary for the realization of the Olympics. In addition, every NOC needed its own revenue sources, inasmuch as it was responsible for making possible the participation of its country's delegation in events promoted by the IOC, even though the host city's OCOG was responsible for reducing housing and transportation costs to the greatest extent possible. In order to carry out these functions, NOCs depended primarily on revenues from sponsors who – at that time – would pay for publicity during the Games, advertisements in official printed programs, and commercial billboards in competition and service venues (IOC 2019b).[9]

When the IOC first allowed the commercial use of the Olympic emblem, it delegated the task of administering it to each OCOG (IOC 1973). However, in addition to establishing the need for the IOC to authorize every use, it also prohibited use of the emblem in any country without the permission of the NOC responsible (IOC 1973, rule 53).

OCOGs were also responsible for negotiating broadcasting rights. Beginning with the 1948 London Games, the Organizing Committee attempted to extract revenue for the event's organization through the sale of broadcasting rights (cf. Chapter One). It was only in the 1958 Olympic Charter, however, that this sale became fully regulated. The OCOG became responsible for controlling negotiations, but these were subject to IOC approval. The IOC also determined the use of broadcasting revenues (IOC 1958, p. 30).

The 1966 Olympic Charter (IOC 1966) established that all profits from the Olympic Games would belong to the IOC rather than the organizing country's NOC, as had been established in 1949 (IOC 1949). However, until TOP was implemented, OCOGs and NOCs were still responsible for developing sponsorship and licensing programs and for controlling all associated contracts.

OCOGs' control of the sale of Olympic marketing rights – as well as their dependence on authorization from each country's NOC to use these rights outside the territory of the host country – imposed significant limits on the financial success of Olympic marketing. For sponsors who hoped to use the program internationally, this condition proved to be a significant hindrance: purchasing marketing rights became a drawn out and practically unviable task involving individual negotiations with NOCs from more than 160 countries (Pound 2006; Payne 2012). It was common, over the course of these negotiations, for NOCs to bargain with global sponsors and demand financing for local sports teams. In addition, each country's NOC could, within its own territory, sell commercial rights to competitors of the IOC's global sponsors.

In order to overcome this obstacle, TOP adopted the strategy of joining together all marketing rights belonging to the Olympic Movement – including the IOC, the Winter and Summer Olympics, and all NOCs – in an exclusive four-year packet. The IOC assumed sole responsibility for negotiating these rights and, later, for redistributing revenue to the Olympic Movement. Implementing this strategy, however, was not without conflicts. In addition to internal disputes (see Chapter One) and negotiations with broadcasters and sponsors, the IOC had to reconcile the interests of NOCs and OCOGs to which it had already conceded sufficient political capital to monopolize negotiations involving all of the Olympic Movement's economic capital.

As Payne (2012) and Pound (2006) note, the task of convincing NOCs from more than 160 countries to abdicate their powers in favor of the IOC demanded a great deal of caution. In addition to imposing an automatic loss of political, social, and symbolic capital, removing NOCs from sponsorship negotiations also involved questions relating to economic capital: would TOP be capable of attracting sufficient resources to make up for the revenue that each NOC had previously managed on its own? What risks did working with a heretofore-unknown marketing firm carry? Would resources be distributed on the basis of parity or on a proportional basis? In the case of proportional distribution, would the criteria be based on the number of athletes and medals belonging to a given NOC or on the NOCs' ability to attract sponsors?

The IOC was not inclined to establish TOP through brusque changes in the rules. After all, the fundamental role that NOCs played in maintaining the life of the Olympic Movement and the events it promoted throughout the world could not be ignored. In addition, NOCs are the main bodies responsible for encouraging competition between cities for this type of event. Therefore, the IOC opted to seek adhesion through the consent of the NOCs while also gradually inserting these changes into the Olympic Charter.

Groups adopted different strategies for each specific situation. Small NOCs with relatively unstructured marketing programs were the easiest to convince. In most of these cases, the IOC's offer to pay a minimal fee and to guarantee participation for each athlete sent to the 1988 Olympic Games surpassed these NOCs' individual ability to obtain sponsorship resources (Payne 2012). In the case of

NOCs that already had more structured marketing programs, the IOC negotiated individually based on each NOC's ability to attract sponsorship; in other words, entrepreneurship won out as the central criterion.

> We have had a great deal of difficulty explaining that this is a marketing program that bears a relationship not to the importance of a country within the Olympics Movement (in the form of the number of athletes who participate in the Games or the number of medals won), but only to the desirability of access to the various markets by commercial sponsors.
>
> (Pound 2006, p. 148)

The argument that NOCs could earn significantly more through negotiations centralized under the IOC, instead of individual negotiations, convinced most NOCs to adhere to the new structure. After intense negotiations, 154 out of 167 NOCs recognized by the IOC at the time[10] had joined TOP in time for the 1988 games (Payne 2012).

The United States Olympic Committee (USOC) – which held a strategic position, given that most probable sponsors were housed in its territory – was one of the most resistant NOCs. In addition to losing power, the USOC did not appreciate the idea of money from American companies financing Soviet athletes in the midst of the Cold War.

Although the USOC adhered to TOP, its ongoing dispute with the IOC carries into the present day and has only intensified in terms of broadcasting rights. With almost 50% of broadcasting revenues from television networks in the United States, the USOC has advocated for a greater share of revenues; it has even gone so far as to pressure the United States Congress to approve legislation to reestablish its control of marketing rights (Payne 2012). Internal difficulties at the USOC, however, favored the IOC's control. Currently, the IOC enjoys unquestionable hegemony within the Olympic Movement, although disputes continue.

Negotiating with OCOGs proved more difficult for the IOC than negotiating with NOCs had been. The loss of autonomy in the negotiation process was not the only reason for this difficulty. The IOC offered OCOGs 50% of TOP participation revenues, but in most cases, this represented less value than when OCOGs controlled marketing rights throughout the world. Although OCOGs retained domestic sponsorship rights, TOP's imposition of exclusivity in every product category prevented them from accepting sponsorships from the competitors of IOC sponsors, which had, in many cases, been an important source of revenue.

Although OCOGs were, on the whole, less satisfied than NOCs, their dissatisfaction was easier to manage. When a collective subject whose existence is temporary complicates business, carrying out business dealings beyond the limits of this subject's existence is sufficient to resolve any quarrels. This was precisely the strategy that the IOC adopted: it began to negotiate contracts for more than one event at a time, preferably before the choice of a given host city, and therefore, before the existence of the OCOG associated with that event. At the same time, the IOC gradually introduced rules in the Olympic Charter that made it impossible for a host OCOG to make its own claims on sponsorship rights. Since 2004, the rule governing the rights to the Olympic Games and all associated properties has emphasized the IOC's exclusive ownership of the event and of all associated information, especially "all rights relating to their organisation, exploitation, broadcasting, recording, representation, reproduction, access and dissemination in any form and by any means or mechanism whatsoever, whether now existing or developed in the future" (IOC 2004, p. 17). According to the Charter, the IOC also holds the power to establish criteria to license part or all of these rights, as it sees fit, in any territory, simply by communicating this licensing and by sharing part of the revenues with the respective OCOG. This content is featured in the 2019 Olympic Charter in an even more emphatic way (IOC 2019a).

Thus, the IOC has consolidated its hegemony over the Olympic Games in relation to locally acting institutions. In order to keep the Olympic Movement satisfied by compensating lost revenue to local promoters – and, at the same time, to continue promoting spectacular events – the IOC has progressively transferred some of the costs previously taken on by OCOGs and NOCs to the political authorities of the cities and countries responsible for organizing these events (cf. Chapter One).

Unlike the Olympic spectacle, disputes for commercial rights among institutions acting in different scales of production of football spectacle have always been practically nonexistent. FIFA centralizes its institutional power under its president; as such, the most obvious disputes in this field are always those relating to individual interests or roles.[11]

As FIFA's Statues (FIFA 2019a) establish, the Football World Cup is under FIFA's complete control, and football associations only retain proprietorship of the broadcasting and marketing rights of their own local events. When FIFA's president sees fit, he announces new programs for distributing resources among the three confederations controlling the Council, or increasing income for Associations, or perhaps increasing prize money for Football World Cup participants. Thus, FIFA manages to accommodate diverse interests and ratify all of its proposals via acclamation.

No general regulations govern the functioning of the Football World Cup's Local Organizing Committees.[12] As such, these committees retain sufficient autonomy to gather resources as they see fit as long as they do not threaten FIFA's exclusive sponsorship and broadcasting rights. In addition to local sponsorship, most of these committees adopt the strategy of seeking public financing from their host countries.

Economic capital

Considering this study's theoretical and methodological presuppositions, the commercial success of marketing programs adopted by institutions promoting sport spectacle cannot be attributed exclusively to entrepreneurs like Dassler,

Samaranch, Havelange, Payne, or Pound[13] whose actions would be unviable were it not for a set of favorable objective relationships. These relationships, in turn, are due to the restructuring of the global economy during the 1970s in an attempt to overcome the structural crises of capitalism, a restructuring for which the groundwork was first laid in the 1960s and which continues to the present day.

Among changes to the global economic, social, and political order, Harvey (1989) highlights the incessant search for accelerating time around capital, which holds a particularly important implication for the field under study here: namely, the intensification of the production and consumption of service goods, especially those that have a strictly ephemeral character, such as goods linked to entertainment and spectacle.[14] Harvey notes that the flow of information and vehicles propagating taste and culture play the roles of vital weapons in a competitive battle (Harvey 1989, p. 160). He emphasizes that, oftentimes, investing in the construction of an image can be as lucrative as investing in new industrial and machine-based plans (ibid., 288). When an image's value extrapolates that which is associated with its sale and instead begins to reflect on its capacity to earn capital, create fusions, gain advantages in relation to governmental politics, or even to change cultural values and produce visions of the world, advertising investments begin to consume ever-greater fractions of corporate budgets.

The production of sport spectacle offers perfect opportunities for such investments: on the one hand, "sport products" in search of financing and, on the other hand, "the cultural logic of late-stage capitalism" (Jameson 1992), which together create a market increasingly keen on investing in images and publicity. Two characteristics make sport spectacle especially attractive to this investment market: its strong association with symbolic values and its potential for almost instantaneous consumption.

Broadcasters

None of the 162,000 German viewers who watched the first reproductions of blurry images from the 1936 Berlin Games (IOC 2019b) could imagine the complexity and amplitude of relations that the IOC and FIFA would develop with televised broadcasting, especially after Dassler took over as the leader for this process. Indeed, even those responsible for the initial broadcasts could not fathom their future importance. Currently, the audience for the Olympic Games and the Football World Cup is half of the world's population (IOC 2019b; FIFA n.d.a).

As sole proprietor of all broadcasting rights for the Summer and Winter Olympic Games, the IOC is responsible for selling these rights to media companies throughout the world. Jacques Rogge,[15] IOC president between 2001 and 2013, understood the strategic role that this market played within the Olympic Movement and decided to create a Special Commission for Broadcasting Rights, which he personally oversaw during his presidency (Payne 2012; Rogge 2004).

Although the IOC aims to create ever more significant contracts for Olympic broadcasting rights, the institution understands that it must guarantee a policy based on making these images accessible to the greatest number of spectators possible. In order to guarantee this condition, the Olympic Charter establishes the following fundamental principal: "[T]he IOC takes all necessary steps in order to ensure the fullest coverage by the different media and the widest possible audience in the world for the Olympic" (IOC 2019a, rule 48, 90).

Figure 2.1 shows that revenue from broadcasting rights for the Olympic Games has grown exponentially since the near-bankruptcy of the IOC at the beginning of the 1980s. Whereas rights for the 1980 Olympics – the Summer Games in Moscow and Winter Games in Lake Placid – brought in US$108.7 million, the 2013–2016 quadrennial, which included the 2014 Sochi Winter Olympics and the 2016 Rio de Janeiro Summer Games, brought in US$4.157 billion in revenue.

Tables 2.1 and 2.2 demonstrate the importance of broadcasting rights for both the IOC and FIFA revenues in recent quadrennials. This, in turn, has given the television companies that control each spectacle's largest audience share the power to dictate rules, ranging from the timing of competitions to the location of sport venues as well as the aesthetic patterns of their surrounding areas.

With most of the global audience for the Olympic Games is concentrated in North America, especially in the United States, competition within this market is especially fierce. In the past five quadrennials, North American revenues have accounted for more than half of total broadcasting proceeds for the Olympic Games (see Table 2.3). Broadcasting rights for Europe are in a distant second place, accounting for approximately one quarter of the total, which in turn is roughly equivalent to the total of proceeds from television companies in all other countries.

Since 1988, when the IOC took direct control of negotiating broadcasting rights, the National Broadcasting Company (NBC) has always won contracts for broadcasting the Olympic Summer Games in the United States. US contracts for

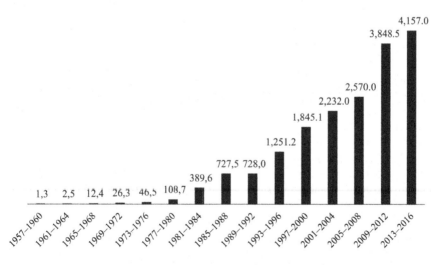

Figure 2.1 Quadrennial broadcasting revenues for Summer and Winter Olympic Games (in US$ millions)

Table 2.3 Broadcasting revenues for the Summer and Winter Olympic Games over the past five quadrennials (in US$ millions)

	North America	*Central America, South America and Caribbean*	*Europe*	*Asia*	*Middle East/ Africa*	*Oceania*	*Total*
1997–2000	1,124	14	422	208	12	65	1,845
2001–2004	1,397	21	514	233	13	54	2,232
2005–2008	1,579	34	578	274	25	80	2,570
2009–2012	2,154	106	848	575	41	126	3,850
2013–2016	2,119	326	941	663	46	61	4,157

Source: IOC (2019b).

* Certain African and Central Asian territories are included under figures for European revenues.

the Winter Games have alternated between the American Broadcasting Company (ABC) and Columbia Broadcasting System (CBS). When the IOC began to adopt the strategy of negotiating more than one event at the same time with contracts for the 2002 Winter Games – thereby eliminating interference from OCOGs – NBC assumed complete control over both the Winter and Summer Games (Payne 2012).

In 2008, in the midst of a recession in the United States, the IOC could not – as it had already done for some time – negotiate broadcasting rights for the 2016 Summer Olympics before the host city had been chosen. In order to assure two quadrennials of financial stability during this time of significant economic doubt, the IOC offered a single package of broadcasting rights for two Summer Games (2016 and 2020) and two Winter Games (2014 and 2018). NBC Universal offered US$4.38 billion, beating out Fox and Entertainment and Sports Programming Network (ESPN) and maintaining its exclusive ownership of Olympic broadcasting rights through 2020. In 2014, this contract was extended until 2032 for US$7.75 billion.

Europe is the IOC's second-most important source for broadcasting revenues. There, the European Broadcasting Union (EBU) – which represents that continent's primary public broadcasters – lost its almost 50-year monopoly to the SportFive marketing agencies in February 2009. SportFive controlled the sale of the 2014 Winter Games and the 2016 Summer Games, and redistributed the broadcasting rights in 40 European countries. Six countries that had previous agreements with the IOC were not included in these negotiations: the United Kingdom, Italy, Spain, Germany, France, and Turkey. In 2015, Discovery acquired pan-European transmission rights across all platforms for the 2018 and 2024 Olympics. Only Russia was not included in this €1.3 billion negotiation.

The sale of television broadcasting rights for the Football World Cup differs from the model of the Olympic Games to the degree that it presents greater regional dispersion, as data for the 2018 World Cup confirms (FIFA n.d.a). Although Asia is the region with the greatest share of audience by numbers (43.7% of the total), the greatest share of audience relative to population is South America (96.6%), followed by Europe (86.1%). The same applies to coverage time, which is greater in South America (29.3% of total coverage time), followed by Europe (18.8%). However, no single country has a share of audience concentration for FIFA events close to that of the United States for IOC events. As such, it is more difficult to centralize power in a single broadcasting network.

Unlike the IOC – which, in its aim to reach the greatest share of audience possible, prioritizes free-to-air TV – FIFA prioritized Pay TV during the 2018 Russia World Cup. Pay TV accounted for 61.9% of total coverage hours, whereas free-to-air accounted for only 38.1%. Audience numbers, however, represented a reversal: 83.7% of hours viewed were on free-to-air TV, whereas only 16.3% were on Pay TV (FIFA n.d.a).

The 2016 Rio Olympics represented a dividing point in Olympic broadcasting history, highlighting changes in media consumption habits. Digital coverage accounted for 243,000 available hours on social media, surpassing traditional television by more than 100%. It attracted more than 7 billion visualizations of Olympic videos (IOC n.d.b), thereby presenting the IOC with both new challenges and new possibilities for commercial exploitation.

The prominence of digital media is a point of convergence between the Football World Cup and the Olympic Games. The Chinese digital platform CCTV obtained 6.5 billion visualizations during the 2018 World Cup, revealing once again the importance of new strategies to address changing habits of consuming broadcasting.

Regardless of how broadcasting rights are divided, the companies who pay so dearly to transmit the events hope to captivate the largest and most long-lasting audiences possible and to profit as much as possible by selling advertisements or by reselling broadcasting rights to other networks. As such, they make certain demands that are met in accordance with the bargaining power that each interested party possesses.

The polemic construction of the Green Point Stadium in Cape Town, South Africa for the 2010 World Cup illustrates the decisive power that broadcasters wield in sport spectacle. To the detriment of two alternative, previously existing venues – the Newlands and Athlone stadiums – FIFA demanded that a new stadium be built on one of Cape Town's limited green spaces (Stuart & Bob 2009; Alegi 2008). As reported in the *Mail & Guardian Online* (Joubert 2007), a FIFA inspector visiting Athlone stadium told a member of the South African government that billions of viewers would not be interested in seeing slums and poverty on television. This statement led local leaders to withdraw their support for existing venues and to opt instead to build a new stadium in the beautiful Green Point neighborhood between the ocean and Table Mountain.

According to Payne (2012), Samaranch's successful 1987 proposal to the IOC to establishing a two-year interval between the Winter and Summer Olympics was also intended to facilitate negotiations for broadcasting rights. This was suggested by Dennis Swanson, then-president of ABC, who argued that paying for the broadcasts for two such large-scale events during the same year wiped out the financial reserves of the US publicity market.

These are only a few examples of the immeasurably decisive sway that broadcasters hold in producing sport spectacle; many others could be enumerated. The most convenient scheduling times for countries with the biggest audiences, or else the best markets for advertisers, can be determinant criteria in selecting host countries. Aesthetic patterns defined by economic capital can direct architecture, mass evictions, or social control around venues. Even the specific sports modalities offered in competitions can – as Bourdieu (1998) noted – result from patterns of taste within a market that finances broadcasting.

Sponsors

The IOC's strategy of bringing all of the Olympic Movement's marketing rights together in a single program has, since the 1980s, offered the business world a unique opportunity to invest in advertising with a global reach. In addition to increased sales, being associated with the Olympic brand allows companies to launch new technologies, demonstrate their accomplishments, and create new habits, customs, and ways of seeing the world.

When TOP was implemented in 1982, the IOC had already managed to bring together nine business "partners," raising US$175 million in the 1998–1991 quadrennial which included the 1988 Seoul Summer Olympics and the Calgary Winter Games (Payne 2012). TOP quickly became the primary reference in global sponsorship programs for FIFA as well as for the IOC. Sponsors became "partners," and brands – such as "the Olympic Games" and "Football" – became franchises. During the 2013–2016 quadrennial, which included the 2014 Sochi Winter Olympics and the 2016 Rio de Janeiro Summer Games, the IOC's revenues through TOP surpassed US$1 billion (Table 2.1). By the same token, FIFA's marketing revenues for the Football World Cup surpassed this value by the more than 50% during the 2011–2014 quadrennial, which included the 2014 Brazil World Cup[16] (Table 2.2).

In its aim to maintain and increase the success it had achieved with TOP, the IOC set a new challenge to itself: to discover what aspects of the Olympic brand were most valuable. The aims of businesses willing to pay millions of dollars to associate their names with the Olympic brand became a central question for the IOC (Payne 2012).

It was not difficult to identify the elements that compose the essence of Olympic branding, such as symbolism, strong images, and rituals. These elements, linked to Olympism since its beginnings, had been carefully reinforced for more than a century (see Chapter One). All that remained was for the IOC, together with the business world, to learn the best way to manage them. This was the IOC's intention when it undertook one of the world's largest market research studies: to understand what characteristics made the Olympic brand the most valuable on Earth, and what situations could threaten its value.

The results of the IOC's study reinforced the initial idea of a combination of distinct and seemingly opposed universes that could be associated with sport: on the one hand, ethical, moral, and humanitarian values; on the other, commercial dynamism and modernity. Based on this finding, the study proposed four synthesized expressions in a strategy to add to the brand's value: "the values of hope"; "dreams and inspiration"; "friendship and fair play"; and "joy in effort" (Payne 2012, p. 114). Later, these expressions were brought together in a widespread TV marketing campaign, consisting of advertisements that, using the slogan "Celebrate Humanity," showed emotionally weighted scenes of competitions with strong symbolic appeals, without clearly identifying either the entity or the event they represented. The intention was to emphasize the values of Olympism and to stoke the interest of major corporations in associating themselves with the Olympic brand. In the words of Dick Pound: "What we are selling, what sponsors and broadcasters wanted, and what the public demanded, were precisely these ethical values that differentiate the Olympics from professional entertainment sports" (Pound 2006, p. 16).

Just as the IOC's study had revealed the values of Olympism as the most potentially valuable assets that the Olympic brand could offer to sponsors, it also revealed elements that could be undesirable to businesses' reputations, as well as situations that could expose investments to risks. For example, it became clear that "badly managed" advertising campaigns, or associating Olympism with products considered to be "incompatible with the Olympic spirit" – such as tobacco, alcoholic beverages, or intimate hygiene products – could make the brand appear banal. In this sense, the process of selecting partners and forms of utilization for the Olympic brand became subject to increasingly rigorous and regulated criteria.

Based on the study's findings, the IOC developed strategies to assure the reliability of each business and to guarantee exclusive rights. "Partners" were not inclined to invest their money in situations in which they felt that these rights were threatened (Pound 2006, p. 157). Among various concerns that could put relations with partners at risk, those related to so-called "ambush marketing" stood out.

> Official Olympic marketing partners provide substantial resources to the entire Olympic Family, while at the same time promoting the ideals of Olympism. Consequently, they, and no other commercial entities, should benefit from their Olympic involvement. Ambush marketing occurs when an unauthorised commercial entity implies an association with the Olympic Movement without a marketing agreement with an appropriate Olympic.
>
> (IOC n.d.a, p. 13)

FIFA, equally concerned with guaranteeing its own financial wellbeing, also considered it crucial to guarantee its partners exclusive marketing rights.

> Ambush marketing can be defined as prohibited marketing activities which try to take advantage of the huge interest and high profile of an event by creating a commercial association and/or seeking promotional exposure without

the authorisation of the event organizer. . . . The reason that FIFA considers prohibited marketing as a priority in its brand protection work is that it puts FIFA's commercial programme directly at risk by trying to devalue official sponsorship.

(FIFA n.d.b, n.p.)

As Payne (2012) notes, the success of the IOC's marketing program was not due to expanding the number of associated businesses, but rather reducing them to a select group of partners who were ever more demanding in relation to returns on their investments. One of the factors that Payne points to in explaining TOP's success is the renewal of 90% of its contracts, which implies maintaining an almost constant group of partner businesses.

Thirteen businesses are TOP partners for the 2020 Tokyo Summer Games: Coca-Cola, Daw, GE, Samsung, Panasonic, Omega, P&G, Atos, Visa, Alibaba Group, Toyota, Intel, and Bridgestone. Of these, this first nine have been partners since the 2012 London Olympics. Eight of the Tokyo partners have already signed contracts, together with Alianz, for the 2024 Paris Games, and five have guaranteed their partnerships through the 2028 Los Angeles Summer Olympics. McDonald's is the only partner from the 2016 Rio de Janeiro Olympics that will not be present in Tokyo: in 2017, it cancelled its contract with the IOC, originally scheduled through 2020, thereby breaking a partnership of almost 40 years.

The Football World Cup is not significantly different. Currently, FIFA has six commercial partners: Adidas, Coca-Cola, Hyundai-Kia Motors, Visa, Qatar Airways, and Wanda Group. The first four were also partners in the 2010 and 2014 World Cups in South Africa and Brazil, respectively. Only two of the partners from these two events – Emirates and Sony – did not retain their contracts for the 2018 World Cup in Russia. In addition, two of FIFA's partners – Coca-Cola and Visa – are also partners in the IOC's TOP program.

FIFA recommends giving advertising preference to its sponsors during official World Cup broadcasts and gives them the right to bar commercials from their competitors thereby making the FIFA television universe even more restrictive. However, FIFA does not have such rigorous criteria as the IOC for choosing partnerships associated with its brand. For example, the official partnership between Budweiser and FIFA during the 2014 World Cup was the subject of polemical debates. Pressured by Ambev – the distribution company that owns the Budweiser brand – FIFA demanded that Brazil's Congress permit the sale of alcoholic beverages inside stadiums, even though this practice is normally forbidden in the country.

If the product that FIFA and the IOC sell their partners consists of the exclusive rights to use their brands within a certain space, the value of contracts with these organizations is directly related to their ability to guarantee that this exclusivity will not be violated. Such guarantees imply measures and rules of prevention that almost always extend FIFA and the IOC's reach, affecting the lives of inhabitants of host cities, as we will see in the second part of this book.

Cultural capital

The exercise of power across different forms of social organization has been a recurring object of study for thinkers throughout history. Although these reflections are derived from distinctly different perspectives, many thinkers have pointed to a strong relation between knowledge and conditions that make the maintenance or transformation of a given order of domination viable. Gramsci (1971), for example, sees the true force of a system of domination as residing not in the violence of the dominant class or the coercive power of its state-sponsored apparatus, but rather in the acceptance by dominated people of a conception of the world belonging to those who dominate them. He attributes great importance to culture, ideology, and politics as fundamental dimensions of power relations among social classes. Bourdieu (1991), meanwhile, sees power as related to classificatory systems that are accepted as legitimate, and, consequently, the struggles to define these systems. Foucault (1977) shows how, through a genealogy of power and knowledge, there is no neutral knowledge: all knowledge is political precisely because it is formed through power relations.

In recent decades, a supposedly rational and objective knowledge of social problems has been activated so as to promote the discourse of "consensual" solutions that legitimate authoritarian postures of public management within the molds of neoliberal thinking. Numerous authors have criticized the role of experts in constructing discourses that, in the name of consensus in discussions relating to territory, legitimate a radical substitution of political space by business space. Such critics include Žižek (1998, 1999a, 1999b), Rancière (1995, 2001), and Swyngedouw (2010).[17]

Three specific types of competence have been mobilized in relations between the production of sport spectacle and the production of the city in order to legitimate such strategies. First, a type of cultural capital is triggered within the field in which theories and practices of urban planning are produced. After all, sustaining the aims of cities that compete to host mega-events depends on an expertise capable of representing a dominant reality in which attracting investments is the only way to confront the consequences of globalization. This type of expertise, which helps to convert the attraction of mega-events into a political project, will be examined further in Chapter Four.

Within the field in which sport spectacle is produced, two other kinds of expertise are triggered so that these spectacles occur in accordance with the patterns expected by the institutions that promote them, as well as their partners. A first group of competencies acts to elaborate the candidature project, whereas the second group is dedicated to lobbying the electoral college of the IOC on behalf of candidates. However, these players have not always participated in the game. Reexamining some of Bourdieu's (1993) provocations, it is worth investigating when and under what conditions these subjects began to exist in a dominant position within the field; in other words, when and how they began to acquire the power to define results.

Although the presence of experts had already featured in the production of sport spectacle, the constitution of an international network specifically specializing in producing mega-events only became evident beginning with the 2000 Summer Olympics in Sydney, with the creation of the Transfer of Olympic Knowledge (TOK) program. Created through the Sydney Organizing Committee for the Olympic Games (SOCOG), as well as other entities and businesses connected to that event, the TOK program's objective was to teach how to host successfully an Olympics "of excellence." There are indicators that the crisis surrounding the 1996 Atlanta Olympics (cf. Chapter One) may have inspired this initiative.[18]

The IOC also created an independent company called Olympic Games Knowledge Services (OGKS) with the goal of sustaining TOK. Created in 2002 and based in Switzerland, the OGKS was first directed by Craig McLatchey, the former secretary general of the Australian Olympic Committee. One of his first tasks was to conduct a seminar in Brazil regarding candidature for the Olympic Games. This seminar – the first of its kind in the world – was proposed by the Brazilian Olympic Committee (BOC) and resulted in Rio de Janeiro's candidature to host the 2012 Summer Games. At the same time that the OGKS was created, the IOC also encouraged the creation of Events Knowledge Services (EKS), a group whose sole owner was also McLatchey. The EKS was the first consulting business to specialize exclusively in mega-event production.

In 2005, the IOC decided to concentrate control of the transfer of knowledge entirely within itself, substituting the OGKS with the Olympic Games Knowledge Management (OGKM) program, which works with OCOGs and candidate cities to transfer knowledge and assess candidatures (IOC 2016).

In parallel to the internal structure created by the IOC, a network of consultants began to develop in every city that had hosted the Olympics. This network was present during candidature processes as well as during the organization of the event itself. Tables 2.4 and 2.5 show how some of the main groups of consultants acted in cities that were selected to host recent editions of the Summer Games as well as these consultants' links to the IOC. Table 2.4 focuses on the group of specialists who worked on candidature projects and on preparing cities to receive the Olympic Games. These include specialists in urban design, installation architecture, governance, information technology, marketing, security, and finances, all of whom began to act especially prominently beginning with the 2000 Summer Olympics. Table 2.5 shows lobbyists dedicated to creating a brand of candidatures for cities in order to capture votes in the IOC's restrictive electoral college. This group promotes positive images of selected cities for members of the IOC and the media and prepares discourses and settings for making persuasive presentations during the selection process. The 2020 Agenda (IOC 2014) proposed reducing consultants' activity, but it did not succeed in diminishing their role in the process of selecting host cities for the 2024 Summer Olympics.

It is worth noting that both Tables 2.4 and 2.5 only examine cities selected to host the Summer Olympic Games. If failed candidates had also be considered, we would see that, since they entered the market, none of these businesses have been absent from any competitions to host the Olympics. It is also important to observe

Table 2.4 Principal consultants for Olympic Host City projects since 2000 and their connections to the IOC

Consultants	IOC	Sydney 2000	Athens 2004	Beijing 2008	London 2012	Rio 2016	Tokyo 2020	Paris 2024	LA 2028
PwC	•	•	•	•	•	•			
MI Associates	•	•	•	•	•	•			
Hill Knowlton Strategies	•		•	•	•				
Atos	•		•	•	•	•	•	•	•
EKS	•	•	•	•	•	•			
John Baker		•	•	•		•			
Intelligent Risks Pty Ltd		•	•	•	•	•	•		
Simon Balderstone	•	•	•	•	•	•	•		
Diane Bernstein	•	•	•	•	•		•		•
Panos Protopsaltis	•		•	•	•	•	•		•
McKinsey					•	•			
Populous		•			•	•		•	
AECON					•	•			•

Source: Created by the author based on information available on official company and IOC websites.

Table 2.5 Principal lobbying consultants for Olympic Host Cities since 2000 and their connections to the IOC

Consultants	IOC	Sydney 2000	Athens 2004	Beijing 2008	London 2012	Rio 2016	Tokyo 2020	Paris 2024	LA 2028
PwC	•	•	•	•	•	•			
MI Associates	•	•	•	•	•	•			
Françoise Zweifel	•				•	•	•		
Mike Lee (Vero Communications)	•				•	•		•	
Nick Varley (Seven46)					•	•	•	•	
Michel Payne	•				•	•			
Scott Givens (FiveCurrents)	•				•	•			
Jon Tibbs (JTA)			•	•					•
Doug Arnot					•	•			•

Source: Created by the author based on information available on official company and IOC websites.

that host cities for the 2024 and 2028 Summer Olympics were chosen through a single selection process, thereby making it impossible for any consulting company to work on two candidacies at the same time.

In Table 2.5, we can see that – with the exception of JTA, active since the 2004 Athens Olympics – firms that concentrate on lobbying or candidacies mostly began to act during the 2012 London Games. Because these companies exercise their services during the candidature period, their work can be considered as beginning at least seven years before a given event, which is the interval between the selection of a host city and the actual Olympic Games. In other words, most of their activity began in 2005.

This insistent presence of the same consultant groups across all candidacies with any chance of success – together with normatization under the IOC and FIFA – has produced such standardized candidate files that selection has become almost impossible and is based exclusively on technical criteria.

In this way, private institutions (Candidature Committees) coordinate candidature projects based on the discourse of competence of a select group of experts, often without regard for social necessities and with the objective of reconciling the interests of those who support them.[19] These projects are guaranteed and agreed upon through contracts with political authorities before those who are truly affected (namely, the communities involved) perceive the full dimension of the commitments that their political leaders have made.

Concerned with promoting candidacies and validating action strategies, the IOC has wagered increasingly on the transfer of knowledge. The 2003 Study Commission on the Olympic Games, the objective of which was "to analyse the scale and scope of the Games" (Pound 2003), made eight relevant recommendations. These ranged from imposing standardized management across certain areas, such as planning and technology, to suggesting the development of long-term relationships with specific technology providers. These recommendations restricted the consultant market even further and guaranteed monopolies on a specific venues market to a select group of providers. This monopoly is reflected in these providers' negotiations with host cities and, consequently, in rising event costs, although the justification for the 2003 study was exactly the opposite: namely, cost reduction.

The existence of this network of specialists has, therefore, exercised a double role of assuring the promotion of competitions for mega-events among cities and guaranteeing that these events take place according to the standards and requirements established by the IOC and its "partners." Acting together, they not only possess the power to influence the elections of host cities; they also define these cities' projects.

In addition, the strengthening of this field of consultancy opens another powerful possibility of the movement of capitals relating to the Olympic Movement; namely, the consultancy market which can culminate in situations in which consultants become "partners." Such is the case of Atos, an Information Technology firm that, having consulted for the organization of the Barcelona Summer Olympics, guaranteed its contract as an official TOP "partner" from the organization of the 2004 Athens Games to the 2020 Tokyo Summer Olympics. Atos also consults potential Football World Cup host cities, having worked with the winning candidates Germany for the 2006 Cup, South Africa 2010, and Brazil 2014.

Partial considerations

Although FIFA and the IOC obtain them through different means, both organizations' revenues have been sufficient to attend to the interests of institutions involved in the promotion of sport spectacle. However, these revenues appear almost insignificant when compared to the investments demanded of the production of cities for these outcomes.

In this sense, both FIFA and the IOC have emphatically adopted the strategy of transferring financial responsibility away from organizers to the local and national governments responsible for hosting (cf. Chapter One). It is here that the convergence between the field of producing sport spectacle and the field of producing the neoliberal city converge. In seeking out agents capable of guaranteeing physical and operational conditions for the realization of spectacles, the institutions responsible for the production of sport mega-events find bureaucratic apparatuses in the host cities and countries to carry out these feats in exchange for media exposure and the legitimization of their capability to host major projects which, under normal circumstances, would have difficulty being approved, as we shall see in the second part of this book.

In order to sustain the billion-dollar revenues shown in Tables 2.1 and 2.2, FIFA and the IOC depend on a kind of clockwork moved by three basic "gears": broadcasters who seek exclusive transmission rights in every territory; "partners" who seek exclusive sponsorship in their product category; and cities who gain exclusivity by hosting the events. Maintaining the value of the brand (whether of the Olympics or FIFA) and thereby gaining from their relationship with the institution that owns the brand depends on the constant and balanced turning of these gears. The more valuable the brand, the greater the dispute will be among cities to associate themselves with it so as to maintain a position in the center of the global media. As such, a valuable brand increases the bargaining power of the institution that owns it as well as its ability to make demands of the cities competing to associate themselves with it. Subsequently, the production of the event itself becomes even more spectacular. The more spectacular the production of the event, the more efficiently it will meet the expectations of its "partners": the dispute for marketing rights and exclusive broadcasting rights will be greater, bringing in a higher number of spectators, which, in turn, will further increase the value of the brand, and so on. If one of these gears should stall, the others will likely follow suit, threatening to collapse the entire clockwork. This is clear in the IOC's concern with cancelled candidatures in the recent selection processes for Summer and Winter Olympic host cities.

Concern in maintaining a smoothly running clockwork can also be seen in the IOC's policy of always entering into contacts with open television channels, even when this implies losing greater opportunities for income through contracts with closed channels. This policy both strengthens the IOC's institutional discourse – in which it presents itself as democratic and dedicated to providing free access to its events – and also keeps the clockwork turning. Restricting the number of spectators means reducing the reach of the spectacle's marketing and, consequently, the projection of host cities and their marketing partners. This, in turn, implies a reduced dispute for these exclusive rights, thereby reducing the value of the Olympic brand in each of these areas.

Within disputes relating to the production of sport spectacle, the great capacity for action among marketing "partners" stands out. In addition to their direct actions within the field of production of sport spectacle through sponsorship programs, they also have the capacity for indirect action, inasmuch as they dictate the rules of the field of production of televised spectacle and may even act in the consulting field. These conditions bestow a special power to this sub-field which acts in the economic field.

Notes

1 Portions of this chapter first appeared in the book *O Poder dos Jogos e os Jogos de Poder: Os interesses em campo na produção da cidade para o espetáculo esportivo* (de Oliveira 2015), published by Editora UFRJ. The English translation is by Raphael Soifer.
2 Here, I alert readers to the constant possibility of these forms of capital being converted into other forms.
3 Currently, the IOC's rules establish conditions for the recognition of outside institutions (IOC 2019a), but statutes published as early as 1920 already determined conditions for the recognition of NOCs (CIO 1920).
4 The criteria for the composition and election of the Executive Committee has been subjected to successive alterations in accordance with disputes and changes in the correlation of forces acting in the IOC. One example of these disputes was the process surrounding Samaranch's final reelection, which resulted in a change in the Olympic Charter (IOC 1995), increasing the age limit for mandatory retirement from 75 to 80 years of age. Currently, a member of the Executive Committee is elected to a four-year mandate with the possibility of only one further consecutive reelection. After serving two terms, a member can only run for the Executive Board again after a two-year leave. However, this leave period is not necessary when said member is running for IOC president (IOC 2019a). The retirement age for members is set at 70 years, but the possibility of an extension to 74 years exists.
5 Until 1999, the IOC president was elected to an initial eight-year mandate and could be thereafter reelected to four-year terms. It was only in the second of two Olympic Charters, published in 1999 (IOC 1999), that reelection was limited to a single four-year mandate.
6 All associations responsible for organizing and supervising football in their respective countries can become FIFA members after going through the admission process (FIFA 2019a). Requirements for admission include presenting an organizational statute in accordance with FIFA's Statutes as well as agreeing to FIFA rules and guidelines. As of 2019, FIFA had 211 associates.
7 FIFA members on the same continent are organized into confederations.
8 FIFA's Secretary General, appointed by the president and approved by the Executive Committee, joins the organization by means of a contract governed by the laws of private employment.
9 To understand the IOC's different advertising strategies over time, see Chapter One.
10 Currently, the IOC recognizes the existence of 206 National Olympic Committees.
11 See, especially, Jenning (2007).
12 For example, the Social Contract of Brazil's Local Organising Committee for the World Cup was registered with the Rio de Janeiro state chamber of commerce in 2008 as a limited society controlled by two partners: the Brazilian Football Confederation (CBF), and its then-president, Ricardo Teixeira. No official information about this company or its organizational format was made available to the public.

13 The personal trajectories of Host Dassler, João Havelange, Antonio Samaranch, Michael Payne, and Richard Pound are elaborated in Chapter One.
14 See also Debord (2002).
15 The Belgian doctor and count, Jacques Rogge, succeeded Samaranch as IOC president in July 2001, a role in which he remained until September 2013. His own sporting activities began in yachting, an area in which he competed in the 1968, 1972, and 1976 Olympics. Rogge was president of the Belgian Olympic Committee between 1989 and 1992 and of the European Olympic Committee between 1989 and 2001. He became a member of the IOC in 1991. Rogge was president of the Olympic Games Coordination Commissions for the 2000 Sydney Summer Games and the 2004 Athens Summer Games. From the time he joined the IOC, he grew close to Samaranch and enjoyed Havelange's support. In 1998, based on Samaranch's recommendation, he joined the IOC's executive board. Samaranch's support of Rogge in the 2001 IOC presidential elections disappointed Dick Pound (Pound 2006), who, as leader of the marketing program that revolutionized the IOC, expected to be seen as Samaranch's natural successor. In Pound's opinion, his opposition to increasing the IOC's retirement age from 75 to 80 years of age – an increase that made Samaranch's final reelection possible – contributed to Samaranch's decision not to support his candidacy. See also Rogge (2004).
16 FIFA's final 2010 report (FIFA 2011) does not distinguish between revenues from global partners and from domestic sponsors.
17 The territorialization of practices relating to the production of sport mega-events will be explored in Part Two.
18 This statement takes as evidence both temporal simultaneity and the emphasis that the IOC gives to the necessity of controlling host cities after its negative evaluation of the 1996 Atlanta Games.
19 In addition to interests in the camp of production of sport spectacle, which have already been presented in this chapter, other interests relating to the production of the city will be addressed in Chapter Four.

References

Alegi, P 2008, "A Nation to Be Reckoned with: The Politics of World Cup Stadium Construction in Cape Town and Durban, South Africa", *African Studies*, 67.3, pp. 397–422.
Bourdieu, P 1991, *Language and Symbolic Power*, trans. G Raymond & M Adamsom, Polity Press, Cambridge.
Bourdieu, P 1993, "How Can One Be a Sports Fan?" in S During (ed) *The Cultural Studies Reader*, Routledge, London and New York, pp. 339–356.
Bourdieu, P 1998, *On Television*, trans. PP Ferguson, The New Press, New York.
Bourdieu, P & Wacquant, LJD 1992, *An Invitation to Reflexive Sociology*, The University of Chicago Press, Chicago.
Comité International Olympic (CIO) 1920, *Statuts*, IOC, Lausanne.
Comité International Olympic (CIO) 1921, *Statuts: reglements et protocole de la célébration des Olympiades Modernes et des Jeux Olympiques Quadriennaux*, IOC, Lausanne.
Debord, G 2002, *Society of the Spectacle*, Black & Red, Detroit.
Dezalay, Y & Garth, BG 1996, *Dealing in Virtue: International Commercial Arbitration and the Construction of a Transnational Legal Order*, The University of Chicago Press, Chicago.
Fédération Internationale de Football Association (FIFA) 2011, *Financial Report 2010*, FIFA, Zurich.
Fédération Internationale de Football Association (FIFA) 2015, *Financial Report 2014*, FIFA, Zurich.

Fédération Internationale de Football Association (FIFA) 2019a, *FIFA Statutes: June 2019 Edition*, FIFA, Zurich.

Fédération Internationale de Football Association (FIFA) 2019b, *Financial Report 2018*, FIFA, Zurich.

Fédération Internationale de Football Association (FIFA) 2019c, *Financial and Governance Report 2015*, FIFA, Zurich.

Fédération Internationale de Football Association (FIFA) n.d.a, *2018 FIFA World Cup Russia™: Global Broadcast and Audience Summary*, FIFA, Zurich, viewed 15 September 2019, <https://resources.fifa.com/image/upload/2018-fifa-world-cup-russia-global-broadcast-and-audience-executive-summary.pdf?cloudid=njqsntrvdvqv8ho1dag5>

Fédération Internationale de Football Association (FIFA) n.d.b, *Brand Protection: Prohibited Marketing Activities (Ambush Marketing)*, viewed 15 October 2019, <www.fifa.com/about-fifa/marketing/brand-protection/prohibited-marketing-activities.html>

Foucault, M 1977, *Discipline and Punish: The Birth of the Prison*, Random House, New York.

Gramsci, A 1971, *Selections from the Prison Notebooks*, eds. Q Hoare & GN Smith, International Publishers, New York.

Harvey, D 1989, *The Condition of Postmodernity: An Enquiry into the Origins of Cultural Change*, Blackwell Publishers, Oxford.

International Olympic Committee (IOC) 1946, *Olympic Rules*, IOC, Lausanne.

International Olympic Committee (IOC) 1949, *Olympic Rules*, IOC, Lausanne.

International Olympic Committee (IOC) 1958, *The Olympic Games: Fundamental Principles Rules and Regulations General Information*, IOC, Lausanne.

International Olympic Committee (IOC) 1966, *The Olympic Games: Fundamental Principles Rules and Regulations General Information*, IOC, Lausanne.

International Olympic Committee (IOC) 1973, *Olympic Rules and Regulations*, IOC, Lausanne.

International Olympic Committee (IOC) 1995, *Olympic Charter: In Force as from 15th June 1995*, IOC, Lausanne.

International Olympic Committee (IOC) 1999, *Olympic Charter: In Force as from 12th December 1999*, IOC, Lausanne.

International Olympic Committee (IOC) 2004, *Olympic Charter: In Force as from 1 September 2004a*, IOC, Lausanne.

International Olympic Committee (IOC) 2014, *Olympic Agenda 2020: The Strategic Roadmap for the Future of the Olympic Movement*, IOC, Lausanne.

International Olympic Committee (IOC) 2016, *Factsheet Olympic Games Knowledge Management (OGKM)*, IOC, Lausanne, viewed 10 July 2019, <https://stillmed.olympic.org/media/Document%20Library/OlympicOrg/Factsheets-Reference-Documents/OGKM/Factsheet-OGKM-July-2016.pdf>

International Olympic Committee (IOC) 2019a, *Olympic Charter: In Force as from 26 June 2019*, IOC, Lausanne.

International Olympic Committee (IOC) 2019b, *Olympic Marketing: Fact File 2019 Edition*, IOC, Lausanne.

International Olympic Committee (IOC) n.d.a, *Brand Protection: Technical Manual on Brand Protection*, IOC, viewed 15 September 2019, <www.gamesmonitor.org.uk/files/Technical_Manual_on_Brand_Protection.pdf>

International Olympic Committee (IOC) n.d.b, *Marketing Report: Rio 2016*, IOC, Lausanne.

Jameson, F 1992, *Postmodernism, or, the Cultural Logic of Late Capitalism*, Duke University Press, Durham.

Jenning, A 2007, *Foul!: The Secret World of Fifa*, Harper Collins, New York.

Joubert, P 2007, "Green Point Gamble", *Mail & Guardian Online*, 12 January, viewed June 2010, <https://mg.co.za/article/2007-01-12-green-point-gamble>

Payne, M 2012, *Olympic Turnarounds: How the Olympic Games Stepped Back from the Brink of Extinction to Become the World Best Known Brand*, Infinite Ideas Limited, Oxford.

Pound, RW 2003, *Olympic Games Study Commission: Report to the 115th IOC Session*, IOC, Prague, viewed 3 June 2019, <https://stillmed.olympic.org/Documents/Reports/EN/en_report_725.pdf>

Pound, RW 2006, *Inside the Olympics: A Behind-the-Scenes Look At the Politics, the Scandals, and the Glory of the Games*, John Wiley & Sons, Toronto.

Rancière, J 1995, *La mésentente politique et philosophie*, Editions, Paris.

Rancière, J 2001, "Ten Theses on Politics", *Theory & Event*, 5.3.

Rogge, J 2004, *The Olympic Games: Athens to Athens 1896–2004*, Orion Publishing Co, London.

Stuart, K & Bob, U. 2009, "Venue Selection and the World Cup: A Case Study of Cap Town", in U Pillay, R Tomlinson & O Brass (eds) *Development and Dreams: The Urban Legacy of the 2010 Football World Cup*, Human Science Research Council (HSRC), Cape Town.

Swyngedouw, E 2010, "Post-Democratic Cities for Whom and for What", in *Regional Studies Association Annual Conference*, Pecs, Hungary, May.

Žižek, S 1998, "For a Leftist Appropriation of the European Legacy", *Journal of Political Ideologies*, 3.1, pp. 63–78.

Žižek, S 1999a, *The Ticklish Subject: The Absent Centre of Political Ontology*, Verso, London and New York.

Žižek, S 1999b, "Carl Schmitt in the Age of Post-Politics", in C Mouffe (ed) *The Challenge of Carl Schmitt*, Verso, London.

3 The rules of the game[1]

Introduction

In making an analogy of play to create the concept of a field, Bourdieu and Wacquant (1992) highlights certain points of approximation between the two. The field, like a card game, includes wagers, which are produced through competition between players. It also includes trump cards, which prevail over other cards and change in relative value in each game. These trump cards would be equivalent to different types of capital, which have different values attached to them in each field or at different times within the same field. Here, too, certain cards operate that are effective in all games, even though their relative value is determined by the type of game; as such, they are the fundamental kinds of capital, both economic and cultural. However, in constructing this analogy, Bourdieu makes the caveat that, inasmuch as the field is not the deliberate product of a creative action, the "rules" that apply within a field are neither explicit nor codified. Players in the field agree to join simply in order to play rather than by means of a contract.

The existence of rules constitutes a very important factor that is common to all concepts of play. "All play has its rules. They determine what 'holds' in the temporary world circumscribed by play" (Huizinga 1980, p. 12). When the field constituting an object of study is that in which sport spectacle is produced, play is no longer merely an analogy; instead, it is the basic element of that field's articulation. In this case, the principle of rules within play becomes one of the few truths presented as unshakeable; this principle therefore takes on such symbolic force that it spills over from inside the field of production of sport spectacle into the entire network of this field's relations.

As in games, rules in the field of production of sport spectacle are absolute and indisputable. Some rules govern the functioning of each game, while others regulate the lives of athletes or other players who act in them, and still others determine the relationship of the field to other fields, including the field of production of the city. Everyone involved with the game must accept these rules in order to enter into the "field."

As seen in Chapter One, the rules that govern the field of sport spectacle did not always exist. They were carefully constructed and modified by disputes carried out over the course of more than a century. Today, they constitute a sophisticated system expressed through the Olympic Charter of the International Olympic Committee (IOC), the Statues of the Fédération Internationale de Football Association (FIFA), and a network of recommendations, manuals, codes of conduct, guarantees, contracts, and even specific tribunals. At the same time in which these rules guarantee the field's autonomy, they also serve as mechanisms to conserve the position of dominant groups within these bodies.

In agreement with Elias (1986), I do not consider rules to be static. Instead, they are produced so as to attend to determined functions then transformed when these functions are lost or when the rules no longer apply to them. As such, this chapter seeks to map the principle rules and instances of arbitration governing the production of sport spectacle. The perspective established in this chapter privileges the analysis of judicial instruments that make this field's control over the city viable.

Rules and arbitration that apply to the entire Olympic Movement

As members of the Olympic Movement, the IOC and FIFA maintain certain judicial instruments, even though these instruments were created by the IOC and continue to function under its control. Such is the case, for example, of the Olympic Charter, the Court of Arbitration for Sport (CAS), and the World Anti-Doping Code (WADA). In carrying out their principle tournaments – namely, the Olympic Games and the Football World Cup – the IOC and FIFA produce another network of specific rules.

Olympic Charter

The *Olympic Charter* represents the codification of the fundamental principles of Olympism and of the rules adopted by the International Olympic Committee. It oversees the organization, actions, and functioning of the Olympic Movement and establishes conditions for the realization of the Olympic Games. Among other aspects, the Olympic Charter functions as a statute for the IOC and establishes rights and obligations in relations between the three principal constituents of the Olympic Movement – the IOC, International Federations (IFs), and National Olympic Committee (NOCs) – as well as between these constituents and the Organizing Committees for the Olympic Games (OCOGs).

The Olympic Charter was first published in 1908, entitled "Annuaire du Comité Internacional Olympique." Currently, the term "Olympic Charter" is used indiscriminately in reference to all editions, although it first appeared as the publication's general title in 1978 (IOC 1978). Some earlier editions are divided into different documents instead of forming a single body; the names of these documents include "Charter of the Olympic Games," "Olympic Rules and Regulations," "Statutes of the International Olympic Committee," and "Fundamental Principles."

Since the 2004 edition (IOC 2004), the Olympic Charter has been organized into six chapters. As its contents have grown increasingly generalized, it has undergone few alterations in recent editions and has taken on an almost constitutional character. Questions that were highlighted in previous editions – such as anti-doping measures or details of electoral processes of IOC constituents – have since been restricted to specific documents. Within the Olympic Charter's recurring contents, certain aspects stand out, such as the supreme authority of the IOC, its power over countries and cities, and the protections and rights of usage associated with the Olympic brand as well as more general pronunciations relating to the selection and responsibilities of host cities.

Especially noteworthy among the small changes that the principal document has undergone in recent years are those relating to dispute resolution. These changes reinforce the ample powers already conferred to the IOC, its Executive Board, and the CAS. Other rules emphasize the financial responsibilities of host cities and exempt the IOC from any such responsibilities in the case that hosting rights are revoked for any given event. The Charter has also incorporated new discourses, such as those relating to the environment (IOC 1991) and to sustainable development (IOC 1996), both of which took on more significant repercussions beginning with the 2008 Olympic Games, and to the legacy of the Games (IOC 2004), an aspect that only began to feature in candidature documents for the 2012 Olympics. Beginning in 2016, Olympic Charters also began to feature certain recommendations for the 2020 Olympic Agenda. After the simultaneous announcements of Paris and Los Angeles as hosts for the 2024 and 2028 Games, respectively, new changes were incorporated into the 2019 Olympic Charter (IOC 2019).

All of the Olympic Movement's member organizations – including institutions commercially linked to the Movement or cities or countries that aspire to host the Games – must accept the Olympic Charter in its entirety. Therefore, they must also accept, unquestioningly and with no restrictions, the IOC's supreme authority as well as the jurisdiction of the CAS.

Court of Arbitration for Sport (CAS)

In 1981, shortly after being elected IOC president, Juan Saramanch proposed the creation of a specific jurisdiction for sports with the objective of resolving international disputes. In 1982, a working group was created to elaborate the statues of what became the *Court of Arbitration for Sport* (CAS). In 1983, the IOC officially ratified the statues of the CAS; these statutes took effect in June 1984 (CAS n.d.).

As an independent institution that is nonetheless financed by and created to serve the IOC, the CAS is charged with resolving judicial litigation relating to the Olympic Movement. It is the only judicial institution authorized for these ends. Its arbitration has the same weight and effect as the judgements of common tribunals and is based either on IOC and FIFA rules or – in last instance – on Swiss legislation. In addition, the CAS also emits consultative opinions on judicial questions relating to sport events and implements non-permanent tribunals (i.e., *ad hoc* Divisions of the CAS) during the realization of major sporting events, such as the Olympics or the Commonwealth Games.

In order for a dispute to be submitted to the CAS, both sides must enter into written agreement to abide by its arbitration. This agreement can be inserted into a contract or into the regulation of the relevant sport organization. Thus, all of the Olympic Charter's signatories are subject to the decisions of the CAS, as are any organizations that have established contracts with the IOC or with FIFA.

Specific rules for the Olympic Games

Beginning with the structural changes introduced in the two editions of the Olympic Charter published in 1999[2] (IOC 1999a, 1999b), there has been a tendency toward separating its contents into specific, more detailed documents, thereby constituting an increasingly complex network of norms and decisions that define any aspect relating to the Olympic Games. These documents have maintained their structure over the course of multiple Olympiads and have undergone a restructuring process only twice in the past two decades: first, with the publication of the "Olympic Games Study Commission" report in 2003; and second, with the 2014 publication of the "Olympic Agenda 2020."

The Olympic Games Study Commission and the rhetoric of legacy

The Olympic Games Study Commission (the Commission) was created in 2001 by then-IOC president Jacques Rogge, with two objectives: proposing solutions to aid in managing the size, complexity, and cost of realizing the Olympic Games and evaluating how they might become more agile and efficient.[3] The commission was composed of IOC members, as well as 40 "experts," and was directed by Dick Pound, the former vice president of the IOC, who signed the final report (Pound 2003) consisting of 117 recommendations.

This report – composed as part of the effort to overcome problems that the Olympic Movement faced following the marketing crisis of the 1996 Atlanta Summer Games, as well as the corruption scandal stemming from the choice of Salt Lake City as host of the 2002 Winter Games[4] – presents a strong emphasis on the necessity of strengthening the control mechanisms that the IOC holds over host cities from the beginning of their candidacy until the realization of the event itself. The significant amount of space given to recommendations relating to the Transfer of Knowledge, as well as the central role of Evaluation and Coordination Commissions in considerations for implementing these recommendations, confirm these concerns.

The Commission's two central objectives – which are clearly laid out in the report's introductory paragraphs (Pound 2003) – reveal the paradox of its undertaking: to reduce the cost of realizing the Olympic Games while, at the same time, maintaining their spectacular character.[5] Despite the discourse of not passing any costs on to cities beyond those necessary to guarantee the organization of the Olympics, the Commission considered any alternative that implied reducing the universal appeal or grandiosity of the event to be inadmissible. The task of suggesting measures to reduce investments in major urban projects was also difficult; after all, the motivation of cities in competing to host mega-events has always been connected to the politicians and enterprises who sought legitimacy by carrying out these projects.

Within this paradoxical logic, the Commission found it almost impossible to recommend actions that produced significant impacts on the costs of events. The report adopted some practical recommendations, such as those restricting the number of athletes and other accredited persons. These measures had a specific effect on the operational costs of events, but – given the scale of infrastructural and installation costs that host cities and countries took on at that time – they were fairly insignificant.

The Commission also recommended the use of provisional or flexible instal- lations for competitions as well as the use of hotels to accommodate the press rather than a specially constructed Media Village. It is worth emphasizing that, because of the highly specific technological demands that provisional installations require – and on which a small number of companies generally hold a monopoly – these installations do not cost less than more permanent ones. The Commission's preference for provisional installations was based instead on its attempt to avoid operational costs after the competitions; in other words, its concern in not leaving behind abandoned or underutilized constructions, the operational costs of which would serve as eternal proof of the misuse of public funds. Furthermore, Olym- pic projects that followed this report practically ignored the recommendation of accommodating members of the media in hotels.

According to the Olympic Games Study Commission's final report, the result that best channeled its objectives and led to a fundamental change in the Olympic Movement's philosophy was the 2003 Olympic Charter's definition of a new role for the IOC: namely, "to take measures to promote a positive legacy from the Olympic Games to the host city and the host country" (IOC 2003, p. 12). The appearance of a "legacy" in the 2003 Charter, based on partial results of earlier studies, was linked to recommendations to standardize and separate the costs of the Olympic Games into two budgets: first, the operational costs of the event, administered by the Organizing Committee for the Olympic Games (the OCOG Budget); and second, expenditures on installations, infrastructure, environmen- tal impact, etc., which would be the responsibility of different spheres of pub- lic administration (the non-OCOG Budget).[6] Within this division, the OCOG's budget was considered to be the official cost of the event, whereas expenditures from the non-OCOG budget were no longer included as event costs; instead, they were called legacy costs, although they were still calculated in the Candidature File.

As a result of the 2003 Olympic Charter, the official IOC documents that guided candidature procedures for cities aspiring to host the Olympic Games began to direct competitors to focus their discourse on the idea of legacy. The production of both "tangible" and "intangible" legacies became the main argument that cities presented in the race to host mega-events; "legacies" took on a clear centrality in official documents, academic books, periodicals, and other communications.

This centrality, which had already begun during preparations for the 2008 Olympic Games, took on greater force in the documents for London's candidature for the 2012 Olympics and assumed unmistakable importance during preparations for the 2016 Rio de Janeiro Summer Olympics. The Candidature File for Rio de Janeiro to Host the 2016 Olympic and Paralympic Games (Rio 2016 Candidate City n.d.) repeats the word "legacy" more than 200 times over the course of 420 pages, including maps and photographs; in this sense, it is emblematic.

With the rhetoric of legacy, the costs of the Olympic Games were considered to be less than what was really invested in their realization, and what had previously been seen as costs became advantages. In fact, the only significant reduction in expenditures as a result of the Commission's report was simply an accounting operation that transferred part of total costs to another budget connected to this legacy. It is worth noting that the 2008 Beijing Olympics – the first to be directly influenced by the report – cost an estimated US$40 billion, the most expensive Olympic Games to date.

Olympic Agenda 2020

As shown in the first chapter, crises have functioned as major catalysts for changes promoted by the IOC. As in 2003, when it created the Olympic Games Study Commission, the Olympic Movement underwent a period of major difficulties during preparations for the 2016 Rio de Janeiro Games. The first major symptom of this crisis – which the IOC has yet to overcome – was when five candidate cities abandoned their bids to host the 2022 Winter Games. The IOC first sought to overcome this crisis by convoking 14 working groups in 2014 and charging them with presenting concrete proposals "safeguarding the Olympic values and strengthening sport in society" (Bach *in* IOC 2014, p. 4). The final report of these working groups, which contains 40 recommendations, was entitled *Olympic Agenda 2020: The Strategic Roadmap for the Future of the Olympic Movement* (IOC 2014). Approved in an extraordinary session of the IOC and held in Monaco in December 2014, the Olympic Agenda 2020 determined an overhaul in relations between the production of sport spectacle and the production of the city.

The most significant recommendations of the Olympic Agenda 2020 related to candidature processes to host the Olympic Games. Under a new selection process, first implemented in selecting a host city for the 2024 Games, the IOC established three stages of candidacy that follow an initial invitational phase for cities interested in hosting. In this new initial phase, cities do not have to commit to hosting the games; instead, it is merely an opportunity for the IOC and interested cities to exchange information. In the first two stages of the selection process, the Executive Board selects cities that will pass on to the next stage. The final stage includes the designation of final candidates by the Executive Board, followed by the selection of a host city by the IOC's Congress.

As in the Olympic Games Study Commission's report, the discourse of legacy, sustainability, and governance holds a central place in the text of the Olympic Agenda 2020. Here, however, the discourse explicitly links the Olympic project to the necessities of host cities and their development projects. Thus, the new evaluation of candidates focuses on a methodological analysis of risk and opportunity. The IOC takes on the role of suggesting corrections in candidature projects so as to aid each city's bid in meeting these demands more adequately.

Other Agenda 2020 recommendations represent initiatives directly connected to valorizing the Olympic brand, including: the implementation of an Olympic Channel; the development of a global marketing program for product licensing[7]; and the increased flexibilization of the use of the Olympic brand for non-commercial purposes.

After the publication of the Olympic Agenda 2020, a candidature can be presented directly by a representative municipal authority, a Candidature Committee, or by the National Olympic Committee (NOC) of the country in question. However, each country is limited to one candidate city at most, a choice which must be supported by the relevant NOC.

In 1999, when the process of selecting host cities was divided into two stages (IOC 1999b), two documents were introduced to establish the guidelines for candidature procedures: the *Candidature Acceptance Procedure* and *Candidature Procedure and Questionnaire*. These documents applied to the choice of host cities for the 2008, 2012, 2016, and 2020 Olympic Games. With the restructuring of candidature under the Olympic Agenda 2020, three new documents establishing rules for the selection process substituted the previous two. These documents marked the process of selecting a host city for the 2024 Olympic Games, which also led to the choice of a host city for 2028. The first of these documents, *Olympic Games Framework* (IOC 2015a), enunciates the structure and "new philosophy of candidature;" the second, *Candidature Process* (IOC 2015b), elucidates the selection process; and the third, *Candidature Questionnaire* (IOC 2015c), explains the themes of each stage of selection, questions relating to them, and guarantees demanded of potential host cities. In addition to presenting candidature proposals in accordance with the IOC's established guidelines, cities selected to host the Olympic Games must also sign a "Host City Contract." All of these documents clearly articulate the importance of the host city and country's acceptance of the Olympic Charter and the IOC Code of Ethics, both in terms of regulations relating to candidature and others relating to the contract.

Olympic Games Framework

With the primary objective of increasing the number of aspiring host cities for the Olympic Games, the Olympic Agenda 2020 established that the IOC would begin the process of selecting a host with an open invitation to all NOCs, cities, and countries interested in bidding. During this phase, the IOC establishes a dialogue with possible candidates to whom it offers a series of services including material and technical support, with the objective of crafting proposals in accordance with IOC-defined standards. The *Olympic Games Framework* was presented as the first step in this dialogue, as it constitutes a grouping of information that the IOC offers to NOCs as part of this new, invitational phase.

The first edition of the Olympic Games Framework for the selection of the 2024 Olympic Games host city (IOC 2015a) is dedicated to promoting consensus regarding the idea of the "unique opportunity" of hosting the Olympic Games or of merely participating in the bidding process. Examples presented throughout the document illustrate the different dimensions of potential "benefits" (economic, social, environmental, spatial, and sport-related) of hosting the event and their effects on a number of different scales (city-wide, regionally, and nationally). Next, the Framework lays out the new guidelines established by the Olympic Agenda 2020 and presents a general overview of the requirements necessary for hosting the Summer Olympic Games. Finally, the document presents two annexes; the first contains the competition schedule for the 2016 Rio Games, while the second shows the results and methodology of an IOC research project regarding awareness and appeal of the Olympic Games and the Olympic brand. The main guidelines in the Olympic Games Framework (IOC 2015a) are based on this research, which aims to identify fundamental aspects of the valorization of the Olympic brand.

Candidature process

The *Candidature Process – Olympic Games 2024* (IOC 2015b) contains further information on bidding to host the 2024 Olympic Games. The document describes, in significant detail, the procedures, rules, and principles of selecting a host city as well as the requirements that every candidature must satisfy.

According to the document's instructions (IOC 2015b), candidature must occur through three stages which are integrated into a single process. Throughout this process, the IOC monitors each city involved on an individual basis, offering specific orientations relating to each proposal so as to create a perfect alignment between each city's urban development plan and the IOC's institutional expectations. A city's Candidature File should address nine total themes. At each stage, candidates submit part of the Candidature File consisting of three themes; based on these documents, the Evaluation Commission presents a report to the Executive Board. After evaluating these reports, the Executive Board decides whether or not each given candidate will progress to the next selection phase.

The themes of the first stage are Vision, Games Concept, and Strategy. In this phase, the IOC demands that cities build national support for their candidature, both from the stakeholders involved in the project and from the public. The second stage features three other themes: Governance, Legal [Issues], and Venue Funding. Candidate cities approved in this stage receive an individual feedback workshop regarding the opportunities and challenges facing their projects. The third and final stage develops the themes of Games Delivery, Experience, and Venue Legacy. The evaluation of this stage includes a visit by the Evaluation Commission to each candidate city as well as another report highlighting opportunities and challenges. This report is published and sent to the IOC's members and other interested parties and made available to candidates, who have the right to respond to comments made in the report. Two months after a Candidate City

Briefing to the IOC and International Federations, the Executive Board designates the candidatures to be submitted to the IOC Congress for the final selection of a host city.

The *Candidature Process* (IOC 2015b) presents two new instruments introduced by the *Olympic Agenda 2020: Rules of Conduct for the Candidature Process – Olympic Games* and Opinion Polls. The Rules of Conduct are annexed to the *Code of Ethics* and must be observed by everyone involved with a given candidature, including third parties. Opinion Polls are part of the new initiatives of political control for host cities. Although Opinion Polls carried out by Candidature Committees were already commonplace in earlier candidature processes, they now have a new format. Two Opinion Polls are conducted in candidate cities during two distinct phases, under the total control of the IOC, which hires specialized companies to conduct them and to define each poll's methodology. Each poll must also feature a list of political parties, including their political strength, position in relation to the Games, and reasoning behind their position. This list, which was already required in previous candidature processes, now must also take into account the number of positions that each party holds across all levels of government.

The document (IOC 2015b) also establishes parameters for the structure of support services,[8] for "international federation engagement," to address "financial, legal, and commercial matters," and makes explicit the rules and limitations of the use of the Olympic brand as well as procedures permitted during the promotion of a given city's candidacy.

The end of the document contains the *Acceptance of the Candidature agreement*. The Candidature Committee, city, and NOC involved in bidding to host the 2024 Games were required to sign this agreement as a condition of entering into the Candidature Process. The agreement establishes a pledge on the part of all signatories to accept, without restriction, all aspects of "the *IOC Code of Ethics, Rules of Conduct for the Candidature Process Olympic Games 2024* and all other rules, instructions and conditions which may be established by the IOC Executive Board" (IOC 2015b, p. 50). The agreement also notes that the resolution of any disputes related to candidature processes will be determined by the Court of Arbitration for Sport and that its decisions hold power over any other legal forum or court.

Candidature questionnaire

The *Olympic Games Candidature Questionnaire* is the document published by the IOC to guide the elaboration of Candidature Files of bids to host the Olympics. It brings together all of the themes addressed in the three stages of the candidature process, the questions relating to each of these themes individually, and the guarantees required by the IOC. The edition for the selection of a host city for the 2024 Olympic Games (IOC 2015c) contains 222 questions distributed in three questionnaires – one for each stage of candidature – and requires 51 guarantees.

The questionnaire for the first stage of candidature contains 66 questions organized around five points: Vision and Games Concept, Legacy and Long-Term Plan Integration and Alignments, General Infrastructure and Capacity Analyses, Country Analyses, and Financing Analyses. In this stage, cities must present a general vision of their project for venues as well as accommodations for the public. It is also at this time that the IOC analyzes each city's capacity in terms of infrastructure and existing services, as well as the social, economic, judicial, and political scenario of each country and the strategy adopted in each bid to finance the games. In order to guarantee their place in the next stage, candidates must guarantee their project's alignment with the IOC's priorities, as shown in the *Olympic Agenda 2020* (IOC 2014), and with their cities' long-term development plans. They must also show how they will attend to the necessities of hosting the Olympics.

At this stage, the IOC requires seven guarantees involving all levels of government. In general, these guarantees refer to a city's commitment to fulfill all of the obligations determined by the *Olympic Charter* and the *Host City Contract*. In addition, the IOC requires a guarantee that all levels of government support the candidature, respect environmental restrictions, will be involved with the IOC's marketing programs, and guarantee funding compatible with that expected by the IOC. Here, it is worth noting the recurring emphasis on the guarantee to free access and movement within the country for all people credentialed by the IOC.

The questionnaire for the second stage of candidature contains 23 questions organized around three central points: Governance, Customs and Immigration, and Sports and Venue Funding. These questions focus on information relating to institutional support for the candidacy from all levels of government and other institutions as well as the legal structure required for the event's realization in terms of migrations and customs, control of advertising space and the prevention of ambush marketing, and regulation of the work force. In addition, cities must make explicit the specific capital expenditure required to stage the Games as well as defining financing responsibilities both by private initiative and at all levels of government.

After the *Olympic Agenda 2020*, budgets for the Olympic Project were reorganized. The operational costs of the event remain part of the OCOG budget, and investments in competition and non-competition venues (such as accommodations, media, and broadcasting service support systems) remain part of the non-OCOG budget. However, investments in infrastructure as well as those in transportation and the environment are now part of a long-term development plan for the city; the relevant budget is no longer part of the Candidature File as it had been previously. Although these investments are not part of the official budget, the IOC still requires guarantees that they will be financed.

At this stage, the IOC requires 37 guarantees. For the first of these, the Candidature Committee, the NOC, and the candidate city must sign the Host City Contract in case the city is ultimately selected. Agreeing to this contract implies renouncing any other previously established agreements with third parties that might contradict the IOC's interests. The text also requires a guarantee of property rights and protection for the Olympic brand and reiterates that all parties must submit to the authority of the CAS. The other guarantees, which must be signed by the relevant authorities or by private entrepreneurs, relate mostly to assuring the legal means necessary to hold the games in accordance with the interests of the IOC and its partners; controlling taxes and the prices of services offered to the OCOG, NOCs, or to the general public; and guaranteeing financing for investments in competition and non-competition venues administered by both public and private entities. In addition, the IOC requires guarantees relating to health, security, accessibility, decisions of the World Anti-Doping Agency (WADA), as well as sustainability, and the functioning of infrastructure including energy, telecommunications, and transportation.

The questionnaire relating to the third stage presents 133 questions that focus on a detailed presentation of the city's Olympic and Para-Olympic projects as well as the operation of these events. These questions also offer the opportunity to reformulate, update, or confirm responses to questions from previous stages. They put a special emphasis on the risks and opportunities of hosting, the sustainability of solutions offered, the impact of the games, and the legacy of venues.

The seven guarantees required at this stage relate mostly to assuring that accommodations and transport systems will meet conditions required by the IOC and to certifying financing sources to cover possible financial damages to the OCOG, such as in the unlikely event of cancellation of the Games.

The Host City Contract

Immediately after a host city is announced, the main obligations agreed to in the Olympic Charter and other candidature documents are detailed and ratified by means of a judicial contract between the IOC, the selected host city, and the host NOC.

Until the selection of Rio de Janeiro to host the 2016 Summer Games, this contract was a single, confidential document.[9] In accordance with the recommendations of the *Olympic Agenda 2020*, the contract's contents, consisting of two distinct sections – *Host City Contract Principles*, and *Host City Contract Operational Requirements* – were disclosed before the selection process for the 2024 Games. The first section contained separate versions for cities chosen to host the 2024 Games (Paris) and the 2028 Games (Los Angeles), respectively. (IOC 2017a, 2017b) The second (IOC 2018a) had a single version that applied to both cities' contracts.

The obligations of the entities responsible for organizing the Olympic Games are organized: first, by the terms of the Host City Contract; second, by the terms of the Olympic Charter; and third, by the application of the interpretation of principles of Swiss law. In the five months following the execution of the contract, the host city and host NOC are required to create an Organizing Committee for the Olympic Games (OCOG) which must follow the contract through a binding joinder agreement.

The OCOG has 18 months from its creation to present two documents that lay out details of its planning and actions undertaken in organizing the Games: the Games Foundation Plan and the Games Delivery Plan. All of the commitments contained in the candidature documents and established in the Games Delivery Plan are also part of the Host City Contract. (IOC 2017a, 2017b, p. 10)

The *Host City Contract Principles* establish the bases for the contract, as well as the organizational and financial responsibilities attributed to each signatory (the host city, NOC, and OCOG), and the IOC's contribution in carrying out a successful Olympics. The document also lays out rules for coordination between the IOC and other parties, responsibility for the organization of the Paralympic Games, key areas of operation and deliverability, and central requirements for receiving the Olympic Games. These include: respect for the Olympic Charter and the promotion of Olympism; sustainability, legacy, and security; impediments to realizing events that might have a negative impact on the success of the Games; and several points protecting the Olympic brand, prohibiting the unauthorized commercial use of the event, and guaranteeing Olympic partners' satisfaction as well as relating to the quality of media and broadcast support services.

The *Host City Contract Operational Requirements* establish all of the necessary conditions for the successful functioning of the Olympic Games in accordance with the interests of the IOC and its partners. Most of these requirements are related to specific themes, which were previously presented in 28 distinct technical manuals. The host city, host NOC, and the OCOG must also submit to all updates, amendments, and modifications of these requirements, regardless of when they may occur, as well as possible changes in the Olympic Charter.

Previous candidatures were also charged with obeying potential future changes in the *Olympic Charter* or in the IOC's operational requirements, but in these cases, they were only bound by alterations that did not imply new financial commitments for the host city. However, the new documents do not contain any clear restrictions on new financial commitments for cities, although they present the possibility of host cities creating new arrangements with the IOC or – in last instance – submitting the matter to the CAS, if the city is unduly burdened (IOC 2017a, §30.3, §51.2).

The contract documents present little new content in terms of determining candidature rules. Based on the fundamental recognition of the IOC's supreme authority, they reinforce and elucidate previously defined obligations, especially those relating to the quality and functioning of installations and infrastructure. The Host City Contract also emphatically highlights financial commitments and indemnities for deficiency in relation to the Olympic family or third parties contracted by the Olympic movement as well as commitments relating to the adoption of legal measures to protect the property of the Olympic brand; facilitating aspects of customs and migrations; and protecting against ambush marketing, including control of the public space and aerial space of host cities.

All of the contract's documents are based in Swiss law, and all disputes regarding their validity, interpretation, or performance – as well as any laws involving the host city, NOC, or OCOG, or any other member of the Olympic family – can only be decided by the CAS or, in last instance, by a Swiss ordinary court.

The IOC Code of Ethics

The IOC Ethics Commission was first mentioned in the 1999 *Olympic Charter* (IOC 1999a). Denunciations of corruption involving the choice of a host city for the 2002 Winter Games[10] led to the creation of this commission which, among other measures, created the *IOC Code of Ethics*.

The 2018 edition of the IOC Code of Ethics, updated in July 2019 (IOC 2018b), was accompanied by 11 documents containing provisions for its implementation. Organized around eight themes, the Code of Ethics addressed issues ranging from respect for the general principles of Olympism to the behavior of those involved in any candidature process. The Code also included statutes and implementing provisions of the IOC Ethics Commission (ibid.).

Provisions for the implementation of the IOC Code of Ethics contain various directives relating to the election of the IOC's presidents, "rules concerning conflicts of interests affecting the behavior of Olympic parties," and rules of conduct governing the candidature processes for hosting the Olympic Games. The rules of conduct established for candidature processes for hosting the 2024 Games (IOC 2018b) determined that any breach of the commitments established in the candidature process would constitute a violation of the rules of conduct. In addition, they implemented the necessity of registering all consultants for candidature projects with IOC. Any service rendered to the candidate NOC or city would need to be registered on a list connected to the city in question. This registry is granted by IOC to consultants who commit, in writing, to uphold "the IOC's ethical principles, the Olympic Charter, the *IOC Code of Ethics* and its Implementing Provisions, especially the *Rules of Conduct* for Continuous Dialogue with Interested Parties and the Rules Concerning Conflicts of Interests" (IOC 2018b, art. 2, p. 42).

All member institutions of the Olympic Movement, all people connected to the Movement, and all participants in the Olympic Games were now required to guarantee that they would uphold the Code of Ethics. This also applies to candidate cities, their representatives, and all others involved in the process as well as OCOGs and their officials.

The Olympic Games Knowledge Management (OGKM)

The *Transfer of Olympic Knowledge* program (TOK) was created by the IOC at the end of the 1990s to add further guarantees to the satisfactory realization of the Olympic Games (cf. Chapter Two). The program, first established in conjunction with the Sydney Organizing Committee for the Olympic Games (SOCOG) in preparation for the 2000 Sydney Summer Games, aimed to gather knowledge related to organizing the Olympics and to transfer it to OCOGs and political authorities in host cities. The program systematizes information from earlier activities considered to represent "best practices" in educational material which it then presents to forthcoming host cities.

In addition to the TOK program, the *Olympic Games Knowledge Service* (OGKS) was developed in partnership with Monash Ed, an Australian consortium based at the University of Monash which also featured several prominent Australian business executives (IOC 2016). In 2004, the IOC became the sole owner of the OGKS, which it substituted in 2005 with the *Olympic Games Knowledge Management* program (OGKM) (ibid.). The services offered by the OGKM include debriefings, workshops, furnishing reference materials relevant to the Games, and maintaining a digital platform with a database of TOK programs.

While the Olympic Charter, together with the instructions and requirements for the elaboration of Candidature Files and Host City Contracts, impose conditions for executing the Olympic Games, the OGKM program describes methods used in earlier editions of the event to successfully implement these requirements.

The Coordination Commission

In 1993, the IOC established (IOC 1993) the *Olympic Games Coordination Commission* in order to administer relations between the OCOG and other members of the Olympic Movement. This commission – initially composed of representatives from the IOC, IFs, and NOCs and later expanded to include a select number of athletes – was charged with monitoring the process of the OCOG, assisting in its mission, and helping to guarantee the connection between the OCOG and other institutions involved in producing the Games. The Coordination Commission also evaluated the organization of the Olympic Games and held additional authority conferred by the IOC Executive Committee to which it was required to submit reports on a regular basis. This function expanded progressively and now includes the tasks of inspecting infrastructural and competition spaces, establishing specialized work groups for specific areas, and making recommendations to the IOC regarding necessary improvements.

Although the Coordination Commission is directly subject to the final decisions of the Executive Committee, it holds authority to define alterations in the organization of the Games. Therefore, its power extends beyond members of the Olympic Movement inasmuch as it has the capacity to validate or annul political strategies that directly affect the production of the urban space.[11]

Changes and continuations within the new rules

The central objective of the changes instituted by the Olympic Agenda 2020 (IOC 2014) was to make candidature more attractive. Although all of the documents associated with the Agenda underwent significant alterations, these related more to conduct and to the organization of the candidature process than to overall themes and content. The requirements and guarantees that the IOC demanded of host cities in order to carry out the Games to its satisfaction – and to the satisfaction of its partners – remained the same, although the new process led to the selection of host cities that could satisfy these demands without having to make major investments.

The change of the concept of "host city" to "host of the Games" – introduced in the 2019 Olympic Charter[12] (IOC 2019) – makes more candidatures viable inasmuch as it establishes the possibility of a greater distribution of the economic and social impact of organizing the event over a larger territory. This new concept can include more than one city, region, or even country, although it also runs the risk of making relations between the IOC and these different spatial scales more complex.

Establishing three selection stages under the exclusive control of the Executive Board – which also holds the power to establish new rules at any given moment – indicates an attempt by the IOC to prevent any candidature projects that might risk putting the value of the Olympic brand in danger to reach the final selection by IOC members. After all, the Executive Board has a more significant commitment to upholding the IOC's objectives than any other member of the electoral college.[13]

Projects that exploit the possibilities of legitimizing major projects that accommodate local interests – such as, for example, Rio de Janeiro's candidature for the 2016 Summer Olympic Games – may damage the image of the Olympic games, and this damage may take significant time to repair. Although the IOC does not intend to make the satisfaction of local coalitions unviable – these, after all, are responsible for building cities' interest in hosting the Games – it has perceived the importance of subjecting coalitions to rigorous control. The recommendations of the *Olympic Agenda 2020* all tend toward this direction.

To summarize, although the discourse of cost reduction is central to the recommendations introduced in the *Olympic Agenda 2020* – as it also was for the Olympic Games Study Commission's recommendations – the regulatory apparatus that the IOC has developed over the course of more than 100 years to guarantee its supreme authority over the Olympic Movement continues intact, and none of the recommendations hint at any structural changes. The imperative of submitting to the Olympic Charter and the decisions of the IOC and its associated bodies – especially the CAS – is fundamental in all of the new documents.

Rules regarding the production of football spectacle

Although it is linked to the Olympic Movement, and therefore subject to the jurisdiction of the Olympic Charter and of CAS as well as the supreme authority of the IOC, FIFA establishes its own specific rules for the production of football spectacle. In reference to FIFA's relationship to host countries of the Football World Cup, these rules are far removed from the sophistication and complexity of those that the IOC has established for the Olympic Games.

The rules that conduct the football world are the FIFA Statues, and, as is the case with the IOC, the CAS is also the maximum judicial power for resolving disputes related to FIFA, followed by FIFA's Congress, Council, and the Ethics, Disciplinary, and Appeal Committees, respectively. According to FIFA's Statues, national associations, clubs, and club members cannot submit disputes with FIFA or with other associations, clubs, or club members to any common tribunals. Instead, such disputes must only be submitted to CAS or to another arbitration tribunal established for this specific end.

While the IOC has progressively worked to make all of the commitments it demands for hosting the Olympic Games clear and public during the candidature phase, FIFA's attitude in relation to World Cup hosts was not at all clear until after preparations for the 2014 World Cup in Brazil. The rules for the functioning of the 2014 World Cup (FIFA 2011) were only published three years before the tournament was held; contracts with host cities were only signed in 2011 and maintained in secret. Only one of these locations – São Paulo – was divulged in 2012 by means of a judicial order. There is no known guide nor document with the requirements for the bidding and hosting nor Bid Book for Brazil's candidature to host the 2014 World Cup.[14]

FIFA began to change its strategy in 2011 when it announced the formation of the *Independent Governance Committee*, as well as four other task forces charged with proposing reforms to the organization's Executive Board and Congress. Concern with attrition caused by constant criticism "for its lack of good governance and transparency, reinforced by a sequence of allegations and incidents of misconduct by football officials"[15] (Independent Governance Committee to the Executive Committee of FIFA 2012, p. 4), led to this impetus for new reforms, which were organized by four categories: a review of FIFA's statues; the Committee of Ethics; transparency; and legal enforcement.

In general, *FIFA's Statutes* have not undergone many alterations throughout their history. They pertain mainly to the functioning of the field itself; in other words, they concentrate mostly on FIFA's functioning and organization, on the other institutions it recognizes, and on the tournaments realized under its authority. Although these documents establish rules of conduct for relationships between FIFA officials and host countries, the actual regulations governing these relations are not very clear.

As a result of the recommendations of the Independent Governance Committee, FIFA's Statues were altered in the 2013 and 2016 editions (FIFA 2013, 2016). The 2019 edition (FIFA 2019a) did not present any significant alterations in relation to 2016. Changes in 2013 focused on the election of host countries for the Football World Cup, which until that point had occurred through a secret vote in the Executive Committee that was not governed by any defined criteria or rules. The new candidature process established in 2013 (FIFA 2013) – which entered into effect for the selection of a host for the 2023 Women's World Cup – is similar to the IOC's pre-Olympic Agenda 2020 process for choosing a host for the Olympic Games. The Council[16] establishes requirements for bidding and hosting, as well as rules and criteria for selection; candidate countries then present a Bid Book to FIFA's General Secretariat, which is responsible for creating a public report. Based on this report, the Council chooses up to three finalists, and FIFA's Congress renders a final decision. All documents relating to this process are now divulged on FIFA's official website.

Among the changes made in 2013 (ibid.), it is worth noting the emphasis placed on discourses of ethics and the recognition of women and human rights, all of which are clearly intended to bolster the symbolic valorization of FIFA's brand. These alterations also introduced the possibility of FIFA's Congress removing the president, vice president, and other members of the Executive Committee.

In accordance with the recommendations of the Independent Governance Committee, and in response to new scandals that FIFA faced in 2015,[17] the 2016 edition of FIFA's Statutes (FIFA 2016) introduced further changes. These included more significant alterations relating to governance and transparency, while the most significant overall change was the reorganization of functions within the organization. The Executive Committee, which had heretofore exercised executive functions, became the Council, which also served as FIFA's strategic and supervisory body. The General Secretariat, which had previously been FIFA's administrative body, took on the role of executive, operational, and administrative organ under the supervision of the Council. The Bureau of the Council[18] was created in order to make efficient decisions. FIFA's 2016 Statutes also introduced measures regarding transparency: more clarity in rules and decision-making processes; the selection of Council members by election, instead of by appointment; terms limits for FIFA's president and for Council and Commission members, consisting of three consecutive or alternating mandates (12 years); and the divulgation of the individual compensation of FIFA's highest executives, including the president. The Statutes reinforced measures relating to FIFA's autonomy, as well as to diversity, human rights, and the promotion of women in football. Thus, after a delay of more than a decade, FIFA tried to introduce the kinds of regulatory alterations that the IOC first undertook in the 1990s.

The code of ethics

While the IOC had concerned itself with introducing a Code of Ethics in the Olympic Charter published in June 1999 (IOC 1999a), FIFA only introduced its equivalent in 2004. The FIFA Code of Ethics established rules for the conduct of players, agents, and assistants, as well as coaches, trainers, club directors, and others responsible for technical, medical, and administrative issues within FIFA and its associated confederations, associations, leagues, and clubs. This code did not, however, directly address relations between FIFA and host countries for the World Cup; at most, it established control mechanisms for behavior among the organization's officials.

As a further result of the recommendations of the Independent Governance Committee, the 2018 FIFA Code of Ethics (FIFA 2018) also contained alternations, which emphasized, among other areas: potential misconduct by directors, violations affecting the institution's image, and financial responsibilities.

The introduction of pecuniary fines, in addition to previously determined sanctions for violations, was the most notable innovation in this edition.

FIFA's 2019 Code of Ethics (FIFA 2019b) also contained new alterations, the most significant of which was perhaps the reinsertion, in Articles 27 and 28, of the term "corruption," which had been removed from the 2018 edition. Additionally, the 2019 Code underwent changes that either amplified or eliminated time limits for certain sanctions and increased the time frame for certain injunctions.

Partial considerations

In its emergence as an autonomous social universe capable of producing a judicial apparatus that is relatively independent of external constraints, the field of production of sport spectacle not only guarantees its own autonomy but also reveals itself to be capable of imposing its own judicial constraints within the territories that receive its events.

The IOC and FIFA – hegemonic subjects in this field – utilize distinct tactics and follow different trajectories, but both move toward the goal of maintaining the grandiosity of the spectacles they produce and the satisfaction of sponsors and broadcasters, the clients who sustain them. In order to achieve this goal, both organizations have adopted the strategy of controlling the cities that finance the spectacles they sell. FIFA may sell its brand more aggressively, but the IOC has organized and prepared the field in order to exercise autonomy and control.

The similarity between themes in the two institutions' regulatory apparatuses reveal how the sophisticated system developed by the IOC – in addition to building a model for FIFA's actions – has validated the naturalization of its organizational demands. The IOC's strategy of entering into agreements with cities and countries during the candidature phase stymies the mobilization of communities most affected by the impact of the Olympic Games. Significant political and institutional changes take place before the selection of a host, when the possibility of the Games is still treated as speculation, or else amidst the euphoria of the declaration of victory, thereby bypassing greater social attention. FIFA's lesser clarity during the candidature period implies more polemical reactions at the time of selection to the political and institutional changes mandated by the institution. After all, these changes only take place when the ample mobilization of capital directed toward preparing the event is already at the center of society's attention. In Brazil, FIFA's practices had negative repercussions for the IOC's strategy inasmuch as they led to lines of questioning that could otherwise have been forgotten.

In any event, the progressive normatization on which the IOC depends naturalizes, to a certain extent, FIFA's demands while also leading to confusion in distinguishing between the two. The rules that the IOC produces contribute to softening negative reactions to the legislative changes that FIFA demands. In this sense, Brazil's experiences, which involved the simultaneous production of events under the auspices of both institutions, offer a unique opportunity for observation, as we will see in Part Two.

The growing sophistication of control mechanisms that the field of the production of sport spectacle exercises in relation to the city contains a contradiction within itself, insofar as, at peak efficiency, this sophistication makes projects involving high economic and social costs possible. Under these circumstances, negative reactions of the inhabitants of territories that are candidates to host these events become a threat to the very existence of the field.

Returning to the arguments made by Elias (1986) – namely, that rules are not static – we can see that the regulatory system developed by sport spectacle maintains itself in constant transformation, instead of presenting itself as completed. Rules that have lost their function or no longer achieve their aims are eliminated or transformed. Facing new challenges implies incorporating new discourses, such as those of legacy and sustainability.

Although this regulatory framework claims a universal character in its application, its repercussions are not felt in a homogeneous way, nor does it produce the same repercussions in all spaces and times, as we will see in Chapter Six. It is worth investigating how structural conditions and disputes inside each territory and moment confer more specific or general forms of application or repercussion.

Notes

1 Portions of this chapter first appeared in the book *O Poder dos Jogos e os Jogos de Poder: Os interesses em campo na produção da cidade para o espetáculo esportivo* (Oliveira 2015), published by Editora UFRJ. The English translation is by Raphael Soifer.
2 See Chapter One.
3 See Rogge (2004).
4 See Chapter One.
5 See Chapter Four.
6 This subject is discussed in greater detail by de Oliveira (2017).
7 The exploitation of production licenses was strictly limited to the responsible OCOG.
8 IOC Assistance and Services include: the Olympic Games Candidature Coordination (OGCC), the Candidate City Workshops, the Olympic Games Observer Programme, the Official Debriefing of the Olympic Games, support from IOC sponsors, the Dedicated Candidate City online platform, the Olympic Multimedia Library, and the Protection of the Wordmark.
9 In the case of Rio de Janeiro, the Host City Contract (IOC 2009) was only made public long after it had been signed.
10 See Chapter One.
11 For example, in the case of the 2016 Summer Games in Rio de Janeiro, the Coordination Commission's endorsement of changes in the Olympic project was fundamental to legitimating the "Marvellous Port" project, which will be discussed further in Chapter Four.
12 See Chapter One.
13 All members of the IOC participate in the electoral college that makes the final selection of the host of the Olympic Games. For more on the organization and composition of the IOC and its Executive Board, see Chapter Two.
14 I attempted to communicate via email with the Local Organising Committee (LOC) and Brazil's Sports Ministry, but I had no success. After many searches, I found fragments of the archive containing 11 items signed by Brazilian authorities, guaranteeing

their approval of the country's candidature and promising to produce legal measures similar to those demanded by the IOC.
15 See, for example, Canton of Zug (2010), and Jennings (2007).
16 Initially, this task fell to the Executive Committee, which was substituted by the Council in 2016.
17 See Chapter Two.
18 See Chapter One.

References

Bourdieu, P & Wacquant, LJD 1992, *An Invitation to Reflexive Sociology*, The University of Chicago Press, Chicago.

Canton of Zug 2010, *Translation of the Order on the Dismissal of the Criminal Proceedings of May 11, 2010, in the Investigation Against Fédération Internationale de Football Association (FIFA)*, viewed 5 April 2019, <http://pt.fifa.com/mm/document/affederation/footballgovernance/01/66/28/60/orderonthedismissalofthecriminalproceedings.pdf>

Court of Arbitration for Sport (CAS) n.d., *History of the CAS*, CAS, viewed 5 April 2019, <www.tas-cas.org/en/general-information/history-of-the-cas.html>

de Oliveira, NG 2017, "Sports Mega-Events and Rhetoric of Legacy, an Accounting Operation Becomes Discourse", in C Vainer, AM Broudehoux, F Sánchez & FL Oliveira (eds) *Mega-Events and the City: Critical Perspectives*, Letra Capital, Rio de Janeiro.

Elias, N 1986, "An Essay on Sport and Violence", in N Elias & E Dunning (eds) *Quest for Excitement: Sport and Leisure in the Civilizing Process*, Basil Blackwell, Oxford, pp. 179–190.

Fédération Internationale de Football Association (FIFA) 2011, *Regulations: 2014 FIFA World Cup Brazil™*, FIFA, Zurich, viewed 5 August 2019, <https://img.fifa.com/image/upload/kjltl3stnwglycokws2s.pdf>

Fédération Internationale de Football Association (FIFA) 2013, *FIFA Statutes: July 2013 Edition*, FIFA, Zurich.

Fédération Internationale de Football Association (FIFA) 2016, *FIFA Statutes: April 2016 Edition*, FIFA, Zurich.

Fédération Internationale de Football Association (FIFA) 2018, *FIFA Code of Ethics: 2018 Edition*, FIFA, Zurich.

Fédération Internationale de Football Association (FIFA) 2019a, *FIFA Statutes: June 2019 Edition*, FIFA, Zurich.

Fédération Internationale de Football Association (FIFA) 2019b, *FIFA Code of Ethics: 2019 Edition*, FIFA, Zurich.

Huizinga, Johan 1980, *Homo Ludens: A Study of the Play Element in Culture*, Routledge & Kegan Paul, Boston London and Henley.

Independent Governance Committee to the Executive Committee of FIFA 2012, *FIFA Governance Reform Project: First Report by the Independent Governance Committee to the Executive Committee of FIFA*, FIFA, Basel, viewed 8 April 2019, <https://resources.fifa.com/mm/document/affederation/footballgovernance/01/60/85/44/first_report_by_igc_to_fifa_exco[2].pdf>

International Olympic Committee (IOC) 1978, *Olympic Charter: Provisional Edition*, IOC, Lausanne.

International Olympic Committee (IOC) 1991, *Olympic Charter: In Force as from 16th June 1991*, IOC, Lausanne.

International Olympic Committee (IOC) 1993, *Olympic Charter: In Force as from 24th September 1993*, IOC, Lausanne.

International Olympic Committee (IOC) 1996, *Olympic Charter: In Force as from 14th July 1996*, IOC, Lausanne.

International Olympic Committee (IOC) 1999a, *Olympic Charter: In Force as from 17th June 1999*, IOC, Lausanne.

International Olympic Committee (IOC) 1999b, *Olympic Charter: In Force as from 12th December 1999*, IOC, Lausanne.

International Olympic Committee (IOC) 2003, *Olympic Charter: In Force as from 4 July 2003*, IOC, Lausanne.

International Olympic Committee (IOC) 2004, *Olympic Charter: In Force as from 1 September 2004*, IOC, Lausanne.

International Olympic Committee (IOC) 2009, *Host City Contract for the Games of the XXXI Olympiad in 2016: Rio de Jeneiro*, IOC, Copenhagen.

International Olympic Committee (IOC) 2014, *Olympic Agenda 2020: The Strategic Roadmap for the Future of the Olympic Movement*, IOC, Lausanne.

International Olympic Committee (IOC) 2015a, *Olympic Games Framework: Produced for the 2024 Olympic Games*, IOC, Lausanne.

International Olympic Committee (IOC) 2015b, *Candidature Process: Olympic Games 2024*, IOC, Lausanne.

International Olympic Committee (IOC) 2015c, *Candidature Questionnaire: Olympic Games 2024*, IOC, Lausanne.

International Olympic Committee (IOC) 2016, *Factsheet Olympic Games Knowledge Management (OGKM)*, IOC, Lausanne, viewed 10 July 2019, <https://stillmed.olympic.org/media/Document%20Library/OlympicOrg/Factsheets-Reference-Documents/OGKM/Factsheet-OGKM-July-2016.pdf>

International Olympic Committee (IOC) 2017a, *Host City Contract Principles: Games of the XXXIII Olympiad in 2024*, IOC, Lausanne.

International Olympic Committee (IOC) 2017b, *Host City Contract Principles: Games of the XXXIV Olympiad in 2028*, IOC, Lausanne.

International Olympic Committee (IOC) 2018a, *Host City Contract Operational Requirements: June 2018*, IOC, Lausanne.

International Olympic Committee (IOC) 2018b, *Code of Ethics and Other Texts IOC, Lausanne: 2018 Edition, Updated in July 2019*, IOC, Lausanne.

International Olympic Committee (IOC) 2019, *Olympic Charter: In Force as from 26 June 2019*, IOC, Lausanne.

Jenning, A 2007, *Foul!: The Secret World of Fifa*, HarperCollins, New York.

Pound, RW 2003, *Olympic Games Study Commission: Report to the 115th IOC Session*, IOC, Prague, viewed 3 June 2019, <https://stillmed.olympic.org/Documents/Reports/EN/en_report_725.pdf>

Rio 2016 Candidate City n.d., *Candidature File for Rio de Janeiro to Host the 2016 Olympic and Paralympic Games*, 3 vol., Rio 2016 Candidate City, Rio de Janeiro.

Rogge, J 2004, *The Olympic Games: Athens to Athens 1896–2004*, Orion Publishing Co, London.

Part 2

Production of sports spectacle on a local scale

4 Two converging fields

The production of the city and the production of sport spectacle[1]

Introduction

The growing complexity of relations between agents who participate in the production of sport spectacle[2] has, in turn, exerted increased pressure on the conditions of this field's organization and, consequently on the costs involved in producing such spectacles. In addition to the resources required for constructing sporting venues, infrastructure, and functional and comfortable accommodations for spectators, athletes, partners, and others involved in organizing these events,[3] mega-event budgets must also account for security expenditures as well as for other services associated with the events' execution.

To the extent that the complexity of producing mega-events continues to multiply, it becomes increasingly difficult to compare costs linked to their production. Several factors contribute to this difficulty, especially variations in different forms of organizing the budget, which are often controlled by the institutions responsible for promoting the events. Significant investments may be measured or omitted in accordance with the format of a given budget, as we saw in Chapter Two.

In addition, regardless of the strategy adopted for a given budget, certain costs may never be computed, such as those related to the value of lands utilized for sporting venues and infrastructure or those relating to the adaptation of permanent or temporary event structures for legacy purposes. As such, it is difficult to find official data on the definitive final costs of a mega-event. Organizers do not always account for their final expenditures in the official Organizing Committee of the Olympic Games (OCOG) reports released after mega-events are completed. Finally, costs regularly exceed those presented in the budgets of candidature files, thereby impeding total expenditures from being considered in final evaluations.

Without ignoring these limitations, however, we can identify a recent rise in costs related to the production of mega-events. The 1976 Montreal Summer Olympics cost approximately US$1.5 billion (COJO 76 1978), while the 1984 Los Angeles Summer Olympics cost approximately US$470 million (LAOOC 1985). Meanwhile, the cost of hosting the Summer Olympic Games in the twenty-first century tends to exceed US$10 billion.

The most emblematic case of this increase was the 2008 Beijing Summer Olympics, which cost US$40 billion dollars.[4] The 2012 London Games received

£9.3 billion (approximately US$14.9 billion in 2012) from the Public Sector Funding Package (DCMS 2012; NAO 2012); this figure still does not account for certain important costs covered by the public sector, nor does it consider the budget for operational costs, which were financed almost entirely by OCOG earnings.

Brazil's Federal Court of Accounts (TCU) (TCU 2017) calculated the costs for the 2016 Rio de Janeiro Olympic Games at 43.7 billion *reais* (approximately US$14 billion in 2017). The 2014 Football World Cup in Brazil cost nearly 27 billion *reais* (approximately US$15 billion in 2014) (CGU n.d.). The Organizing Committee for the Tokyo 2020 Olympics (Tokyo 2020 n.d.) presented a total budget of US$12.6 billion.

Despite the incremental growth of costs associated with the organization of sport spectacle, the Fédération Internationale de Football Association (FIFA) and the International Olympic Committee (IOC) have continuously sought to free themselves from the burden of actually having to produce such spectacles. Both institutions aim to steer the bulk of marketing revenues to their own upkeep and to that of entities affiliated with them; in doing so, they have transferred a progressively greater share of financial responsibilities to host cities and countries.[5] Without a doubt, the ambitions of hegemonic groups in the field of production of sport spectacle is not enough to produce such spectacles in and of themselves. Instead, spectacles' viability depends on the existence of favorable structural conditions, which are created when subjects acting within the field of the production of the city work toward this end in order to validate their own strategies. Beginning in the 1980s, a line of thought began to emerge that established an agenda in which market-oriented logic determined the theories and practices of urban planning. This line of thought proved to be perfectly suited to FIFA's and the IOC's goals.

Burbank, Andranovich and Heying (2001) maintain that two conditions are necessary for the development of an urban planning strategy based on attracting mega-events: first, the desire among elite groups to change a given city's image, and second, the existence of an "urban regime." Stone (2008) identifies this "urban regime" as a set of informal agreements between political leaders and actors from the private sector that guarantees certain conditions of government, taking into account both macroeconomic pressures and the different abilities of public and private agents. Like Stone, other authors address similar empirical situations through other approaches and the use of different nomenclatures. Examples include: the "growth machine" defined by Logan and Molotch (1987); Elkin's (1987) "entrepreneurial regime;" or Mollenkopf's (1983) "pro-growth coalitions." In fact, all of these share a common focus: namely, the practices and strategies of different actors, which are articulated through a line of thought that Harvey (1989a) calls "urban entrepreneurialism" and that has become hegemonic within the field of urban planning since the mid-1980s.

By considering the strength that these ideas have acquired in the field within which the city is produced, this chapter seeks to identify the main actors – acting in support of and supported by these ideas – who have dominated this field in its convergence with the field of production of sport spectacle. What elements have conferred the status of player to individual and collective subjects within these pro-growth coalitions? What are the roles that these subjects play within the game? What motivations drive these subjects to join forces by forming coalitions? What are their principle strategies and disputes? Based on the assumption that these projects, which emerge from the entrepreneurial discourses of local forces, can only come to fruition through articulations, alliances, and disputes across and between scalar levels, my research adopts a cross-scale perspective to search for answers to these questions.

The attraction of mega-events and urban entrepreneurialism

The technology and information revolutions, the reorientation and relocation of labor, the financialization of the global economy, and the intensification of competition are all recent alterations in the global order that can be linked to the phenomenon of globalization,[6] the inexorability of which has been used to justify ideas of urban entrepreneurialism. This model of urban management is associated with a profound reconfiguration of the hierarchies and scales of power, which Swyngedouw (1997) sees as one of the defining elements of contemporary society.

The challenges that competition imposes on a global scale, together with the supposed "inability" of nation-states to offer alternatives to these challenges, have been among the main arguments that reputable urban planning professionals[7] have offered to prop up theories that invert scales of power and see local governments as protagonists promoting economic development. Thanks to the efforts of these professionals, as well as certain multilateral agencies,[8] such ideas began to serve as the basis for a hegemonic model of urban management employed throughout the world. It follows that the need to insert the city into a highly competitive global production environment became the central argument spurring the race between governments to access the global market and different forms of capital. Sporting mega-events showed themselves to be among the most powerful possibilities in exercising this newfound protagonism.

Given the profound alterations in social-spatial relations that the reorganization of capitalism on a worldwide scale has caused in the last three decades (Harvey 1989b) – in terms of the role of the public sphere, as well as in habits, customs, and the repositioning of culture – disputes over spectacle are especially suited to competitions between places seeking to attract different forms of capital. After all, as Debord noted, since at least the 1960s, spectacle has become modern-day society's most profitable commodity.

> As indispensable embellishment of currently produced objects, as general articulation of the system's rationales, and as advanced economic sector that directly creates an ever-increasing mass of image-objects, the spectacle is the leading production of present-day society.
>
> (Debord 2002, pp. 10, 15)

Sport spectacle, as the most attractive contemporary mega-event, has great potential to promote the international visibility of host cities and countries as well as to boost major construction projects for infrastructure, sporting venues, and urban renewal. Such characteristics make sport spectacle especially well-suited to development strategies, the principal goal of which is to attract capital.

Logan and Molotch (1987) identify two key groups for the production and maintenance of the "growth machine": political and business leaders. Among politicians, the most ardent defenders of economic developmentalism are those who hold elected office; whereas among business leaders, urban property financiers and real estate promotors prove to be especially keen. Media and other institutions that serve the public also join these protagonists, whereas cultural institutions play important supporting roles.

In the following pages, I will analyze the logic and strategies of these agents within coalitions built around attracting mega-events. Throughout my analysis, the city of Rio de Janeiro, which hosted consecutive editions of the two largest contemporary mega-events in the 2014 Football World Cup and the 2016 Summer Olympics, will serve as an important example.

For the purposes of this research, Logan and Molotch's (1987) considerations serve as an excellent starting point, as do the formulations of Burbank, Andranovich and Heying (2001). However, the specificities of this kind of coalition, as seen in its convergence with the field of production of sport spectacle in the beginning of the twenty-first century, will lead us to consider subjects who the aforementioned authors do not consider and to question the importance of certain subjects they emphasize.

Politicians

Elected politicians and other state bureaucrats hold symbolic capital that can be used as leverage in pro-growth coalitions and can help unite the diverse agents involved in them. In addition, they are responsible for coordinating projects and for making decisions regarding the inversion and control of public resources.[9] Their role in articulating, channeling, and amplifying economic forces involved in these coalitions is especially crucial (Mollenkopf 1983; Stone 2008).

Within a strategy that aims to create a favorable environment for the valorization of capital, public investments in infrastructure, communications, urban renewal projects, and other actions that reflect the quality of services are a prescription for success. When the production of sport spectacle becomes the central issue around which pro-growth coalitions are organized, the demands of the international institutions responsible for such mega-events will, in turn, legitimize this prescription.

Despite the evidence of conflicts and disputes between different groups acting in the heart of pro-growth coalitions on a city-wide scale as well as in articulations with other scalar levels, political leaders are responsible for managing appearances of cohesion and consensus not only within these coalitions but throughout the society that surrounds them. After all, as Mollenkopf (1983) writes, all coalition members have their own interests within the coalition, but the strength of the coalition lies in its capacity to eliminate disagreements.

> Like-minded private elites did not join together to manipulate public policy toward their own ends. To the contrary, this study argues that political entrepreneurs arduously built progrowth coalitions out of conflicting interests, mass as well as elite, and that each element had its own reasons for joining forces. It also argues that the successes of these coalitions increased rather than decreased disagreement over the content of progrowth politics.
>
> (Mollenkopf 1983, p. 19)

These leaders also promote legislative, political, and institutional changes to support the creation of a business-friendly environment. Businesses connected to the production of sport spectacle are not only those led by groups involved in the coalition and the investors whom they aim to attract; instead, a business-friendly environment must also extend to institutions that promote spectacle.[10]

Considering the crucial position that these players occupy, it is possible to understand the other coalition members' efforts to elect politicians whose objectives are in tune with their own strategic positions. The control of government programs and actions, as well as the organization of administrative structures, is what effectively is in dispute in the electoral processes. In certain cases, the objective of elite business leaders goes beyond shaping a given city's management model for business; such elites also aim, to the fullest extent possible, to manage the city themselves.[11]

The great media visibility that mega-events command tends to confer political and social capital sufficient to attract the adhesion of the political representatives of cities, regions, and countries to pro-growth coalitions. The possibility of carrying out large-scale urban transformations – the viability of which will also confer political capital across all scales of power – guarantees that such leaders will remain in these coalitions.

Other motivations, which vary from place to place, may also reinforce the mobilization of political leadership from different scales of government. In Barcelona, for example, while municipal authorities used the 1992 Summer Olympics to obtain financing to carry out a major transformation of the city, the regional government took advantage of the opportunity to promote Catalan nationalism, and the Spanish government saw the Games as a chance to showcase Spain as a modern country and an important member of the European Union. A similar desire to communicate ideas of modernity and power also mobilized political leaders in authoritarian countries, such as China in 2008 or South Korea in 1988. Likewise, the desire to show the world a "unified" or "modern" image of post-apartheid South Africa was the principal motivation of South African leaders who sought to host the 2010 Football World Cup (Bass 2009). In other cases, such as in Brazil, the large volume of private economic capital involved in financing political campaigns[12] established links between politicians and other coalition members that were strong enough to guarantee the commitment of politicians.

As other works have demonstrated,[13] the interests of private actors almost always prevail in pro-growth coalitions. This only occurs thanks to the articulation of agents connected to political power who – by consolidating their own interests – also make the interests of other coalition members viable. Generally speaking, it is impossible for a coalition that aims to attract mega-events to be established without involving political leaders from all levels of government. Even in the case of the 1984 Los Angeles Summer Olympics, for which the candidature and organization were entirely the responsibility of the private sector (Burbank, Andranovich & Heying, 2001), the involvement of political leaders proved necessary.

Private entrepreneurs

In general, establishing a business-friendly environment in a city tends to lead, directly or indirectly, to gains for all major business leaders acting locally. However, some of these stand out for their ability to gain larger profits; consequently, they act more decisively within pro-growth coalitions. Among these business leaders, land speculators, real estate promotors, land grant holders, and those involved in the service industry are especially noteworthy. In certain places, real estate contractors also play an important role.

Frequently, the same businesses profit from different areas of a single operation, such as speculating, carrying out public works, and providing services. Thus, the division between business segments that I present in what follows is intended for strictly didactic purposes. Considering the standout position that speculators and real estate promotors assume within pro-growth coalitions, I will explore their actions in greater detail.

Speculators and real estate promotors

The valorization of land and of major developers has been the most immediate consequence of major development projects related to sport spectacle. Although most host cities experience real estate valorization throughout their territory, the spatial concentration of Olympic projects in clusters tends to valorize these areas in a markedly different way than other parts of the city. In addition, businesses that act in these areas also tend to receive other kinds of advantages, such as the flexibilization of zoning laws as well as fiscal and credit-based benefits.

Attracting private investment has been a central justification for politicians who join pro-growth coalitions. In this sense, public-private partnerships (PPPs) have become important instruments in making major urban development projects viable, regardless of the motivations of a given coalition. When these coalitions organize around preparing for sporting mega-events, the urgency imposed by inflexible event timetables always results in a significant investment of public funds which are intended to attract potential partners more quickly. The vast quantity of public resources invested in land, infrastructure, and financing are generally justified through the promise of future returns, while such results are far from guaranteed. Although pro-growth coalitions adopt different strategies, over the course of the last three decades, the interest of both real estate developers and speculators have always been taken into consideration in defining public policies related to sport spectacle.

The pro-growth coalition behind the organization of the 1992 Barcelona Summer Olympics, which included three spheres of public administration (central, autonomous, and local), has been held up as a paradigm for success in the articulation of private investment. This coalition expropriated land and promoted infrastructural work with public funds but, in order to guarantee profitability for private investments, ignored the city's pre-existing housing deficit and renounce any plans to house low-income people (COHRE 2007).

The organization of the 1996 Atlanta Summer Olympics was perhaps the most expressive case of the power of real estate promotors in the Olympics. Atlanta's candidature to host the Games – promoted by a group of businesspeople led by Billy Payne, a real estate lawyer – won over political leaders by promising that financing for organizing the Games would be entirely private. With the clear objective of promoting the city's real estate market, Atlanta's Olympic project also received significant public investments, especially for acquiring land and building infrastructure for development projects. The event was organized through a three-way agreement between Atlanta's mayor office, the Metropolitan Atlanta Olympic Games Authority (MAOGA) – a public authority created by the Georgia state government – and the Atlanta Committee for the Olympic Games (ACOG). MAOGA was given the power to buy and sell land, to borrow and lend money, to form its own police force, and to distribute major construction contracts. However, MAOGA delegated a significant part of its power to ACOG, a private organization that was also run by Billy Payne and his team. In return, ACOG assumed control of all major decisions relating to the 1996 Games.[14] The demolition of 2,000 public housing units to open space for new real estate developments near the Olympic installations was especially representative of the actions of Atlanta's Olympic entrepreneurs. According to the Center on House Rights and Evictions (COHRE 2007), 1,195 units within the Techwood and Clark Howell public housing developments were destroyed to give way to 900 mixed-use units, of which only 360 were reserved for low-income populations. The income levels necessary to afford these new properties were ten times higher than the median income of families who lived there before the demolition.

In Sydney, a vast area of public land was utilized for Olympic construction and associated developments. Overall, the organization of the Olympics in that city had a negative impact on the availability and price of housing (COHRE 2007), and developments related to the Games did not take public housing needs into account.

The representation of Athens as the cradle of Olympism conferred a special symbolic appeal to the city's candidature to host the 2004 Games. This, in turn, legitimized the use of public funds to finance almost all new infrastructure associated with the event. Stavrides (2017) identifies the PPPs established in Athens for the Olympic Games as presenting an opportunity for a very small number of people to become very rich. He emphasizes that changes to the Master Plan of Athens, allowing the city to undertake the modernizing project associated with the Olympics (see Chapter Six), were among the central pillars that sustained this opportunity.

Chinese political leaders used the objective of building confidence and attracting foreign investors to China as their main argument to build significant public support for Beijing's candidature to host the 2008 Olympic Summer Games. Although this support was based on a belief that sacrifice on the part of some would be necessary to benefit the majority with a greater quality of life (COHRE 2007), evidence shows that the primary beneficiaries of the 2008 Beijing Games were private entrepreneurs, especially real estate speculators who benefitted from the valorization of properties near revitalized areas (Broudehoux 2007). The Center on Housing Rights and Evictions (COHRE 2007) pointed to real estate developments – both commercial buildings and luxury residences – as being central to the high number of evictions relating to the organization of the Beijing Olympics. COHRE (2007) also notes other motivations linked to the valorization of land, including major infrastructure projects as well as sporting and cultural venues.

London's candidature to host the 2012 Summer Games overestimated the participation of private initiatives in financing infrastructure and venues. It also significantly underestimated the need for financing from the public sector, which resulted in additional implementation costs of £5.9 billion in public funds (House of Commons 2008). In addition, the cost of buying land for London's Olympic park as well as the unplanned financing of part of the Olympic Village, were not accounted for in the £9.298 billion Public Sector Funding Package. The Department for Culture, Media and Sport (DCMS) justified disregarding these expenditures by arguing that the sale of houses and plots of land to real estate developers would minimize overall effects on the public budget (House of Commons 2012). Thus, it fell to the London Legacy Development Corporation – a municipal business responsible for commercializing the Games – to attract investments in the Olympic Park and produce the promised returns. However, it was still unclear, in terms of value and time, if the real estate market would have the appetite to make the necessary investments (House of Commons 2013).

The simultaneous organization of the 2016 Summer Olympics and the 2014 Football World Cup in Brazil, which were said to have sufficient private financing, were marked by contracts with PPPs involving all of the actors in pro-mega-event coalitions. Two major partnerships highlight the concentration of power among a small number of real estate developers and land speculators within these coalition.

The choice to locate Rio de Janeiro's Olympic Park in the Barra da Tijuca neighborhood was, ipso facto, enough to make Carlos Carvalho Hosken – a pioneering real estate developer who owns more than 10 million square meters of land in Barra da Tijuca – the primary beneficiary of all investments carried out there. After all, the proximity of the Park, which was built on land owned by the government of the Rio de Janeiro state, led to the major valorization of privately-owned land throughout Barra da Tijuca. In joining construction firms Odebrecht and Andrade Gutierrez to form the consortium behind the PPP that won construction rights for the Olympic Park, Carvalho Hosken assumed an even more privileged position. Under the PPP contract, signed in 2012 and valued at 1.35 billion *reais* (US$770 million), the consortium took on the responsibility of building the Rio Media Center (RMC), the Main Press Center (MPC), a hotel, three Olympic Training Center pavilions, and various infrastructure projects. In return, the consortium was paid through a pecuniary consideration worth approximately 37% of the contract as well as real estate considerations for the rest of the cost. This involved the transference of property rights for 1.18 million square meters of public lands (75% of the Olympic Park's total area) for luxury condos after the conclusion of the Games. Venues located within the Olympic Park – including the Olympic Aquatic Stadium, the Olympic Tennis Center, and the International Broadcast Centre (IBC), among others – were not included in the PPP contract; Rio de Janeiro's municipal government took responsibility for their construction, using funds from Brazil's federal government (Rio 2016 2012). The later inclusion of the IBC in the contract was balanced by the Rio municipal government's promise to raise the allowance for future constructions in the area through alterations in local zoning laws. Although public authorities claimed that the construction of Olympic venues carried out by private sector partners counted as private investment, a mathematical calculation, using the value of this construction minus associated territorial concessions and the size of the area transferred, shows that the much-vaunted contribution of the private sector was nothing more than a land grab. Consortium members bought public land at US$411.00 per square meter, slightly more than one-third of its value, which at the time could exceed US$1200.00 per square meter. Finally, as the owner of the land on which the Olympic Village was constructed, Carvalho Hosken was also guaranteed construction rights for apartments destined for high-income populations. These units, originally destined for Olympic athletes, were constructed using infrastructural assistance provided by Rio de Janeiro's municipal government and financed through loans with interest rates subsidized by Brazil's federal government (Rio 2016 Candidate City n.d.).

Porto Maravilha (the "Marvelous Port" revitalization project in Rio de Janeiro's port district) is located 30 kilometers away from the Olympic Park but was also justified through the execution of the 2016 Olympics, even though it was not connected to any Olympic venue. Through a single PPP contract, the Porto Maravilha Urban Operation Consortium (*Operação Urbana Consorciada –* OUC) consolidates construction and maintenance projects of 5 million square meters of land, 75% of which is public property, and also includes the privatization of public services. The PPP establishes fees for construction exceeding basic land use through Certificates of Additional Construction Potential (*Certificados de Potencial Adicional de Construção –* CEPACs). CEPACs, which serve as real estate deeds regulated by the Commission for Market Values, can be negotiated multiple times before they are joined together as a single lot. As it happens, 6.4 million of the available CEPACs – corresponding to an area of 4 million square meters – were sold together as a single lot for 3.4 billion *reais* (equivalent to US$2.2 billion at the time) to Caixa Econômica Federal (CEF), an entirely publicly-owned bank. This purchase was made with resources from the federal government's Severance Indemnity Fund (*Fundo de Garantia por Tempo de Serviço do Trabalhador –* FGTS). CEF took responsibility for 8 billion *reais* (equivalent to US$5 billion) in costs for revitalization projects in the port district. To complete this payment, which was made to the development companies responsible for constructions in the area, CEF received CEPACs, together with public land throughout the area, through a transference between federal, state, and municipal governments. Thus, it fell to CEF to take on the risks of transferring CEPACs and lands to private enterprise; if the market lost interest, it would also be CEF's responsibility to pay for losses with money from the public indemnity fund. A chart published on Urban Development Company of Rio de Janeiro's Port Region official website (*Companhia de Desenvolvimento Urbano da Região do Porto –* CDURP) shows that, eight years after CEF bought the CEPACs, 91.21% had not yet been resold.

The Football World Cup has less capacity than the Olympic Games to mobilize capital to competition and non-competition venues. Furthermore, it relies on a spatial distribution that disperses sporting venues throughout a given host country's territory. As such, there are smaller benefits for real estate speculators and developers. For the most part, these benefits relate to the valorization of property near football stadiums or new infrastructure. Only in a limited number of cases have pro-growth coalitions in host cities managed to justify major urban reform projects. In this sense, the case of the construction of Arena Pernambuco – located in the city of São Lourenço da Mata, part of the Recife metropolitan region in northeastern Brazil – for the 2014 Football World Cup is especially symbolic. A consortium consisting of two businesses linked to the Odebrecht construction group formed a PPP that won rights to construct Arena Pernambuco and to manage it for 33 years through administration concessions. The PPP for Arena Pernambuco also included a transfer of 2.47 million square meters of public lands to partner businesses for a development project known as the "City of the Cup." The project was made possible through an alteration in São Lourenço da Mata's Municipal Code, converting a Special Social Interests

Zone (*Zona de Especial Interesse Social* – ZEIS) into a Special Urbanization Zone (*Zona de Urbanização Preferencial*). The companies that formed the private consortium also obtained the rights to establish a specific Master Plan for their project, which enjoyed complete autonomy in relation to São Lourenço da Mata's Municipal Master Plan.[15]

In Tokyo, the All Japan Real Estate Association released a report in 2015 on the relationship between the Olympic Games and the real estate industry (All Japan Real Estate Association 2015). The report contained six recommendations for guidelines establishing urban policies that result in greater support from political leaders for creating a business-friendly environment. These recommendations include controlling unoccupied buildings and urban agricultural land, which is also connected to two other recommendations: mapping of landowners and of urban real estate. The report argues that, in order to prevent disasters, measures must be taken to control ruined structures and buildings considered to be precarious. In order to make these measures viable, the Association presents itself as a potential collaborator in creating conditions for large-scale evictions and establishes a role for the Association's offices in contributing to these objectives, including through supporting behavioral controls in public spaces.

The removal of undesirable neighbors, always a central strategy among pro-growth coalitions for increasing land valorization, becomes more efficient when a coalition's main purpose is to attract mega-events. Planning for infrastructure and sporting venues is often intentionally used to justify evictions so as to present spaces that fall within the aesthetic patterns established by investment capital.

The COHRE has studied the impacts of mega-events on housing between 1988 and 2008. According to the group's final report (COHRE 2007), the case of Beijing – in which 1.5 million people were evicted in preparation for the 2008 Summer Games – was the most emblematic. The report notes the 720,000 people were evicted during the organization of the 1988 Seoul Olympics. Furthermore, 68,000 were evicted for the Atlanta 1996 Games and 2,700 were removed for the 2004 Athens Games. In Athens, the Roma population suffered the most direct effects of these removals.[16] Although other cases – like Sydney in 2000 and Barcelona in 1992 – did not show this same propensity for forced mass evictions, COHRE found that housing values increased in both locations (COHRE 2007). Researchers noted that, in Barcelona, low-income populations were effectively expelled from central areas of the city through climbing property and rental prices (Capel 2005; Broudehoux 2007).

In London, Raco and Tunney (2010) note the difficulties that 201 small businesses faced when they were compelled to move from the area where the Olympic Village was constructed. They argue that forced eviction represents a transference of benefits from these businesses to development agencies and real estate firms. In Brazil, the National Popular Committee on the World Cup and Olympics sent a video to the United Nations (ANCOP 2013) showing 250,000 forced evictions related to the 2014 World Cup and the 2016 Olympic Games.

The organization of the 2020 Summer Olympics in Japan has also promoted forced evictions. Additions to the new National Stadium have resulted in the expulsion of dozens of homeless people who lived in a nearby park as well as in the forced dislocation of 200 mostly elderly public housing tenants whose homes near the new stadium site were slated for destruction (Suzuki, Ogawa & Inaba 2017).

Construction firms

The economic capital mobilized in constructing venues, accommodations, and infrastructure tends to turn business leaders from the construction sector into some of the most ardent defenders of pro-mega-event coalitions. In many cases, they assume an active participation in the definition of public policies. In addition, discourses of urgency and the need to honor commitments made on an international scale lead to other advantages for sector, ranging from fiscal and credit-related[17] benefits[18] to the establishment of exceptional legal measures allowing them to public funding.[19]

Governments throughout the world have argued that the speed and efficiency demanded by preparations for mega-events justify transferring public responsibilities to private construction firms. This was the argument that the city government of Seoul used during preparations for the 1988 Summer Olympics in adopting the "joint redevelopment" method (COHRE 2007), which gave construction companies and land owners the responsibility of "cleaning" pre-existing settlements from the urban terrain so as to clear the way for urban reconstruction. This transference of responsibilities freed city authorities from having to involve themselves directly with the bothersome task of carrying out evictions; furthermore, it paved the way "for the increased (extralegal) use of private eviction companies which employed 'thugs' to get rid of existing residents" (COHRE 2007, p. 86).

In other places, political leaders have adopted systems of building that give private investors contracted to construct sporting venues the right to operate these venues for a significant period of time. Broudehoux (2007) argues that this system – which allowed venues built for the 2008 Games to be converted into leisure and commercial spaces for foreign visitors – privatized constructions built through public financing, thereby creating a new, exclusionary space within Beijing's urban landscape.

Similarly, the aforementioned administrative concessions contract for the revitalization of Rio de Janeiro's port zone (the *Porto Maravilha* project) also included a transference of public services, giving private firms operation and maintenance rights for a period of fifteen years. Officially, the *Porto Maravilha* project was authored by Instituto Pereira Passos (IPP), a publicly owned institute charged with implementing strategic projects on behalf of Rio de Janeiro's municipal government. However, the essence of its contents reproduces almost entirely the planning proposal contained in the "Urbanistic Report for the Operation of the *Porto Maravilha* Urban Consortium." This report was prepared by the New

Port Consortium *(Consórcio Porto Novo)* – composed of the construction firms Odebrecht, OAS, and Carioca Engenharia – which, within a year, was declared to be the only bidder capable of carrying out construction projects and administering services in Rio de Janeiro's port district.

The participation of constructors in defining public policy was also observed in Barcelona. The importance of the construction industry in Spain was a key criterion to define priorities in urban transformation project in that city.[20] Observing the Barcelona's housing policy during the period from 1982 to 1992, COHRE (2007) noted that public housing policies were used to counteract the cyclical crises in the construction sector rather than to address social needs.

It is common for mega-events to exceed budgetary projections. This is reflected in the construction contracts. In addition to the aforementioned benefits, contractual additions based on changes to or the inclusion of new projects that attend to the interests of pro-growth coalitions also contribute to these cost increases. The £9.3 billion (approximately US$14.9 billion in 2012) investment from the Public Sector Funding Package in London more than tripled the US$4.04 billion estimated in London's candidature budget without accounting for certain important public expenditures. (DCMS 2012; NAO 2012) The total cost for the 2004 Athens Games, estimated at close to US$8 billion in the city's candidature file (Athens Bid Committee n.d.), increased to US$16 billion. In Beijing, the initial US$15.9 billion budget (Beijing Olympic Bid Committee n.d.) skyrocketed to US$40 billion. Although the final costs of the 2016 Rio de Janeiro Games were divulged at US$14 billion (TCU 2017), close to estimated cost in Rio's candidature file (Rio 2016 Candidate City n.d.), many of the projects connected to that budget were not executed, such as the promised clean-up of Guanabara Bay.

In almost all of these processes, construction rights are concentrated among a small number of firms. In Brazil, where major business owners have played a significant role in the historical formation of the construction sector, five businesses have formed a variety of different consortiums and monopolized almost all contracts relating to the production of sporting mega-events as well as the benefits connected to other partnerships. In addition to contracts for the Olympic Park and *Porto Maravilha*, the Odebrecht firm also participated in consortiums to rebuild Maracanã Stadium and construct Rio's Bus Rapid Transit (BRT) system, two of the most important projects for the 2016 Olympics. Odebrecht was also involved in building four stadiums for the 2014 World Cup, including Arena Pernambuco. Andrade Gutierrez, another construction firm connected to the Olympic Park, was also involved with Maracanã and three additional stadiums. Finally, Carvalho Hosken still reigns supreme over all developments in the Barra da Tijuca neighborhood.

Private partners

Businesses that administer services through special concessions always find pro-growth coalitions useful in increasing their holdings. High costs of maintenance and the discourse of greater efficiency that private enterprise supposedly offers in comparison to public administration have long served as justification for granting long-term concessions to private firms for sporting venues and infrastructure produced with public resources. In every mega-event host city, private enterprise has taken over airports, stadiums, sporting venues, transportation systems, and even public parks; these, in return, have become inaccessible to the majority of the population that, by paying taxes, funds their construction.

Normally, funds that the state raises through concessions are far less than the resources spent on construction projects, yet the funds that private partners earn through administering services tend to surpass the fees that they pay for such rights. For example, Horne and Whannel (2016) observed that when London's Olympic Stadium was rented to the West Ham Football Club, the contract required a one-time payment of £15 million from West Ham in addition to annual payments of £2.5 million. These values, however, are far from sufficient to cover the £250 million in public funds invested in construction projects specifically tailored to West Ham's needs. In addition, the contract allows West Ham up to £12 million in additional profits per season, far exceeding the club's expenditure on rent.

The case of Brazil's Mário Filho Stadium (universally known as Maracanã) is similar. Maracanã hosted the opening and closing ceremonies of the 2016 Olympics, as well as the final match of the 2014 World Cup. The PPP contract signed by the Maracanã S/A consortium – which won administrative rights for the management, operation, and maintenance of the stadium complex – was initially set at 35 years. The consortium, controlled by Odebrecht, was scheduled to make 35 annual payments of 4.5 million *reais* to the Rio de Janeiro state government, invest approximately 500 million *reais* in demolishing pre-existing constructions, and build leisure venues and infrastructure intended to make the future commercialization of the stadium complex viable. After a tumultuous period of protests against privatization and in defense of preserving venues intended for public use, a judicial order suspended the projected building project. Without additional construction, the contract's value to the state over the course of 35 years would be a total of 157.5 million *reais*, far below the 1 billion *reais* (US$500 billion in 2013 when work on the stadium was completed) that the state had paid Odebrecht to renovate Maracanã. In 2017, the legality of the contract was challenged in court, and in 2019, the partnership was suspended when Odebrecht failed to make its annual payments. It is worth emphasizing that the commercial viability study that proposed demolition and new construction was conducted by IMX Holding S/A, one of the initial members of the Maracanã S/A consortium, the sole candidate for the contract.

In addition, the architecture of sporting venues is constructed to attract private partners: for example, in search of such "partnerships," football stadiums are converted into multiuse areas that can be adapted to shopping malls, or centers for business, entertainment, or conventions. Broudehoux (2007) cites the case of Beijing's National Aquatics Center, which was designed as an entertainment palace complete with a wave pool, artificial beach, gym, ice skating rink, movie theatre, stores, and restaurants as well as other spaces that can be transformed into professional sports stadiums or private health clubs.

The service industry

The service industry stands to make gains from mega-events beyond its significant participation in PPPs. Hotel and entertainment industries are the main beneficiaries of FIFA's and the IOC's demands for reception and accommodations. Benefits offered to investors in this sector[21] include tax forgiveness and subsidized interest rates, which are associated with relaxed zoning standards for the construction of new developments or the reform of existing structures.

Producers of representations of the real

Urban projects adapted to the impulses of the global economy also demand updating representations of that which is understood by "city," especially representations that reorient material practices in urban restructuring processes. It is here that subjects responsible for the production and reproduction of different forms of seeing the world carry special importance.

Media, consulting companies, and institutions that represent certain groups of specialists play a central role as subjects capable of producing representations of the real: in other words, of producing and reproducing visions of the world (Bourdieu 1991), manipulating tastes and opinions, and orienting thoughts and actions. So, too, do all other subjects who act in the field of cultural production. It is they who conduct processes that legitimize and (re)affirm the orientation of actions. They are also the main arbiters of internal disputes within coalitions that sustain the "growth machine" (Logan & Molotch 1987).

Technical competence and the institutions that represent it

Constructing the hegemonic position that a given worldview holds within a field depends on the production and legitimization of arguments and diagnoses that justify this vision and provide it with the support it needs. Ideas do not possess their own strength; instead, the strength they acquire is related not only to the authority with which they are enunciated but also the existence of subjects who – in searching to validate their own interests – become capable of incorporating the strategies that these ideas articulate.

For Bourdieu (1991), symbolic power, as a condition of the unrecognizable form of other kinds of power, possesses this capacity to construct the real through the simple fact of enunciating it. It transforms not only worldviews but also actions made in the world and even the world itself. Therefore, symbolic power has "almost magical power which enables one to obtain the equivalent of what is obtained through force (whether physical or economic), by virtue of the specific effect of mobilization" (Bourdieu 1991, p. 170).

When Bourdieu examines this almost "magical" power which exerts authority by bringing things into existence through the simple act of enunciating them in public, he calls attention to the fact that this power depends not only on the recognition of whoever enunciates it but also on the principle of belonging to a group to which it is directed. In other words, whatever is enunciated must be based on the group's objectivities to obtain recognition.

Symbolic power in the field of production of sport spectacle involves electing a network of experts who establish a prescription for victorious candidatures in the disputes to host events related to the field or who determine necessary practices for executing events defined as "successful." It can only be viable to the extent to which a worldview is produced and accepted in the field of production of the city that is capable of sustaining both disputes among cities for the rights to host these events and the aspiration to carry them out in accordance with such orientations. Meanwhile, a worldview can only be imposed when it is connected to the dispute for a monopoly on the power to form beliefs and recognition, which is formed specifically within the field in which cultural capital takes a determining role.

Establishing the hegemony of competitive policies within the field in which the city is produced relies on invoking technical supposed neutrality. A marketplace of consultors who create models and discourses based on scientific authority bolster this supposed neutrality as they diagnose, prescribe, and establish consensuses. It was not by chance that the urban transformations that Barcelona underwent in preparation for the 1992 Summer Olympics – as well as the political gains associated with these changes – became the definitive paradigm for urban entrepreneurialism.

Conflicts of interests may occasionally occur within the heart of pro-growth coalitions, such as conflicts related to the spaces prioritized for investments and, consequently, the groups of individuals who stand to benefit most. In these cases, specialists who retain the authority to speak "for the good of the city" produce technical feedback and, whenever possible, present and create proposals that reconcile and satisfy the interests of all coalition members even if this increases the quantity of public resources involved.

The articulation of specialists during the process of legitimizing Rio de Janeiro's *Porto Maravilha* project illustrates this situation especially well. The reform of Rio de Janeiro's port district has long been a concern of certain groups that sustained the city's pro-mega-events coalition. However, the *Candidature File for Rio de Janeiro to host the 2016 Olympic and Paralympic Games* (Rio 2016 Candidate City n.d.) did not propose locating any Olympic venues in the city's port district. Instead, the *Porto Maravilha* project was based strictly on providing services for ships docked in the port with the objective of supplementing the paucity of accommodations available to the public and reinforcing the local hospitality industry's attempts to adjust to IOC demands. Given that *Porto Maravilha* involved nearly US$5 billion in investments, political leaders needed a stronger justification for implementing the program. This, in turn, led to the decision to transfer the Media and Referee Villages to the port district. In 2010, one year after the Rio de Janeiro city council voted to approve the urgent implementation of *Porto Maravilha*, the Institute of Architects of Brazil (IAB), in partnership with Rio de Janeiro's mayor's office, organized the seminar "The Olympics and the City: The Rio-Barcelona Connection," which sought the IOC's approval for this proposed transfer. The seminar brought together representatives from federal, state, and city governments with others from the IOC and Brazilian Olympic Committee, local consulting firms, and other institutions as well as select academics. Jordi Borja, Manoel de Forn y Foxá, and Pasqual Maragall, all of whom hold significant cultural and political capital due to the Barcelona paradigm,[22] were guests of honor. In addition, national and foreign companies supported the event and helped to strengthen its articulation in the national media and other institutions.[23] The IOC's final verdict, supporting the transference, was never carried out but served the objective of legitimizing the *Porto Maravilha* project and accommodating interests in the pro-growth coalition.

The noteworthy presence of designer architecture firms in projects linked to sport spectacle throughout the world demonstrates the power that this select group of professionals exerts in defining priorities for public investment. In seeking to present an image of modernity and sophistication, city leaders pay vast sums for projects connected to firms including Santiago Calatrava (Spain), Norman Foster (UK), AECON (UK), PTW (Australia), and Koolhaas (Netherlands), among others. They are also willing to invest significantly more to guarantee the spectacular character of these firms' projects.[24]

The media

As the primary sector responsible for spreading ideas, the media is essential in constructing a consensus to sustain projects steered by pro-growth coalitions. In a context in which the production of signs and images constitutes a source of power (Harvey 1989b; Debord 2002), the media holds the ability to modify power relations within different fields.

Bourdieu (1998) considers the field of journalistic production as a space of opposition between two forms of logic and two principles of legitimization: one based on the profession's values and the other on sales, revenue, and audience. He observes that although journalism – like literary, scientific, or artistic fields – operates according to its own cultural logic, it differentiates itself from these other fields because it is more closely subjected to the verdicts of the market. As such, it contributes to reinforcing, within the heart of all other fields, the value of what can be commercialized.

The commercial support of the media occurs through the sale of printed and digital materials or advertising space, which depends on the audience or the number of readers. The media therefore must strengthen its consumer market or else enter new markets so as to expand its reach and ability to accumulate. In addition to promoting economic growth and strengthening this internal market, sport spectacle augments local media and projects it into other scales, thereby attracting new advertisers, readers, and spectators.

On the other hand, media markets expand mainly through new partnerships and increased distribution networks, which occur through purely political processes. As such, it has been very common for the support for certain political projects to be offered in trade for partnerships. In certain situations, political leaders or their families control media or distribution networks;[25] in others, media bosses are involved in business ventures that connect them to other interest groups in pro-growth coalitions.

These players adopt two principal strategies to advance the interests of pro-growth coalitions. First, they act to spread the idea/strength of the city spectacle as competitive by means of subtle, well-constructed, and recurring discourses, preferably drawing on related areas of expertise. Second, and perhaps more powerfully, they work to shape the themes and issues that, progressively and subtly, produce public opinion (Bourdieu 1998) by constructing agendas based on the selected facts, groups, and individuals they deem fit to control communications. Thus, they create an environment in which the city, the country, and the world appear to constitute a public sphere that is completely depoliticized and incomprehensible and that cannot be approached through critical reflection. The absence of political debate, in turn, creates a completely favorable environment for urban management practices that benefit the coalition.

Partial considerations

Observing players who align themselves within pro-growth coalitions structured around the production of sporting mega-events reveals the competition among different complementary strategies that, in their reciprocal and multi-scalar execution, move the gearwork that articulates local and localized interests within the city.[26]

We can also identify a more ample pattern in the agreements made between the public and private agents in pro-growth coalitions when such coalitions are attached to the production of sport spectacle. However, certain patterns only reveal themselves in this specific kind of coalition, whereas others seem to construct specificities of their materialization in determined territories, thereby revealing themselves to undergo variations based on the effect of place.

In general, the production of spaces adequate for capitalistic accumulation has been the principal objective of maintaining the "growth machine" in motion no matter where it has been constructed. The standout role that elected politicians take in pursuing this objective can be seen in coalitions organized around the production of sport spectacle; these, in turn, demonstrate very emphatically the imperative of cross-scale articulation among these players.

Although other pro-growth coalitions also influence land valorization through changes to zoning laws and infrastructure projects, sporting mega-events occur in clusters, thereby facilitating their concentration in a relatively limited number of areas. One strategy that has been systematically utilized to amplify this kind of valorization is the dislocation of vulnerable communities. Pro-mega-event coalitions plan construction strategically for locations in which such communities are located so as to make this task easier. In turn, the discourse of efficiency and urgency helps neutralize attempts at resistance.

Private partners and the service industry are especially privileged segments in pro-mega-event coalitions thanks to the countless possibilities that mega-events offer for taking advantage of venues and services financed with public resources. In addition, pressures to offer certain services during mega-events in a quantity that far exceeds the city's normal demands elevates the benefits available to the sectors that produce these services, thereby further whetting the appetites of potential coalition members. This is especially relevant in cities without a completely developed tourism infrastructure, as has been the case in Rio de Janeiro.

The noteworthy participation of major construction firms in defining public policy and their direct involvement in managing territory deserves special emphasis in countries with less government accountability, such as Korea, China, and Brazil.

Specialists are called in cities slated to host mega-events in order to snuff out potential conflicts and maintain cohesion among different groups involved, although they cannot completely stifle all forms of dissent.[27] Brazil's experiences demonstrate the necessity of recruiting international experts whose names confer legitimacy to projects that are, in fact, produced and driven by technicians, corporate institutions, politicians, and local consulting firms or else by major domestic corporations that act locally (see Chapter Six).

In this way, the gearwork that sustains the "growth machine" in cities stays well lubricated with the legitimacy it has acquired through commitments made on a global scale, produced through candidature documents and the tangle of rules and contracts that steer the field of production of sport spectacle (cf. Chapter Three). Inasmuch as this process is driven by local and localized interests, it also aids the movement of a more substantial gearwork that also sustains the very field that maintains it (cf. Chapter Two).

The positions and strategies of the agents who participate in this gearwork are neither fixed nor definitive; they can change according to structural conditions and the positions of every actor in the field. At any given moment, certain important actors may simply stop participating, or else new actors may be incorporated into the field. The repercussions of these positions and strategies outrun the churning of the "growth machine." They can also reflect the continuity – or the collapse – of the system's reproduction.

Notes

1 Portions of this chapter first appeared in the book *O Poder dos Jogos e os Jogos de Poder: Os interesses em campo na produção da cidade para o espetáculo esportivo* (Oliveira 2015), published by Editora UFRJ. The English translation is by Raphael Soifer.

2 See Chapter Two.
3 The IOC demanded 16,000 beds in the Olympic Village for the 2024 and 2028 Games (IOC 2018) as well as the capacity to house 41,001 stakeholders, members of the Olympic family, and partners. These parameters also applied to the two previous editions of the Olympic Summer Games.
4 This number is based on fragmented information of all costs related to the preparation of the event. It considers operational costs as well as investments in venues, infrastructure, and the environment.
5 See Chapter One.
6 Here the word "globalization" is used, following Bourdieu (2000), in the sense of a form of representation of reality intentionally produced as a strategy to impose a world order based on the legitimization of neoliberal thinking. In Bourdieu's words, globalization "is a myth. [. . .] It is the main weapon in the battles against the gains of the welfare state" (Bourdieu 2000, p. 34).
7 Manoel Castells, Jordi Borja, Manuel de Forn y Foxá, Michel Piore, Charles Sabel, Michael Storpel, Philip Coke, and Gianfranco Battazzi are among the most important authors who defend these principles.
8 Especially the Inter-American Development Bank (IADB), the World Bank, the International Monetary Fund (IMF), and UN-Habitat.
9 In the production of sport spectacle, this responsibility is often transferred to private initiatives. During the candidature period for mega-events, the participation of consulting firms and OCOGs in defining projects is especially noteworthy.
10 See Chapter Two.
11 See Chapter Six.
12 Although corporate financing of electoral campaigns has been illegal in Brazil since 2016, shareholders of major real estate development and promotion firms have always been major contributors to political campaigns, whether as private citizens or corporate entities. For example, financial records maintained by the Regional Electoral Court in Rio de Janeiro state show that, during the 2012 elections, the Brazilian Democratic Movement Party (PMDB) and its candidate, incumbent mayor Eduardo Paes, received equal donations worth US$300,000 from the construction firms OAS, Carvalho Hosken, and Cyrela. All of these companies were involved in major publicly funded construction projects for mega-events. In addition, Carvalho Hosken made a donation worth US$88,000 directly to the campaign of Eduardo Paes.
13 For example, see Logan and Molotch (1987), Stone (2008), Elkin (1987), Mollenkopf (1983), Burbank, Andranovich and Heying (2001).
14 To better understand the power relations between ACOG, MAOGA, and Atlanta's mayor's office, see COHRE (2007), and Burbank, Andranovich and Heying (2001).
15 To learn more about the City of the Cup in Pernambuco Arena, see de Mello (2014).
16 See also Stavrides (2017).
17 As seen previously, most infrastructure and venue construction for mega-events is completely financed by public funds or through publicly subsidized loans.
18 In Brazil, for example, the tax breaks granted to FIFA and its partners through the General Law of the World Cup also applied to construction firms responsible for projects associated with mega-events. See Chapter Six.
19 See Chapter Six.
20 According to COHRE information, approximately 20% of male workers in Spain were involved in the construction industry, 12% of the Spanish workforce was directly involved in the construction, and six out of ten of the construction companies most important in the world were Spanish.
21 See Chapter Six and Ramos (2019).
22 During the candidature and organization period for the 1992 Barcelona Games, Manoel de Forn y Foxá served as coordinator of the city's Strategic Development Plan, Pasqual Maragall was the mayor, and Jordi Borja was vice mayor.

23 See Chapter Five to know the role of Jordi Borja and Manoel de Forn y Foxá in Rio de Janeiro Bids to host Olympic Games.
24 See Broudehoux (2007).
25 Currently, the world media market is dominated by a small number of conglomerates supported by vast fortunes. The political influence of some of these international groups can be seen throughout the world. Examples include: the Rupert Murdoch Group; Silvio Berlusconi's Mediaset; Anne Cox Chambers, from the United States; the Spanish group Prisa; Brazil's Globo organizations; and ORT, a Russian state-owned television channel.
26 Here, I understand local interests as those related to groups whose centers for decision-making are located within a given city. I understand localized interests as groups located in any part of the country or the world, but whose interests are connected to the territory of a given city.
27 In addition to the aforementioned cases of Denver and Los Angeles whose populations protested public financing for mega-events, it is worth noting Toronto's Bread, Not Circus Coalition; the World Class Cities for All, in South Africa; the No Games movement in Chicago; and Brazil's Popular Committees for the World Cup and Olympics, among others.

References

All Japan Real Estate Association 2015, *Relation Between the Tokyo Olympics and Real Estate Industry Report*, viewed 10 September 2019, <http://tokyo.zennichi.or.jp/wp/wp-content/uploads/2015/06/86de469726a21baec39e050cacf99db81.pdf>

Articulação Nacional da Copa (ANCOP) 2013, *World Cup 2014: Who Wins the Match?* viewed 18 June 2018, <www.youtube.com/watch?feature=player_embedded&v=aAX0 zSfrJK4#at=62>

Athens Bid Committee n.d., *Athens 2004 Candidature File*, vol. 1, Athens Bid Committee Athens.

Bass, O 2009, "Aiming for Africa: Durban, 2010 and Notions of African Urban Identity", in U Pillay, R Tomlinson & O Brass (eds) *Development and Dreams: The Urban Legacy of the 2010 Football World Cup*, Human Science Research Council (HSRC), Cape Town.

Beijing Olympic Bid Committee n.d., *Beijing 2008 Candidature File*, vol. 1, Beijing Olympic Bid Committee, Beijing.

Bourdieu, P 1991, *Language and Symbolic Power*, trans. G Raymond & M Adamsom, Polity Press, Cambridge.

Bourdieu, P 1998, *On Television*, trans. PP Ferguson, The New Press, New York.

Bourdieu, P 2000, *Acts of Resistance: Against the New Myths of our Time*, trans. R Nice, Blackwell Publishers, Oxford.

Broudehoux, AM 2007, "Spectacular Beijing: The Conspicuous Construction of an Olympic Metropolis", *Journal of Urban Affairs*, 29.4, pp. 383–399.

Burbank, M, Andranovich, G & Heying, C 2001, *Olympic Dreams: The Impact of Mega-Events on Local Politics*, Lynne Rienner Publishers, Boulder.

Capel, H 2005, *El modelo Barcelona: un examen crítico*, Ediciones del Serbal, Barcelona.

Centre on Housing Rights and Evictions (COHRE) 2007, *Fair Play for Housing Rights: Opportunities for the Olympic Movement and Other*, COHRE, Geneva.

Comité organisateur des Jeux olympiques (COJO 76) 1978, *Games of the XXI Olympiad Montréal 1976: Official Report*, vol. 1, COJO 76, Ottawa.

Controladoria Geral da União (CGU): portal da transparência n.d., *Matriz de Responsabilidades Copa do Mundo 2014*, viewed 16 January 2014, <www.portaltransparencia.gov.br/copa2014/matriz/>

Debord, G 2002, *Society of the Spectacle*, Black & Red, Detroit.

Department for Culture, Media and Sport (DCMS) 2012, *London 2012 Olympic and Paralympic Games – Quarterly Report October 2012*, DCMS, London, viewed 25 November 2019, <https://assets.publishing.service.gov.uk/government/uploads/system/uploads/attachment_data/file/78251/DCMS_GOE_Quarterly_Report_Q3.pdf>

de Mello, GMS 2014, "Transformações na dinâmica territorial de São Lourenço da Mata: Da Cidade da Copa aos novos empreendimentos imobiliários", masters dissertation, Universidade Federal de Pernambuco, Recife.

Elkin, SL 1987, *City and Regime in the American Republic*, University Chicago Press, Chicago.

Harvey, D 1989a, "From Managerialism to Entrepreneurialism: The Transformation in Urban Governance in Late Capitalism", *Geografiska Annaler, series B, Human Geography*, 71.1, pp. 3–17.

Harvey, D 1989b, *The Condition of Postmodernity: An Enquiry into the Origins of Cultural Change*, Blackwell Publishers, Oxford.

Horne, J & Whannel G 2016, *Understanding the Olympics*, 2nd ed., Routledge, Abingdon and New York.

House of Commons: Committee of Public Accounts 2008, *The Budget for the London 2012 Olympic and Paralympic Games*, Authority of the House of Commons, London, viewed 10 July 2018, <https://publications.parliament.uk/pa/cm200708/cmselect/cmpubacc/85/85.pdf>

House of Commons: Committee of Public Accounts 2012, *Preparations for the London 2012 Olympic and Paralympic Games*, authority of the House of Commons, London, viewed 10 July 2018, <https://publications.parliament.uk/pa/cm201012/cmselect/cmpubacc/1716/1716.pdf>

House of Commons: Committee of Public Accounts 2013, *Preparations for the London 2012 Olympic and Paralympic Games: Post – Games Review*, authority of the House of Commons, London, viewed 10 July 2018, <https://publications.parliament.uk/pa/cm201213/cmselect/cmpubacc/812/812.pdf>

International Olympic Committee (IOC) 2018, *Host City Contract Operational Requirements: June 2018*, IOC, Lausanne.

Logan, J & Molotch, H 1987, *Urban Fortunes: The Political Economy of Place*, University of California Press, Berkeley.

Los Angeles Olympic Organizing Committee (LAOOC) 1985, *Official Report of the Games of the XXIIIrd Olympiad Los Angeles, 1984*, vol. 1, LAOOC, Los Angeles.

Mollenkopf, JH 1983, *The Contested City*, Princeton University Press, Princeton.

National Audit Office (NAO) 2012, *The London 2012 Olympic Games and Paralympic Games: Post-Games Review*, National Audit Office, London, viewed on 5 November 2019, <www.nao.org.uk/wp-content/uploads/2012/12/1213794fr.pdf>

Organizing Committee of the Olympic and Paralympic Games RIO 2016 (Rio 2016) 2012, *Lançamento de pedra fundamental marca o início das obras do Parque Olímpico*, Newsletter 14, viewed 30 June 2012, <www.rio2016.org/noticias/noticias/lancamento-da-pedra-fundamental-marca-o-inicio-das-obras-do-parque-olimpico>

Raco, M & Tunney, E 2010, "Visibilities and Invisibilities in Urban Development: Small Business Communities and the London Olympics 2012", *Urban Studies*, 47, pp. 2069–2091, September.

Ramos, SR 2019, "Copa do Mundo FIFA 2014 no Brasil: da regulação do território às ações voltadas ao turismo", doctoral dissertation, Universidade de São Paulo, São Paulo.

Rio 2016 Candidate City n.d., *Candidature File for Rio de Janeiro to Host the 2016 Olympic and Paralympic Games*, 3 vol., Rio 2016 Candidate City, Rio de Janeiro.

Stavrides, S 2017, "Athens 2004 Olympics: An Urban State of Exception Which Became the Rule", in C Vainer, AM Broudehoux, F Sánchez & FL Oliveira (eds) *Mega-Events and the City: Critical Perspectives*, Letra Capital, Rio de Janeiro.

Stone, C 2008, "Urban Regime and the Capacity to Govern: A Political Economy Approach", *Journal of Urban Affairs*, 15.1, 28 June.

Suzuki, N, Ogawa, T & Inaba, N 2017, "The Right to Adequate Housing: Evictions of the Homeless and the Elderly Caused by the 2020 Summer Olympics in Tokyo", *Leisure Studies*, 37.

Swyngedouw, E 1997, "Neither Global nor Local: 'Glocalization' and the Politics of Scale", in RC Kewin (ed) *Spaces of Globalization: Reasserting the Power of the Local*, The Guilford Press, New York and London, pp. 137–166.

Tokyo Organising Committee of the Olympic and Paralympic Games (Tokyo 2020) n.d., *OCOG and Other Entities Budget (V3)*, viewed 2 December 2019, <https://tokyo2020.org/en/games/budgets/>

Tribunal de Contas da União (TCU) 2017, *Acordão 580 de 2017, Processo n° 026.394/2016-2*, viewed 10 July 2018, <https://pesquisa.apps.tcu.gov.br/#/documento/acordao-completo/*/NUMACORDAO%253A580%2520ANOACORDAO%253A2017/DTRELEVANCIA%2520desc%252C%2520NUMACORDAOINT%2520desc/0/sinonimos%253Dfalse>

5 The host of the games
Playing to win[1]

Introduction

On June 23 and 24, 2017, the heart of Paris was temporarily transformed into a peculiar sporting park for the celebration of Olympic Day. A floating racetrack was installed on the waters of the River Seine, the Place de la Concorde became an open-air velodrome, and a climbing wall was erected on the Pavillon de l'Arsenal. In total, ten Paris landmarks were converted into staging grounds for 33 Olympic and Paralympic events. Over the course of these two days, Parisian residents and visitors had the opportunity to participate in various sporting and cultural activities as well as to come into contact with their favorite athletes. Even Emmanuel Macron, the president of France, took part in some of the sporting events.

Although Olympic Day has been observed for more than a century in different parts of the world in commemoration of the International Olympic Committee's founding on June 23, 1894, the events in Paris took on extraordinary proportions to serve a specific end goal: namely, promoting the French capital's candidature to host the planet's largest sporting mega-event. Converting public urban spaces into a projection of what an Olympic Park could look like for the 2024 Paris Games represented an opportunity to seduce the IOC and, at the same time, build a consensus in support of the candidature among the French populace.

The Paris 2024 candidature was not alone in promoting itself through creative activities with the potential for significant social mobilization. On April 4, 1989, the Atlanta Olympic Committee (AOC) promoted the Olympic Mile which brought 40,000 runners to the city (ACOG 1997). Seeking similar results its bid to host the 1992 Summer Olympics, Barcelona's Olympic Office utilized complementary strategies that were equally creative. First, in order to seduce IOC members, the Office created itinerant exhibitions of its candidature project that it brought to fairs and showcases with major global reach. Second, to consolidate domestic adhesion to the city's Olympic project, it created the Olympic Bus – a large trailer specially made to be converted into an exhibition hall – with the objective of bringing the project to the capital cities of all Spain's autonomous communities (COOB '92 1992).

The capacity of mega-events to promote the images of host cities throughout the world and to legitimize major development projects[2] has led to disputes for hosting rights that tend to be marked by clever strategies.[3] Many cities have entered these disputes, often in recurring cycles,[4] but only a select group has succeeded in winning hosting rights. Of the 68 cities that have competed to host one of the 34 editions of the Olympic Summer Games – from the first modern Olympics in 1896 to the 2028 Los Angeles Olympics – only 23 have been selected. As Horne (2019) notes, hosting rights for half of editions of the Games have been awarded to one of six cities: London (1908, 1944, 1948, 2012); Los Angeles (1932, 1984, and 2008); Paris (1900, 1928, and 2028); Tokyo (1940, 1964, and 2020); Athens (1896 and 2004); and Berlin (1916 and 1936).

Regardless of the promotional strategies they adopt during their candidature processes, cities must attend to two fundamental prerequisites: first, they must gain the IOC's confidence in their ability to carry out the event in accordance with that institution's interests; and second, even under authoritarian regimes, they must create local consensus in support of the candidature project.

What are the fundamental conditions for a given city to consolidate its candidature project to host sport spectacle? How do individual and collective subjects align themselves within and between different scales during the construction of this project? How do decision-making processes establish the main guidelines for these projects? What principal elements must be utilized in order to guarantee success? Based on contemporary discussions that utilize scalar choices to approach social phenomena (Swyngedouw 1997),[5] this chapter will reflect on the trajectory that certain so-called successful cities have taken in their attempts to attract mega-events. The chapter focuses on cities that, in creating projects to attract sport spectacle, have gone on to convert these projects into strategies for promoting economic development.

The construction of a hegemonic project

As shown in Chapter Four, the attempt to create a development strategy based on attracting mega-events is associated with the recent emergence of urban planning theories inspired by business management (Harvey 1989). In accordance with these ideas, the convergence between the production of sport spectacle and the production of the city takes Barcelona's urban restructuring as its principal paradigm. Under the nomenclature of "strategic city planning," the model has been systematized and spread by the intellectuals who led the charge to restructure Barcelona. By understanding the city through the logic of competition and productivity, this model establishes an imperative of collaborative between public entities and private initiative.

Within the frames currently established by the International Olympic Committee (IOC) and the Fédération Internationale de Football Association (FIFA) for the production of sport spectacle, a successful candidature must satisfy two indispensable prerequisites: first, an unprecedented level of collaboration between government authorities operating on different scales of power; and second, the unconditional support of the majority of the city's residents.[6] According to those who defend "strategic planning" as a methodological paradigm for urban management, certain conditions are fundamental to success. Among these, Borja and Castells (1997, p. 94). emphasize:

- Expansive vocation of the city (under way or as a project).
- Existence of urban agents who accept linkage.
- Widespread feeling of growth crisis or of loss of opportunities to permit confrontations between agents connected with the day-to-day conflicts to be overcome.
- Leadership (one person and shared).
- Support of the population

The preliminary articulations of a given city's candidature for hosting sport spectacle mega-events cannot always attend to all of these prerequisites. Oftentimes, even within dominant groups, no articulation is capable of establishing unity. In these cases, the candidature process itself may establish an environment and a context suitable for building a hegemonic project (Gramsci 1957, 1971) that is capable of creating cohesion among different parts of the dominant class and, at the same time, legitimize its dominance; in other words, it can shape the interests and necessities of subordinate groups through consensus.

Unity of the dominant coalition

Because of their strong use of images and their potential to produce concrete interventions in space, sporting mega-events can be carried out by making a significant mobilization of economic, political, and social capital viable. As such, they consolidate a coalition of dominant groups around the idea of growth.[7] However, constructing such a coalition often demands a long and delicate cross-scale (Swyngedouw 1997) articulation of power.

According to the official report of the 1896 Olympic Games (de Coubertin et al. 1897), not even the viability of the first modern edition of the Olympics – which occurred that year in Athens – enjoyed immediate consensus among the leaders of different spheres of public administration. With the Greek treasury facing bankruptcy, concerns over the possibility of raising funds necessary for the Games and organizing an event within such a limited window of time led Greek politicians to oppose the Olympics, despite the fact that, at that time, the IOC did not demand any financial commitments from the host city or country. Baron de Coubertin – the eloquent creator of the modern Olympic Games – managed to convince local leaders (both politicians and other influential figures) that, based on its role in organizing the ancient Games, Greece ought not refuse the honor of inaugurating the modern Olympics, financial difficulties notwithstanding. Invocations of the patriotic pride of the Greek people persuaded the local press and a significant portion of the Greek populace of the symbolic importance of Athens receiving the "rebirth"[8] of the Olympic Games. According to de Coubertin et al. (1897), the 1896 Athens Games were only made possible due to the support of Greece's Prince Constantine, who assumed the leadership of the organizing committee, which he steered resolutely through its most difficult moments.

The shortage of time and resources to meet all of the IOC's demands also proved concerning to local authorities in Seoul, who initially showed themselves to be opposed to that city's candidature to host the 1988 Summer Games. Consensus around Seoul's candidature only began to materialize when the federal government promoted the project as one of national importance both economically and diplomatically.[9]

The reverse process occurred in Rio de Janeiro, whose successive candidatures to host the Olympics (for the 2004, 2012, and 2016 editions of the Games) was a central part of the first Strategic Plan for the City of Rio de Janeiro. (PCRJ 1996) This Strategic Plan was developed in partnership with the consulting firm Tecnologies Urbanes Barcelona S.A. (TUBSA), led by Jordi Borja and Manuel de Forn y Foxá, the principal proponents of the Barcelona model.[10] The 1993–1996 Strategic Plan, entitled "Rio, Always Rio," aimed to follow Barcelona's example; as such, it presented a candidature project for the 2004 Olympic Games as the city's principal development strategy. However, Rio's candidatures for the 2004 and 2012 Games, which were more closely linked to developing an entrepreneurial approach to city government, did not involve other scales of public administration nor garner significant support. In fact, the strategy of attracting the Olympics only began to gather momentum and to find success when, during preparations for the 2007 Pan American Games, the goals of the local government aligned with those of the Rio de Janeiro state and Brazilian federal governments. This alignment came about through the national political project led by President Luís Inácio Lula da Silva,[11] who saw the Olympics and the World Cup as presenting opportunities for Brazil to position itself as an emerging international power. In 2008, images shown throughout the world of Rio de Janeiro commemorating its bid acceptance to host the 2016 Olympics – besting Tokyo, Chicago, and Madrid – symbolized the definitive establishment of a consensus between different spheres of public administration and private enterprise in support of Lula da Silva's project. This massive embrace included: the federal Minister of Sports, Orlando Silva (of the Communist Party of Brazil – PCdoB); the governor of Rio de Janeiro state, Sérgio Cabral (of the centrist Brazilian Democratic Movement Party – PMDB); and the mayor of Rio de Janeiro, César Maia (of the center-right Democratic party – DEM). Carlos Nuzman, then-president of the Brazilian Olympic Committee (BOC), and the presidents of the Commercial Association and Industrial Federation of Rio de Janeiro state were also involved in the festivities.

In some cities, consensus among the leadership of different spheres of public administration and private enterprise has been constructed since the beginning of the candidature process. For example, Sydney's bid to host the 2000 Olympics was a joint undertaking of the state of New South Wales and the Australian federal government, but Sydney's city government immediately offered its support as did both of Australia's main political parties and a significant portion of the country's business leaders (COHRE 2007).

The symbolic appeal of the Olympic Games' returning to their original home united Athenians around the idea of claiming the 2004 Games for their city after losing to Atlanta in bidding to host the 1996 Olympic Centennial Games (ATHOC 2005). Even after the idea of an honorary concession of the 2008 Games was abandoned, the last-minute proposal of submitting a candidature to host the 2004 Olympics won the support of political groups from throughout Greece (ATHOC 2005; Stavrides 2017; COHRE 2007). In addition, the composition of Athens' first Bid Committee, which included some of Greece's most successful business leaders, aimed to emphasize support for the city's candidature among private business leaders (ATHOC 2005).

Horne and Whannel (2016) use London's candidature to host the 2012 Games as an example to demonstrate the enormous power of an Olympic bid in articulating coalitions between traditionally opposed groups. He notes that the Secretary of State for Culture, Media and Sport from 2001 to 2007 was Tessa Jowell, a Member of Parliament for the Labour Party and a Tony Blair loyalist; meanwhile, Sebastian Coe, a former Conservative MP, controlled the Bid Committee and later became president of the London Organizing Committee for the Olympic Games (LOCOG). Finally, the mayor of London from 2001 to 2008 was Kenneth Livingstone, "a left-wing maverick" (ibid. p. 33).

Barcelona's candidature to host the 1992 Olympics, which was articulated through an executive initiative by the city government (COOB'92 1992), also brought together leaders from all spheres of government and private enterprise, although inter-scalar disputes often arose relating to control of the Olympic project (COHRE 2007; Capel 2005). The Spanish national government, led by the Spanish Socialist Workers' Party (PSOE), considered the Olympic Games to be an opportunity to promote Spain on an international level and aimed to control the process according to its own terms; whereas, the autonomous regional government of the Generalitat de Catalunya, led by the conservative Catalan nationalist Convergence and Union Party (CIU), sought to promote Catalonia; and the Barcelona City Council, led by the Socialists' Party of Catalonia (PSC) in coalition with other progressive political groups, sought a complete urban restructuring of the city and claimed autonomy in defining the Olympic project. However, over the course of the city's candidature, these tensions gave way to mutual cooperation (COHRE 2007). In relation to Barcelona specifically, European Union resources helped finance certain urban restructuring projects, revealing that the articulation of the city's project also involved a continental scale. In addition, the noteworthy presence of private investments in Barcelona's project (COOB'92 1992) attests to a commitment on the part of private enterprise to see the project succeed.

Even in Atlanta, where private groups launched the city's candidature to host the 1996 Olympics, the Olympic project involved all scales of public administration. The commitment of different scales of government can be seen in the significant public resources invested in constructing facilities, despite the initial promise that the Games would be entirely privately financed. Burbank, Andranovich and Heying (2001) note that, of the US$2.906 billion spent on facilities for the 1996 Games, 71.5% came from public coffers: US$996 million from the federal government, US$226 million from the State of Georgia, and US$857 million from the Atlanta city government.

In summary, the production of sport spectacle demands unity among dominant groups at the same time as it makes such unity viable in the interest of exercising hegemony (Gramsci 1957, 1971). However, an Olympic project does not achieve hegemony simply through unifying dominant groups. It also must obtain legitimacy in order for domination to be exercised by consent.

Consensus

According to the logic of urban entrepreneurialism, globalization not only challenges cities to position themselves as places for doing business, it also allows cities themselves to become commodities, but only insofar as their production and sale are based on consensus. The business management project for the city represents such a radical negation of the city as a political space that it can only be made viable through consensus (Vainer 2017). The search by businesses for lucrative results demands pragmatism and agility. In order to attend to these demands, time and space for political reflections must be completely eliminated. Those who promote this business model of city management tend to point to two elements that are crucial in building consensus: consciousness of crisis and civic patriotism (Borja & Castells 1997; Borja 1995; Castells 1992). Consciousness of crisis creates circumstances leading to a truce in internal conflicts, inasmuch as overcoming crisis demands collective unity against an external enemy: other cities seeking the same investments.

> The response to these challenges calls for a strategic plan city project. The construction of this project may rest on different factors. In some cities, the sensation of crisis led to a joint reaction on the part of the local government and main economic agents to undertake transformation of the urban infrastructure to facilitate a transition from the traditional industrial model towards the skilled tertiary centre.
>
> (Borja & Castells 1997, p. 93)

The feeling of crisis was an essential element for the creators of Barcelona's strategic planning model, which later materialized as that city's Olympic project. The process of "profound [spatial] degradation" in which the city found itself after Spain's long dictatorship formed the basis of the diagnosis that intellectuals, including Manuel Castells, Jordi Borja, and Manoel de Forn, used to establish a consensus supporting their proposed radical urban reform project (Borja & Castells 1997; Borja 1995; Castells 1992). Spain's young democracy, still instable and undergoing a period of economic crisis, needed to defeat these obstacles so as to offer immediate answers to the urban crisis facing Barcelona.

> The response to the awareness of crisis has been facilitated in some cities by their ability to attract and make use of a major international event. Barcelona has become a paradigmatic example of this.
>
> (Borja & Castells 1997, p. 93)

The same thinkers offered identical arguments as consultants for Rio de Janeiro's Strategic Plan (PCRJ 1996), which resulted in three Olympic bids (2004, 2012, and 2016) as well as the 2007 Pan American Games. At the beginning of the 1990s, Rio de Janeiro found itself submerged in profound political, social, and economic crises. Academics and members of the elite only began to recognize these crises – which had begun to fester in the 1960s when the core Brazil's federal government was transferred to Brasília – in the 1980s, as an economic and fiscal crisis overtook all of Brazil with particularly devastating effects on the Rio de Janeiro metropolitan region.[12] Between 1989 and 1992, the regional GDP contracted 15% and, between 1991 and 1996, the region lost 180,000 industrial jobs (Lessa 2005). In this context, the city's Strategic Plan (PCRJ 1996) presented sporting mega-events as an opportunity to restore the city's economic dynamism, which – along with its status as the federal capital – it had lost decades earlier.

When it is impossible to establish a consciousness of crisis throughout a city, planners create a consciousness of crisis in relation to so-called "degraded" spaces within a city so as to create consensus of a need for renewal. In this sense, the case of London's East End is emblematic. Raco and Tunney (2010) show that London's 2012 Olympic candidature created a narrative of the East End as a "problem place," and that this, in turn, justified the urgent necessity of the neighborhood's physical regeneration. The authors argue that, in adopting this narrative, the Olympic Park project ignored pre-existing conditions in the East End, destroying everyday socioeconomic practices that – even if they didn't fit the patterns of visibility that dominant groups desired – gave life to the neighborhood.

Considering the ephemeral nature of the feeling of crisis, civic pride can make consensus more viable and consistent. Consolidating a generalized "civic patriotism" creates conditions in which anyone who dares question this consensus can be seen as an enemy. This is why those who defend business-style management of the city place such importance on building this feeling.

> Internal promotion of the city in order to instill 'civic patriotism' in its inhabitants, a sense of belonging, a collective wish to participate and confidence in an optimism about the future of the city. This internal promotion must be based on visible works and services, both those of monumental or symbolic character and those directed at improving the quality of public areas and the wellbeing of people.
>
> (Borja & Castells 1997, p. 110)

Participation is what confers this feeling of belonging on a collective grouping. In this sense, the strategic planning model takes up the cause of participation as a necessary element in consensus building. It is fundamental that everyone feel involved and, therefore, responsible for the process. This much-lauded participation, however, occurs in a very selective way. The strength of "stakeholders" invited to participate is always measured so as to guarantee results that satisfy dominant groups, even if the community feels itself to be represented.[13]

Stavrides (2008) emphasizes how the "illusion of participation" was an essential element in constructing civic pride in Barcelona. As he notes (ibid.), the situation in that city was different than in Athens where the absence of any representatives of civil society in the decision-making processes made this "illusion of participation" unviable. The construction of a national identity, threatened by the possibility of failing to honor the commitments the city had made on an international scale, roused civic and patriotic pride in its defense. However, in this case, insecurity substituted confidence in building consensus; as such, it produced an effect similar to the feeling of crisis.

The expectation of a victorious candidature is also a fundamental symbolic element in mobilizing civic pride. Many people who are motivated by the sensation of power, normally associated with the idea of success, defend pro-mega-event projects, ignoring possible impacts that the organization of sport spectacle might produce in their lives. Raco and Tunney (2010) tell of small businesses owners in London whose firms were removed from the East End to give way to the Olympic Park and who admitted to participating actively in the London government's "I Back the Bid" campaign. Those interviewed said that, at first, they believed they would benefit from reforms proposed for the area in which they lived and worked. A similar phenomenon occurred in cities throughout Brazil. Many of those affected by projects related to mega-event organization had taken to the streets to celebrate the country's successful bids to host the 2014 World Cup or the 2016 Olympics and had dreamed of the improvements that might come about as a result of those successes. Michel, who was evicted from his workplace and his home in Rio de Janeiro's Restinga neighborhood, illustrated the situation in an interview I conducted with him.

> I feel like a sucker, because when Brazil won this damn Olympics, I was on the Yellow Line [highway] in my car, honking like an idiot. Now I'm paying for it. Is this what the World Cup is? Is this the Olympic spirit?
>
> (Michel, pers. comm., April 2011)[14]

Authors such as Broudehoux (2007) and COHRE (2007) relate testimony from Beijing residents who not only accepted forcible evictions to make way for Olympic infrastructure but also considered some sacrifices to be necessary to benefit the city.

These facts show how the production of sport spectacle builds consensus in favor of pro-growth coalitions (Elkin 1987). The ability of mega-events to mobilize economic capital carries with it the promise of economic development and, as a result, promises the possibility of overcoming crisis. Furthermore, the inherent symbolic capital that sport spectacle holds brings together elements necessary to spur civic pride.

The localization of investments

Without exception, the lack of transparency, together with civil society's limited participation in decision making, has been a constant feature of candidature processes to host sport spectacle. Meeting behind closed doors, international consultants, national and international sporting institutions, private business leaders, and certain public administrators[15] have defined the essence of candidature projects, which the public can only see after the project has been submitted to the international institutions responsible for selecting mega-event hosts. What varies from place to place, then, is the decision-making power that each of these actors exercises with a given group's specific composition. If the production of sporting mega-events has been utilized as a catalyzing element to spur or expand reurbanization plans, the choice of location of urban interventions in cities that aim to host these mega-events almost always comes about as a result of this correlation of forces and of the interests of each of these actors in every part of urban space.

In general, locations are selected by giving priority to spaces that show themselves to be suited to the accumulation of capital; in other words, spaces that are already valorized, or that have great potential for real estate valorization. The most frequently chosen locations are central areas considered to be "degraded," or areas close to significant cultural or natural landscapes. In the case of Rio de Janeiro's *Porto Maravilha* project and of Barcelona's Montjuïc Olympic Ring, the argument of opening the city center to the sea allowed both of these tendencies to be combined.

The repertory of arguments used in making such selections often repeats. Promoting development and improving living conditions in a city's central area – as in London's East End, Rio de Janeiro's *Porto Maravilha*, and Barcelona's Montjuïc – is among the most frequent of these arguments. Revitalizing spaces close to the sea, such as the Tokyo Bay (Tokyo 2020 Candidate City n.d.), is also a common justification. Another legitimizing factor is the existence of significant portions of public land, as in the cases of Rio de Janeiro and Sydney's Olympic Parks (SOCOG 2001). Finally, a recurring argument is the idea of major city-wide transformations, as in Barcelona 1992, Athens 2004, and Beijing 2008 as well as Rio de Janeiro 2016, all of which incorporated each of the previously elucidated arguments.

In some cities, such as Barcelona, Athens, and Rio de Janeiro, bidders used the strategy of preempting facility construction to strengthen their Olympic candidature. Barcelona's Montjuïc Olympic Stadium, along with a swimming pool, had been built decades earlier in preparation for its candidature for the 1936

Games (COOB'92 1992). Thus, of the 37 competition venues required for the 1992 event, 27 had already been built (ibid.) As soon as the Greek Parliament voted unanimously to submit a candidature bid to host the 1996 Olympic Games, organizers began to construct Olympic facilities at the Athens Olympic Sports Centre (OAKA), next to the already constructed Olympic Stadium. This program aimed to show the government's seriousness in disputing hosting rights for the Golden Jubilee of the Games (ATHOC 2005). In Rio de Janeiro, the strategy of investing in the organization of the 2007 Pan American Games served to justify a renovation of Maracanã Stadium as well as the construction of new facilities in the Barra da Tijuca neighborhood. The goal was to improve Rio's chances in its candidatures to host the 2012 and, posteriorly, 2016 Olympic Games (Rio 2016 Candidate City n.d.) after the city had failed to make the shortlist to host the 2004 Olympics. In spite of these preemptive investments, many facilities have had to be rebuilt or reformed to satisfy the IOC's standards (or FIFA's in cases relating to the World Cup).

The production of sport spectacle almost always reorients city planning. Mega-events allow projects that would normally be unattainable or stymied due to local conflicts to be legitimized and begun anew. In certain cases, such as in Barcelona, urban and infrastructural reform projects for the Olympic Games were aligned with urban planning. However, Barcelona reoriented its priorities to emphasize opening the city to the ocean (COHRE 2007; COOB'92 1992) and abandoned plans to construct public housing in improved areas of the city. In other instances, this reorientation occurred through a more direct intervention in a given city's Master Plan or zoning legislation, as in the cases of Athens (Stavrides 2017) and Rio de Janeiro.[16] These two cities also reoriented their priorities when a majority of infrastructural investment was directed toward areas of significant real estate speculation that had historically received significant public funding. Meanwhile, local political leaders continued to neglect areas that presented greater demands for urban services and where the majority of the population was concentrated.[17]

The Paris and Los Angeles candidatures to host the 2024 Olympics indicated a certain rupture with past models as both cities aimed to utilize pre-existing buildings thereby avoiding large-scale urban restructuring projects. The Paris Candidature File (Paris Candidate City Olympic Games 2024 n.d) pledged that 95% of its Olympic venues would utilize existing buildings, spaces for public use, or temporary facilities. In addition, the candidature guaranteed that all new construction would be aligned with the city's long-term development plans, that no residents would be relocated, and that all commercial and industrial relocations necessary would be negotiated according to terms that favor the owners of displaced properties.

Similarly, in its candidature file (Los Angeles Candidate City Olympic Games 2024 n.d.), Los Angeles pledged not to construct any new permanent venues. Accordingly, the majority of competitions were projected to take place in previously existing facilities (ibid.) complemented by temporary facilities. The location of the Olympic Village, meanwhile, was charted for dormitories at the University of California, Los Angeles (UCLA).

The Tokyo 2020 project (Tokyo 2020 Candidate City n.d.) presented a sort of middle ground. The city's Olympic project consisted of two thematic and operational zones, organized as two rings forming an infinity symbol: the "Heritage Zone," which included the reappropriation of several iconic locations from the 1964 Tokyo Olympics; and the "Tokyo Bay Zone," housing an innovative urban planning project and including new monumental and futuristic architecture. In total, Tokyo's project proposed new construction for 11 of the 33 necessary Olympic venues.

The tendency among recent Olympic projects to change direction follows the recommendations of the Olympic Agenda 2020 (IOC 2014), many of which were incorporated into the 2019 Olympic Charter (IOC 2019). These recommendations aim to guarantee the survival of the symbolic capital that the Olympic Movement has accumulated over the course of more than a century. After the attrition associated with the organization of the 2016 Games,[18] guaranteeing two consecutive events in cities where economic, social, and political costs were less prone to be questioned had the potential to produce favorable conditions for recuperating this symbolic capital. Future demands based on the interests of local groups that support these cities' Olympic projects may still result in tensions leading to changes in the overall process, as has previously occurred in other situations. Although the IOC works constantly to perfect the mechanisms that make its control over cities viable, it cannot guarantee results and, at any given moment, depends on the correlation of forces with locally established coalitions in each of these cities. Faced with an increasingly unstable global context, many intervening occurrences may yet come to bear on the execution of mega-events.

The final competition

The final exposition of candidature projects to host the Olympic Games brings together the collective strength of politicians, business leaders, consultants, athletes, celebrities, and National Olympic Committees (NOCs). Orchestrated by marketing specialists, this spectacle exhibits a perfect scenic ritual in which discourses, gestures, gazes, and even applause are carefully rehearsed so as to capture the unpredictable electoral college of an IOC Session.

The noteworthy recurring presence of a select group of marketing consultants in almost every successful candidature – especially beginning with the 2012 Olympic Games – sets the tone of this spectacle, and reinforces, once again, the role of a specific segment of individuals who hold significant cultural capital: namely, producers of representations who orient behaviors and actions, construct discourses, determine important contacts and articulations, trigger actions, images, and emotions, define ideas/strengths and symbolic appeals, and often, are decisive in defining the results of the selection process.

Producers like Mike Lee (Vero Communications),[19] Michael Payne (the former IOC marketing director), Scott Givens (FiveCurrents), Nick Varley (Seven46), and Doug Arnot (Broadstone Group) played decisive roles in the selections of London and Rio de Janeiro to host the 2012 and 2016 Games, respectively, and their presence in successful candidatures continues.[20] The high consulting fees they charge are usually financed through a combination of public and private resources.

The role that members of NOCs play in this process cannot be minimized. It is they who propose candidatures, command the selection process for the cities that will represent their countries, mediate between these cities and the IOC, guaranteeing that candidatures attend to the IOC's interests, and, together with other interested parties, form the Bid Committee and the OCOG, which NOC members are often responsible for steering.

Organizers who aim to construct a successful candidature rely on especially suggestive discourses. In advertising Athens as the only city capable of offering the 2004 Olympics a "Homecoming of the Games to the country where they were born and the city where they were revived in 1896" (Gianna Angelopoulos-Daskalaki, cited in ATHOC 2005, p. 9), organizers opted for an obvious but convincing discourse. Organizers of Tokyo's candidature to host the 2020 Games exploited natural disasters in a unique strategy to demonstrate Japan's capacity to rebuild quickly (Tokyo 2020 Candidate City n.d.). While Brazilians' joyful receptiveness was central to the symbolic appeal of the Rio 2016 bid, the Tokyo 2020 "Discover Tomorrow" candidature highlighted Japan's technological capacity. Similarly, the "Green Olympics, High-Tech Olympics, and People's Olympics" served as the motto for the Beijing 2008 candidature. (BOCOG n.d.).

The recurring presence of a limited number of consultants in different candidatures can result in a certain standardization – and even predictability – in the symbolic actions these bids utilize. The harmonious integration of antiquity and modernity was a central element of the Barcelona 1992 (COOB'92 1992), Athens 2004 (ATHOC 2005), and Beijing 2008 (BOCOG n.d.) bids. When the Rio 2016 candidature invoked South America's right to host its first Olympic Games, it recalled the argument that the organizers of Barcelona 1992 used to bring the Games to the Iberian Peninsula for the first time. The images used to represent both cities' arguments were nearly identical. In the Rio 2016 bid, an illuminated map showed cities that had already hosted the Olympics, while South America remained in the dark; similarly, the Barcelona campaign showed the Iberian Peninsula in shadows (COOB'92 1992). In Sydney, the passion of local residents for sport was an important element in the city's candidature to host the 2000 Games, it was also central to the Paris 2024 bid.

Whenever possible, candidatures invoke the support of personalities from the sporting world. Previously, when selection procedures were still not very well elaborated, the president of the IOC could support or even appeal on behalf of a specific candidate. Such was the case of Pierre de Coubertin, who claimed the

1924 Olympics for Paris to mark his departure from the presidency of the IOC. Juan Samaranch's eagerness to bring the 1992 Olympics to Barcelona was also fundamental in that city's selection. Various Olympic Games candidatures capitalized on the support of iconic figures like João Havelange, who served as IOC member and as FIFA's president for 24 years, or Pelé, the most celebrated football player of the twentieth century. By the same token, artists and other celebrities from outside the world of sport have been incorporated into marketing campaigns or else used their direct contact with members of the IOC and their families to aid candidatures.

Symbolic elements, such as the short films that well-known director Fernando Meirelles produced for the Rio 2016 candidature emphasizing the warm, fun-loving nature of the city's inhabitants, can play an important role in a bid's success. The video directed by Darryl Goodrich showing the power of sport to inspire children throughout the world was also a key element of the London 2012 candidature.

The symbolic elements that candidatures rely on for their presentation's spectacle generally manage to justify the final outcome of these disputes to the media and spectators. Furthermore, work behind the scenes necessitates the continued presence of large teams of professionals, supporters, and politicians in the cities that serve as the stages for these disputes in the period leading up to the final decision. This process often lasts longer than a month.

Considering the relevant role that political representatives play in building pro-mega-event coalitions, their actions in decisive moments cannot be ignored. When the host for the 2012 Olympics was announced in Singapore in 2005 – a dispute between London, Paris, Madrid, New York, and Moscow – each country sent some of their principal political leaders as representatives. These included Queen Sofia of Spain; Jacques Chirac, the president of France; United States Senator Hillary Clinton; the British Prime Minister Tony Blair; and Mikhail Fradkov, his Russian counterpart. Many people attribute the success of London's candidature to Tony Blair's effort at the end of the campaign.

On October 2, 2009, the most important political representatives of the countries disputing hosting rights for the 2016 Olympics gathered in Copenhagen, which served as the stage for the final decision. With Brazil's president, Luiz Inácio Lula da Silva, were: Barack Obama, president of the United States; José Luis Zapatero and Juan Carlos, respectively prime minister and king of Spain; and Yukio Hatoyama, prime minister of Japan. Before presenting Rio de Janeiro's project, Lula da Silva held a press conference that reverberated in media outlets throughout the world. His subsequent tears of joy when Rio de Janeiro was declared victorious made his political capital clear; in addition to spearheading a project of national political importance, he also successfully demonstrated his "international citizenship":

> Today is the most emotional day in my life, the most exciting day of my life. . . . I've never felt more pride in Brazil. Now, we are going to show the

world we can be a great country. We aren't the United States, but we are get-
ting there, and we will get there.

(Lula da Silva cited in Macur 2009)

Symbolism and emotion are not the only elements invoked in the fierce dispute
among cities aiming to host mega-events: denunciations of vote-buying are also
frequent. In addition to the most evident cases of Salt Lake City 2002 and Rio
de Janeiro 2016 – examined in Chapter One – the selection of Tokyo to host the
2020 Summer Games and of Russia and Qatar to host, respectively, the 2018 and
2022 Football World Cups have also been targets for condemnation of these sorts
of practices.

The lack of disputes for the 2024 Olympics[21] gave the ceremony in which Paris
won hosting rights and during which Los Angeles was named host city for 2028
a formal and even tedious tone. As such, the IOC could not improve its symbolic
and emotional capital by taking advantage of the weight that such ceremonies
tend to confer.

Partial considerations

This chapter shows the priority that countries disputing hosting rights for mega-
events place on candidature projects. As such, it is worth returning to some of
the chapter's early questions so as to inquire how and why a certain grouping of
forces can articulate this type of project, and what kinds of strategies and arguments can transform a project proposal into one with concrete chances of being
executed.

In response to this first question, we must remember, on the one hand, that
producing mega-events represents the possibility of mobilizing global forms of
capital and media exposure and, as such, spurring economic development. On
the other hand, it also presents a policy of risk-taking. Such risks are not only
linked to the growing amount of economic resources that organization and candidature processes demand; they also entail ruptures produced in social space.[22]
In addition, the benefits associated with mega-events are almost always difficult
to measure.

It would be overly simplistic to search for a single answer to explain the complex process in which attracting sport spectacle serves as development policy.
Through diverse scalar combinations, sport spectacle articulates strength in the
grouping and actions of both individual and collective subjects who hold different
interests.

The possibility of a given candidate country's improved positioning in global
economic and political contexts fuels optimism that undeniably contributes to the
construction of consensus, inasmuch as this optimism plays a double role. At the
same time as it stimulates confidence in a more concrete possibility of a victorious
candidature, it also consubstantiates the belief that a victory might contribute to
the country's global repositioning. The enthusiasm of then-president Luiz Inácio

Lula da Silva in seeking to bring the 2014 World Cup and 2016 Olympics to Brazil is especially emblematic. In a perceptive way, Lula da Silva recognized that the media exposure associated with hosting rights would open doors to fulfilling his ambitious project of repositioning Brazil – and with it, himself – on the global political map.[23]

Major corporations with local and localized interests are among the forces that must be mobilized in order to create the necessary consensus for such projects. Companies linked to construction, real estate, tourism, and consulting play especially important roles.[24]

In considering strategies and arguments, a great deal has been speculated regarding the reasons behind a winning candidature's success. Some attribute this success to more localized actions, such as the international prestige that certain leaders – especially those connected to the sporting world – exercise in the campaign. Others search for more structural causes, such as the guarantees or technical quality that a given project offers. It is worth emphasizing that, thanks to the IOC's regulatory apparatus and guidelines – as well as the recurring involvement of a small group of consultants – candidature projects have become so standardized that it is increasingly difficult to choose a host city based strictly on technical criteria.

In any event, it seems unquestionable that the major factor responsible for successful candidatures is none other than the significant ability of certain agents to articulate different forces in a cross-scalar way, thereby unifying the different interests involved in a given coalition. Hiring major consulting firms that specialize in producing successful candidatures and have the competency to transform a network of differing interests into a single, convincing discourse is the culminating factor in this articulation.

Although many candidature processes stem from an entrepreneurial attitude on the part of local political leaders, their success only becomes viable when it attracts support from all spheres of public administration, although their respective levels of involvement vary from case to case.

Successful Olympic entrepreneurialism is the result of a strong grouping of favorable structural conditions, as well as of the combined actions of different public and private agents working together in a coalition based on their interests and articulated on local, national, and international scales.[25] This reinforces the methodological position of my research: namely, that only a cross-scalar approaches can provide an understanding of social phenomena.

Notes

1 Portions of this chapter first appeared in the book *O Poder dos Jogos e os Jogos de Poder: Os interesses em campo na produção da cidade para o espetáculo esportivo* (Oliveira 2015), published by Editora UFRJ. The English translation is by Raphael Soifer.
2 See Chapter Four.
3 Until the 2018 tournament, the guidelines set by the *Fédération Internationale* de *Football Association* (FIFA) for selecting host countries for the Football World Cup were

much less clear. This, in turn, has not inspired creative strategies in disputes to host FIFA events. The most significant of these disputes took place within already-selected host countries among cities that aspired to host tournament games.

4 Here, the most emblematic example is Los Angeles' insistence on submitting a candidature to host the Olympics. Only six years after hosting the 1932 Games, certain groups in the city raised the idea of bringing the games back to Los Angeles. As such, the city bid to host the 1940 Olympics, which were eventually canceled due to World War II. After the war, the city bid to host the 1952 Summer Games after which it did not miss a single Olympic cycle without articulating its aspirations to host the event. Los Angeles was an official candidate for the 1956 Olympics, although it lost out to Detroit as the United States Olympic Committee's official candidate for the 1960, 1964, 1968, and 1972 Games. It was the official American candidate for the 1976 and 1980 Olympics and finally won hosting rights for the 1984 Summer Games (LAOOC 1985). In 2017, Los Angeles submitted its candidature to host the 2024 Olympics; after negotiating with the IOC, the city was selected as the host for the 2028 Games.

5 See Introduction.

6 See Chapter Three.

7 See Chapter Four.

8 See Chapter One.

9 During South Korea's candidacy, widespread expectations held that carrying out the Olympic Games would improve relations between South Korea and North Korea, as well as relations between these countries and the communist bloc as a whole (COHRE 2007; SOOC 1989). However, this improvement only came to fruition 30 years later when North Korea participated in the 2018 PyeongChang Winter Games. The IOC took full advantage of this participation as a form of expanding its symbolic capital.

10 Manoel de Forn y Foxá was the coordinator of the city's Strategic Development Plan, and Jordi Borja was vice mayor during the candidature and organization period for the 1992 Barcelona Games. These two urbanists, who oversaw the implementation of business-style management in Barcelona's territorial transformation, used this model as a paradigm that they spread throughout the world, especially in Latin American cities. See also Chapter Four.

11 Luís Inácio Lula da Silva, Brazil's President from 2003 to 2011, began his career working in a metallurgical factory. He is co-founder and honorary president of Brazil's Workers' Party (*Partido dos Trabalhadores* – PT). In spite of his relative lack of formal education, Lula is perceptive, intelligent, and highly charismatic. In 2009, he held growing sway over the international media and was very open in his ambitions to be a leading global reference.

12 In this respect, see Silva (2006).

13 For a more detailed account of this methodology's application in the production of Rio de Janeiro's Strategic Plan (PCRJ 1996), see Vainer (2017).

14 I heard this account in 2011 when I accompanied the Brazilian Platform for Human, Social, Cultural, and Environmental Rights (DHESCA Brasil) as it visited communities affected by mega-events in Rio de Janeiro.

15 For more on the actions of sporting institutions, see Part One. For further information on the positions of other subjects, see Chapter Four.

16 See Chapter Six.

17 For Athens, see Stavrides (2017), and for Rio de Janeiro, see de Oliveira and Gaffney (2010).

18 See Chapter One.

19 Mike Lee's death in October 2018 left a major lacuna in the world of sports marketing.

20 See Chapter Two.

21 See Chapter One.

22 Here, I understand social space as a multidimensional space (Bourdieu 1991) that, in addition to the economic dimension, also includes social, cultural, political-institutional, and symbolic dimensions.

23 A significant number of references in the international press described Lula's ascension in these terms. To cite only a few examples: in 2009, both *Le Monde* and *El País* named him "Man of the Year" while the *Financial Times* named him one of 50 people who had shaped the 2000s. In 2010, soon after Rio was selected to host the 2016 Games, he received the first-ever Global Statesman Award from the World Economic Forum.

24 See Chapter Two.

25 The final conclusion of Burbank, Andranovich and Heying (2001) was in the same direction. They concluded that, although the concept of an "Urban Regime" is theoretically useful for understanding mega-events in the cities they studied, simply observing the actors involved in local pro-growth regimes was not enough to explain these regimes' results, which often depend on decisions that surpass this scale of observation.

References

Athens 2004 Organising Committee for the Olympic Games S.A. (ATHOC) 2005, *Official Report of the XXVIII Olympiad: Homecoming of the Games*, vol. 1, ATHOC, Athens.

Atlanta Committee for the Olympic Games (ACOG) 1997, *The Official Report of the Centennial Olympic Games*, vol. 1, ACOG, Atlanta.

Barcelona'92 Olympic Organising Committee S.A (COOB'92) 1992, *Official Report of the Games of the XXV Olympiad Barcelona 1992*, vol. 1, COOB'92, Barcelona.

Beijing Organising Committee for the Games of the XXIX Olympiad (BOCOG) n.d., *Official Report of the Beijing Olympic Games*, vol. 1, BOCOG, Beijing.

Borja, J. (ed) 1995, *Barcelona: un modelo de transformación urbana*, Programa de Gestión Urbana, Oficina Regional para América Latina y Caribe, Quito.

Borja, J & Castells, M 1997, *Local and Global: Management of Cities in the Information Age*, Earthscan Publications, London.

Bourdieu, P 1991, *Language and Symbolic Power*, trans. G Raymond & M Adamsom, Polity Press, Cambridge.

Broudehoux, AM 2007, "Spectacular Beijing: The Conspicuous Construction of an Olympic Metropolis", *Journal of Urban Affairs*, 29.4, pp. 383–399.

Burbank, M, Andranovich, G & Heying, C 2001, *Olympic Dreams: The Impact of Mega-Events on Local Politics*, Lynne Rienner Publishers, Boulder.

Capel, H 2005, *El modelo Barcelona: un examen crítico*, Ediciones del Serbal, Barcelona.

Castells, M 1992, "The World Has Changed: Can Planning Change?" *Landscape and Urban Planning*, 22.1, pp. 73–78.

Centre on Housing Rights and Evictions (COHRE) 2007, *Fair Play for Housing Rights: Opportunities for the Olympic Movement and Other*, COHRE, Geneva.

de Coubertin, P, Timoleon, JP, Politis, NG & Anninos C 1897, "The Olympic Games in 1996", in Central Committee in Athens (ed) *The Olympic Games: B. C. 776. – A. D. 1896*, Charles Beck, Athens and H. Grevel & Co., London.

de Oliveira, NG & Gaffney, CT 2010, "Rio de Janeiro e Barcelona: os limites do paradigma olímpico", *Biblio 3w*, Universidad de Barcelona, XV.895, p. 17, 5 Noviembre.

Elkin, SL 1987, *City and Regime in the American Republic*, University Chicago Press, Chicago.

Gramsci, A 1957, "The Modern Prince: Essays on the Science of Politics in the Modern Age", in A Gramsci (ed) *The Modern Prince and Other Writings*, Lawrence and Wishart LTD, London.

Gramsci, A 1971, *Selections from the Prison Notebooks*, eds. Q Hoare & GN Smith, International Publishers, New York.

Harvey, D 1989, "From Managerialism to Entrepreneurialism: The Transformation in Urban Governance in Late Capitalism", *Geografiska Annaler, Series B, Human Geography*, 71.1, pp. 3–17.

Horne, J 2019, "On the Olympic Games: An Afterword", *International Journal of Japanese Sociology*, 28.1, pp. 128–131.

Horne, J & Whannel, G 2016, *Understanding the Olympics*, 2nd ed., Routledge, Abingdon and New York.

International Olympic Committee (IOC) 2014, *Olympic Agenda 2020: The Strategic Roadmap for the Future of the Olympic Movement*, IOC, Lausanne.

International Olympic Committee (IOC) 2019, *Olympic Charter: In Force as from 26 June 2019*, IOC, Lausanne.

Lessa, C 2005, *O Rio de todos os Brasis: uma reflexão a busca de auto-estima*, Record, Rio de Janeiro.

Los Angeles Candidate City Olympic Games 2024 n.d., *Candidature Questionnaire Stage 3: Games Delivery, Experience and Venue Legacy*, Los Angeles Candidate City, Los Angeles.

Los Angeles Olympic Organizing Committee (LAOOC) 1985, *Official Report of the Games of the XXIIIrd Olympiad Los Angeles, 1984*, vol. 1, LAOOC, Los Angeles.

Macur, J 2009, "Rio Wins 2016 Olympics in a First for South America", *The New York Times*, 2 October, viewed 3 November 2016, <www.nytimes.com/2009/10/03/sports/03olympics.html>

Paris Candidate City Olympic Games 2024 n.d., *Candidature File: Phase 3*, Paris Candidate City, Paris.

Prefeitura da cidade do Rio de Janeiro (PCRJ) 1996, *Plano estratégico da cidade do Ride Janeiro: Rio Sempre Rio*, PCRJ/ACRJ/FIRJAN, Rio de Janeiro.

Raco, M & Tunney, E 2010, "Visibilities and Invisibilities in Urban Development: Small Business Communities and the London Olympics 2012", *Urban Studies*, 47, pp. 2069–2091, September.

Rio 2016 Candidate City n.d., *Candidature File for Rio de Janeiro to Host the 2016 Olympic and Paralympic Games*, 3 vol., Rio 2016 Candidate City, Rio de Janeiro.

Seoul Olympic Organizing Committee (SOOC) 1989, *Official Report: Organizing and Planning*, vol. 1, SOOC, Seoul.

Silva, MO 2006, "A crise do rio e suas especificidades", in *IE – Série Seminários de Pesquisa: 2006*, UFRJ, Rio de janeiro.

Stavrides, S 2008, "Urban Identities: Beyond the Regional and the Global. The Case of Athens", in J Al-Qawasmi, A Mahmoud & A Djerbi (eds) *Regional Architecture and Identity in the Age of Globalization*, Proceedings of 2nd International Conference of CSAAR, CSAAR, Tunis, pp. 577–588.

Stavrides, S 2017, "Athens 2004 Olympics: An Urban State of Exception Which Became the Rule", in C Vainer, AM Broudehoux, F Sánchez & FL Oliveira (eds) *Mega-Events and the City: Critical Perspectives*, Letra Capital, Rio de Janeiro.

Swyngedouw, E 1997, "Neither Global nor Local: 'Glocalization' and the Politics of Scale", in C Kewin (ed) *Spaces of Globalization: Reasserting the Power of the Local*, The Guilford Press, New York and London, pp. 137–166.

Sydney Organising Committee for the Olympic Games (SOCOG) 2001, *Official Report of the XXVII Olympiad*, vol. 1, SOCOG, Sydney.

Tokyo 2020 Candidate City n.d., *Tokyo 2020: Discover Tomorrow*, Tokyo 2020 Candidate City, Tokyo.

Vainer, C 2017, "Rio de Janeiro's Strategic Plan: Olympic Construction of the Corporate Town", in L Albrechts, A Balducci & J Hillier (eds) *Situated Practices of Strategic Planning*, Routledge, Abingdon and New York.

6 Force-of-law

Institutional ruptures and realignments linked to the production of sport spectacle[1]

Introduction

Certain contemporary thinkers have identified a profoundly authoritarian character in the consensus that forms around competitive practices frequently adopted by public administrators in response to neo-liberal interpretations of the phenomenon of globalization. Agamben (2005) identifies the state of exception as a paradigm of government in contemporary society that affects even countries seen to be democratic. Žižek (1999a, 1999b) uses the expression "post-politics" to refer to this form of authoritarianism in its association with neoliberal consensus. Vainer (2017) situates these ideas in a discussion of contemporary politics when he refers to the direct democracy of capital, while Swyngedouw (2010) writes of "governance-beyond-the-State" or "[the] zero-ground of politics."

The idea that unifies all of these authors is the emphasis they give to the authoritarian character of neoliberal consensus under the aegis of selective participation. My work contributes to the study of convergences between authoritarian practices in urban management styles inspired by neoliberal thinking and processes of producing the city for sport spectacle.

Carlos Vainer, professor of urban planning at the Federal University of Rio de Janeiro, delivered a lecture at the Urban Social Forum of the City of Rio de Janeiro in 2010 in which he introduced the provocative idea of a "city of exception." Vainer made an analogy between the concept of a "state of exception" and the condition of emergency and depoliticization that mega-events make possible in the cities and countries that host them. Vainer returned to this idea at the International Conference on Mega-events and the City, also in 2010. At this same conference, Stavros Stavrides, professor of the National Technical University of Athens, referred to a sort of "Olympic state of emergency," first introduced in Stavrides (2008), that functioned as a legitimating element in the rapid and serious decision-making processes in preparations for the 2004 Athens Olympics. Also at this conference, I presented the preliminary results of my research into the exceptional legal framework produced in Brazil for the 2014 World Cup and the 2016 Olympic Games. Since then, various publications have used the expression "city of exception" to examine the relations between cities and sporting mega-events.

In attempting to explore this theme more deeply, I have attempted to pose certain essential questions. Can a concept of "city of exception" be based on an analogy between the state of exception and authoritarian acts related to neoliberal planning models? Could this concept be applied to exceptional measures taken in preparation for mega-events? If so, what are the principal arguments that give the concept substance as well as the symbolic elements that sustain it? Finally, what mechanisms must be put in place to make it viable? This chapter aims to examine these considerations in order to contribute to the discussion of cities of exception, though it lays no claims to resolving the topic. Instead, I will seek to understand the ways in which laws of exception relating to the production of sport spectacle are applied in different places and what their repercussions are.

Beginning with the idea of a "city of exception" based on contemporary discussions regarding the negation of politics intrinsic to neoliberal projects, this chapter seeks to analyze – across different scales of public administration – the principal institutional ruptures and realignments that occur as a result of the organization of sporting mega-events in the places that host them. I argue that the political and juridical autonomy that the field of production of sport spectacle has claimed historically (cf. Chapter 1) gives it the power to make specific forms of institutionalism and of exercising power viable. As such, this field creates ideal conditions for the authoritarian character inherent in neoliberal management models to assume its highest degree of sophistication. Here, I consider the urgency of producing a timeline – which many authors present as a determining element in mega-event management – as another instrument that serves this authoritarianism. In other words, I will argue that the convergence between the field of production of sport spectacle and the field of the production of the city offers an ideal empirical object to show how market-oriented planning models engender and, simultaneously, are sustained in intensely authoritarian exercises of power and public management.

Giorgio Agamben's articulations of a theory of the state of exception serve as my initial reference points in sustaining this argument. I also consider certain observations made by Nicos Polantzas, as well as by other authors whose work reveals the authoritarian character of neoliberal planning and public management models.

The state of exception and the authoritarian character of neoliberal consensus

Whenever the Roman Senate got word of something that could put the Republic at risk, it put emitted a *senatus consultum ultimum*. Through this instrument, the Senate convoked, in descending scales of hierarchy, consuls, their substitutes in Rome, praetors, plebian tribunals, or even individual citizens to adopt any means considered necessary to save the state. A *senatus consultum* was based on a decree establishing a state of *tumultus* – an emergency situation in provoked by exceptional conditions – and it tended to give way to the proclamation of *iūstitium*, a legal concept whose meaning recalls "the suspension of rights." According to Agamben (2005), the *iūstitium* provides the basis for the state of exception.

Agamben's (2005) theory, which shows a tendency in contemporary politics for states of exception to be presented as governmental paradigms, is well suited for the debate I intend to undertake here.

> This transformation of a provisional and exceptional measure into a technique of government threatens radically to alter – in fact, has palpably altered – the structure and meaning of the traditional distinction between constitutional forms. Indeed, from this perspective, the state of exception appears as a threshold of indeterminacy between democracy and absolutism.
>
> (Agamben 2005, pp. 2–3)

In order to understand the state of exception, both Poulantzas (1974) and Agamben (2005) opt for a comparative analysis of different processes in which states of exception have been put into practice over a diverse range of temporal and spatial contexts. The historical perspective they adopt in these studies allows them to identify certain regularities that, notwithstanding the structural specificities of each given situation, can aid our comprehension of certain facts presented here.

In his attempts to understand processes of fascistization, Poulantzas (1974) emphasizes the political and ideological character of the crises in which such processes originate and identifies two essential characteristics that help give rise to fascism: first, relations between these processes and political crises and, second, the presence and hardening of internal contradictions within power blocs and across political and ideological planes leading to a crisis of hegemony. In other words, according to Poulantzas, contexts in which no single segment of the dominant classes can impose itself on the bloc of power result in a profound disorganization of forces within this bloc.

Like Poulantzas (1974), Agamben sees exceptional legal measures as fruits of political crises which should be understood as belonging to the realm of politics rather than the juridical-constitutional realm. Agamben identifies the paradoxical situation of these "juridical measures that cannot be understood in legal terms" (Agamben 2005, p. 1). Here, the contradictory circumstance of the state of exception is evident so far as it "appears as the legal form of what cannot have legal form" (ibid., p. 1).

Agamben's theory of the state of exception derives from his determination of its localization (or delocalization) within the field of law. He questions the notion, articulated by certain authors, that exception does not suspend law but rather fills an existing lacuna by regulating unforeseen situations "of necessity." In contrast, Agamben emphasizes the strong subjective character of the word "necessity." He argues that a state of exception does not fill an existing lacuna within the law but "appears as the opening of a fictitious lacuna in the order for the propose of safeguarding the existence of the norm and its applicability to the normal situation"

(Agamben 2005, p. 31). In other words, it implies the "suspension of the order that is in force in order to guarantee its existence" (ibid.).

Agamben therefore questions Carl Schmitt's theory of sovereignty, which seeks to inscribe the state of exception within juridical order with no restrictions. According to Agamben, the paradox of Schmitt's theory of sovereignty derives precisely from the strategy that Schmitt (1921, 1922) uses to articulate the difference between concepts of the state of exception and dictatorship. The archetype of dictatorship that Schmitt uses for the state of exception is associated with the idea of order, whereas the archetype of *iūstitium* that Agamben (2005) utilizes is associated with the idea of chaos and anarchy. The archetype of dictatorship makes viable references to the Roman magistrate within the state of exception; as such, it establishes a distinction between legal norms and the norms of realization.

According to Schmitt's theory, sovereignty maintains the right to decide a state of exception and, through this power of decision, anchors it within juridical norms. In deciding on a state of exception, the sovereign suspends norms so as to create conditions for the state of exception's application: it separates the "norm" from its "application." For Agamben (2005), this separation "introduces a zone of anomie into the law in order to make possible the effective regulation [*normazione*] of the real" (Agamben 2005, p. 38).

Based on this rational, Agamben (2005) seeks to define the state of exception in Schmitt's theory as a place in which the opposition between the "norm" and "its realization" reaches maximum intensity. According to this view, the specific contribution of the state of exception is its use of the syntagm "force-of-law": decrees promulgated in certain cases by executive power especially within a state of exception. Although they are not laws, such decrees take on the force of law, representing a sort of isolation between the "force of law" and laws themselves. According to Agamben, "a 'state of law' in which, on the one hand, the norm is in force [vige], but it is not applied (it has no 'force' [forza]) and, on the other hand, acts that do not have the value [valore] of law acquire its 'force'" (Agamben 2005, p. 38). Thus, the state of exception is that which defines itself through its own anomie (the absence of a norm).

> The state of exception is an anomic space in which what is at stake is a force of law without law (which should therefore be written: force-of-law). Such a force-of-law, in which the potentiality and the act are radically separated, is certainly something like a mythical element, or rather, a *fictio* by means of which law seeks to annex anomie itself.
>
> (Agamben 2005, p. 39)

For Agamben (2005), the singularity of the anomic space in its archetypal condition of *iūstitium*, which unexpectedly coincides with the space of the entire city, leads to a situation of extreme disorder. This contradicts Schmitt's explanation of the archetype of the dictatorship, which implies an order inscribed upon the field of law. In Agamben's view, *iūstitium* seems to question the very consistency of public and private spaces (Agamben 2005). This confusion between public and private and between juridical and non-juridical spheres also implies an impossibility of considering an essential question: namely, "that of the nature of acts committed during the iūstitium" (Agamben 2005, p. 49). The impossibility of framing these acts as either transgressive, executive, or legislative situates them, in terms of the law, in an absolute non-place.

Agamben is not the only author to attempt to apply this discussion of the state of exception to contemporaneity. Žižek (1999a, 1999b) also seeks to discuss the paradox of Schmitt's theory of sovereignty from a viewpoint privileging our current moment, thereby linking the political, ideological, and economic realities of so-called contemporary democracies and the state of exception. For Žižek (1999a, 1999b), neoliberal consensus has caused us to face a form of political degeneration which is no longer simply a "repression" of politics aiming to contain and pacify the "return of the repressed." Instead, it is a much more effective attempt to "close down" politics.

> In post-politics, the conflict of global ideological visions embodied in different parties which compete for power is replaced by the collaboration of enlightened technocrats (economists, public opinion specialists . . .) and liberal multiculturalists; via the process of negotiation of interests, a compromise is reached in the guise of a more or less universal consensus.
>
> (Žižek 1999a, p. 198, 1999b, p. 30)

According to Žižek (ibid.), the essence of the discourse of consensus is made viable through the argument of the necessity of overcoming old ideological divisions and confronting new problems with specialized knowledge, thereby steering deliberations toward peoples' demands and necessities. In fact, the discourse of technique has largely been utilized when public administrators adopt competitive strategies so as to respond to the challenges of a reality that can supposedly be known objectively. This rationalist realism tends to ignore both existing conflicts between different representations of the real and disputed interests within these struggles of representation. In other words, by relying on the rhetoric of knowledge, consensus completely denies the political dimension of social practices.

Rancière (2007), meanwhile, believes that the essence of politics is dissensus; as such, he presents consensus as an element that reduces politics to policy. For him, consensus is the end of politics, rather than the realization of its ends. As he puts it:

> The essence of consensus is not peaceful discussion and reasonable agreement as opposed to conflict or violence. Its essence is the annulment of dissensus as the separation of the sensible from itself, the annulment of surplus subjects, the reduction of the people to the sum of the parts of the social body, and of the political community to the relationship of interests and aspirations of these different parts.
>
> (Rancière 2007, thesis 10, 32)

The construction of consensus as a form of negating politics has been a striking characteristic in places that establish a competitive strategy of attracting sport spectacle as a goal of public policy. Based on issues already presented in this research, the following sections aim to show the authoritarian character of regulatory and institutional transformations that tend to occur across all spheres of public administration in territories chosen to host sporting mega-events with the objective of attending to the interests of the coalitions that sustain this project across multiple scales.

Urban management and mega-events from the perspective of exception

Chapters Four and Five showed how the emergence of the (competitive) strategy of attracting sporting mega-events creates both the arena and the context to produce a reorganization of power structures, (re)unify local dominant classes, construct cross-scale alliances (i.e., across state, national, and international levels), and finally, attract non-dominant sectors, thereby reconstructing possibilities of hegemony (Gramsci 1957, 1971). In other words, although the production of sport spectacle takes on a specific city as its principal stage, it involves a system of cross-scale articulation of forces, interests, and actions that both unify elites and gain the consent of subaltern classes through the construction of consensus.

Swyngedouw (2010) alerts us to the authoritarian character of the so-called "technical" discourse that mobilizes these strategies of competence in response to the inexorability of a neoliberal global economic order. In relation to this same discourse, Swyngedouw (2010) identifies a profound re-definition of "governability"[2] based on a network of relations among actors who share a high degree of consensus and confidence and highly selective standards for participation. Regardless of internal conflicts and divergences in priorities, this regime of governance – which Swyngedouw calls "governance-beyond-the-State" (ibid., p. 4) – concerns itself primarily with policing and control. As such, it accentuates the imperatives of the globally connected neoliberal market even more. For Swyngedouw, competitive strategies do not answer the demands of a global order; on the contrary, these are the strategies that create the symbolically defined conditions for a global urbanism. Although this model of public urban management is legitimated through arguments of increased democracy and participation, it actually serves to annul democracy by creating conditions that Swygnedouw defines as the "ZERO-ground of politics" (ibid., p. 2).

The selective essence of neoliberal planning is evident in the theoretical arguments that some of the model's foremost advocates make when referring to different groups of citizens involved in elaborating Barcelona's strategic plan (Forn y Foxà 1993), in which participation was subject to different degrees of strategic relevance. In his examinations of the elaboration of Rio de Janeiro's first Strategic City Plan (CRJ 1996), Vainer (2017) finds significant asymmetry in the preference given to developers and employer associations, thereby presenting the goal of attracting mega-events as the city's primary development strategy. Vainer analyzes the methodologies and modalities behind the organization of social participation in formulating the Strategic City Plan in order to show how authoritarianism in the entrepreneurial city is created through "civic patriotism," a consensus based on the consciousness of crisis.

The perception of crisis and the desire to overcome it by competing for investments with other cities are both essential elements in building consensus to support proposals that completely deny space to politics. In moments of external disputes, there cannot be space for internal disagreements. As such, pro-growth strategies present the radical reduction of public space as the natural path to victory. The *polis*, in the sense of a place of meeting and conflict, dissensus, and democratic negotiation – in other words, a space of politics – thereby succumbs. In its decline, it cedes to the *city*, the locus of business and consensus (Swyngedouw 2010; Vainer 2017).

Due to its significant capacity to mobilize political and economic capital at the same time as it triggers symbolic elements of seemingly unquestionable legitimacy,[3] sport spectacle promotes discourses of consensus in such a thorough and radical way that the mere idea of an action or omission that might pose an obstacle to the eventual realization of sport spectacle becomes unacceptable. As such, coalitions that utilize mega-events as development strategies have easily managed to convert cities into arenas of business opportunities for major investors. The consensus that forms around these situations does not allow for criticisms, conflicts, or claims of social rights: such attitudes are labelled "conservative" or "anti-patriotic," and political leaders can, without limitation, use the imperative of honoring candidature commitments to justify any type of action.

With the objective of making this business-friendly environment viable, a network of decrees, provisional measures, and legal projects – all of which are instituted in an emergency regime – produce major ruptures across multiple scales in the political institutions of territories that host mega-events. In attempting to understand these processes, I have carried out a survey of the primary legal measures established in different territories that have hosted sport spectacles in recent decades and that have been justified by such events' organizational needs. I have organized this research according to the primary scale of action of the interest groups represented in each case.

Having based my methodology on Bourdieu's concept of the field (cf. Introduction), which I understand as a field of symbolic struggles to transform or conserve the configuration of forces acting in it (Bourdieu & Wacquant 1992; Bourdieu 1991), I have also found it necessary to reflect on certain specificities of these laws' enactment as well as parallel structures of management that have resulted from their implementation. It is worth emphasizing that, over the long process of preparing for a given mega-event, certain segments of established institutions may gain or lose their prominence, depending on the correlation of forces among groups in pro-growth coalitions across different scales of action (see Chapters Two and Four).

Legal frameworks attending primarily to global interests

Chapters One and Three present a genealogy of the rules that govern the field of production of sport spectacle and their contemporary configurations. A significant part of this regulatory apparatus is aimed at guaranteeing the IOC and FIFA's control over the production of cities that host mega-events. FIFA and the IOC exert this control through ruptures and realignments of these territories' juridical and institutional boundaries.

Since the 1970s, when the IOC's Olympic Charter first demanded a legal framework for the production of the Olympic Games (see Chapter One), these political-institutional ruptures have grown deeper and more frequent. This process intensified with the organization of the 2000 Sydney Olympics, following the crisis of Atlanta 1996,[4] which led to a series of alterations in the 1999 Olympic Charter (IOC 1999a, 1999b) and, consequently, alterations in the candidature process (cf. Chapters One and Three).

The primary demands that FIFA and the IOC make of the juridical and institutional limits imposed by countries and cities hosting the events they promote relate to creating special management structures, protecting brands and symbols, preventing ambush marketing, abolishing barriers represented by taxation, customs, and migration, and creating measures related to security and the control of public space.

I will analyze certain aspects of these political-institutional changes here, beginning with changes in Australian federal law and in Sydney's municipal legislation in preparation for the 2000 Olympics. It is worth emphasizing that some of these laws, produced under exceptional circumstances to attend to the interests of stakeholders acting on a global scale, were also adapted to attend to locally active interests.

Exceptional models of governance

The IOC's insistent demands for exceptional models of government to mediate its relationship with host cities and coordinate different spheres of administration in preparations for the Olympic Games are aimed, above all, at streamlining the organization's actions and giving it greater control so that the Olympics takes place in exact accordance with the IOC's expectations.

During the organization of the 1996 Atlanta games, the government of the state of Georgia created the Metropolitan Atlanta Olympic Games Authority (MAOGA), a public body charged with coordinating activities related to the Olympic Games. Yet, MAOGA was limited to acting within a single scale of public administration as well as by its lack of financial resources, and by having to compete for space with Atlanta's city government and with the powerful Atlanta Committee for the Olympic and Paralympic Games (ACOG) (Burbank, Andranovich and Heying 2001; COHRE 2007).

The 2000 Sydney Olympics marked the first Games in which an Olympic authority exercised a significant role in coordinating the event. In fact, the

Olympic Co-ordination Authority (OCA), created by the New South Wales Olympic Co-ordination Authority Act 1995, launched an era of special management structures for the production of sporting mega-events. Created to serve under the controlling authority of the Ministry for the Olympics, the OCA aided the government through its relation to the Sydney Organizing Committee for the Olympic Games (SOCOG). In addition, the OCA accompanied and monitored reports and expenses for construction projects and other services carried out by the government as well as contracts with other government agencies and private enterprise relating to the organization of the Olympic Games. The law that created the OCA gave the agency the authority to buy and disappropriate land, to coordinate and execute projects, and to alter other laws in addition to establishing special conditions for approving projects coordinated by the OCA. However, the Co-ordination Authority Act also established mechanisms by which the Ministry, SOCOG, and other authorities linked to government could control the OCA.[5]

The 2004 Olympic Games in Athens also saw the creation of certain special organizational forms (ATHOC 2005), such as the *Inter-Ministerial Committee' 2004 Olympiad*, coordinated by Greece's Minister of Culture. The Committee, established in 1998, was charged with preparing legal reforms as well as coordinating and monitoring activities related to the organization of the Games. In 2000, the *Inter-Ministerial Committee' 2004 Olympiad* was substituted by the Inter-Ministerial Committee for the Coordination for Olympic Preparation, overseen by Greece's Prime Minister and including a greater number of government ministries. However, these committees were coordinated between already-existing political authorities; thus, they differed in certain aspects from a special management agency, such as in the case of the Sydney Olympic Authority.

As indicated in Chapter One, Beijing's candidature to host the 2008 Olympics did not present a special governing authority for the Games' organization. However, the IOC, in its Final Report on Beijing 2008 (IOC 2010), showed itself to be dissatisfied with the model of governance adopted for the Games due to difficulties in coordinating between various levels of command simultaneously.

The public authority responsible for the 2012 London Games, the Olympic Delivery Authority (ODA), was created by the United Kingdom's *London Olympic Games and Paralympic Games Act of 2006*. Like the OCA, created for the 2000 Sydney Olympics, the ODA held the power to plan urban interventions, acquire lands for purchase or disappropriation, construct, establish contracts and relations with governmental agencies and private enterprise, and take other measures necessary for organizing the Games. However, the Act made it clear that the ODA was subordinate to the ministry for the Olympics and to all other relevant laws, rules, and authorities.

The creation of the Olympic Public Authority (APO) for the 2016 Rio de Janeiro Olympics was accompanied by a tumultuous process that revealed disputes between different scales of government. Article 62 of *Constitution of the Federative Republic of Brazil 1988* establishes that, in relevant or urgent cases, the country's president has the power to adopt provisional measures that are immediately imbued with the power of law. These, however, must be submitted to Brazil's Congress and voted on within 120 days at most; otherwise, they expire. President Luis Inácio Lula da Silva utilized this prerogative in May 2010 to create the APO as an Inter-Federal Public Consortium between Brazil's federal government, the government of Rio de Janeiro state, and Rio de Janeiro's municipal government, through *Provisional Measure 489/2010*. The APO, formed with the objective of coordinating actions between these three spheres of government in producing the 2016 Olympic Games, had the power to define Brazil's Olympic Projects Agenda and to monitor and plan the projects that it included. In situations regarding the timeline or quality of constructions, the APO would have the power to intervene – together with the governmental bodies it included – and to take over planning, coordination, and execution of construction or services falling under the responsibility of any of these spheres of government. Under such "exceptional" situations, the APO would have the authority to draw up contracts or to conduct bidding under special conditions. In order to acquire legal status, however, the APO needed to be ratified by legislative bodies at the federal, state, and municipal levels. Because Brazil's Senate would not ratify *Provisional Measure 489/2010* within the stipulated timeline, the executive branch of the federal government found itself forced to issue another provisional measure, which the senate approved in March 2011 as *APO Federal Law – Law 12.396 of 2011* – (RFB). In addition, although Rio de Janeiro's state legislature approved the consortium without hindrance, the municipal government tried to restrict its potential to act. *APO Municipal Law – Law 5.260/2011* – (CRJ), which ratified the existence of the APO, removed the consortium's right to take over construction projects from the municipal government or to represent the city under any circumstances. The correlation of forces in the city government – which, unlike the federal government, was not endorsed by the IOC – forced Eduardo Paes,[6] the mayor of Rio de Janeiro, to retreat; finally, after countless entanglements,[7] Paes found himself obligated to submit a new law to the city council restoring the APO's original powers. In June 2011, this became a second *APO Municipal Law – Law 5.272-2011* (CRJ). It is worth emphasizing that Paes' office crated also the Municipal Olympic Authority, the nomenclature of which was a clear reference to this dispute with the APO. The law ratifying the APO eventually renamed the organization, which became known as the Municipal Olympic Business (EOM).

After this significant attrition, the APO – which only gained full legal recognition five years before the Olympics – continued to lose power. In principle, *Federal Law 12.396 of 2011* (RFB), which created the APO, did not make the body subordinate to any federal ministry, as had occurred in London and Sydney. However, the APO was initially overseen by the federal Ministry of Planning and later by the Ministry of Sports. Although the text of the law establishing the APO gave the agency extraordinary powers – for example, allowing it to intervene in the work of the governmental bodies responsible for its creation – in practice, it was completely deprived of control over preparations for the 2016 Olympics. The mayor's office of Rio de Janeiro exercised an almost autocratic level of control over these preparations, excluding the APO and Brazil's federal government from most decision-making processes, even those regarding constructions financed with federal resources.

No public authority was created to coordinate the organization of the 2020 Tokyo Olympics. The Tokyo Organizing Committee of the Olympic and Paralympic Games (Tokyo 2020), a public interest foundation established in accordance with Japanese law and directed by former Prime Minister Yoshirō Mori, is responsible for all tasks associated with planning, organizing, and delivering the Games. The Tokyo 2020 Executive Board includes representatives of the Olympic Movement in Japan, as well as business leaders and leaders from metropolitan, municipal, and national governments. In order to guarantee coordination among the public and private authorities involved in organizing the Games, the Executive Board established the Venue, Transport, and Security Committees. Although these committees play a fundamental role in organizing the Games, they do not exist as separate legal entities (Tokyo Candidate City 2020 n.d.). Similarly, the cities selected to host the 2024 and 2028 Olympics – respectively, Paris and Los Angeles – did not present any special management models for coordinating the Games in their candidature bids (Paris 2024 Candidate City n.d; Los Angeles 2024 Candidate City n.d).

Establishing special governance authorities imbued with ample powers to streamline the production of sport spectacle in accordance with the interests of the IOC and its partners makes exceptional conditions possible for disappropriating land, acquiring real estate, and creating contracts involving the use of public funds. To the degree that such conditions create measures that deviate from traditional forms of managing public resources, they also privilege the interests of locally acting coalitions, as seen in Chapter Four. In the cross-scalar disputes involving the creation of the APO in Brazil, disputes for power within the coalition were also at play. In the specific case of Rio de Janeiro, although the law of exception took on "force-of-law" (Agamben 2005), it did not take on a life of its own.

Brand protection, ambush marketing prevention, and easing customs and migration barriers

The IOC and FIFA, in order to guarantee the Olympic Movement's existence and safeguard their partners' commercial contracts, demand that host countries and cities adopt rigorous measures to protect the symbols and brands they own as well as to prevent so-called ambush marketing (see Chapter Two). In relation to the flow of people, the IOC maintains the power to grant Olympic family members, employees, and partners the credentials to enter, remain, and work in host countries without undergoing consular bureaucracy. Meanwhile, FIFA stipulates that athletes, commercial partners, and employees involved in producing the World Cup as well as fans holding match tickets enjoy special privileges – in terms of both timelines and costs – in receiving visas. In relation to the flow of goods and services, both FIFA and the IOC demand exemptions from import taxes on materials and equipment, a demand that FIFA extends to all commercial transactions that it or its partners carry out within host countries.

The new era of legal measures specifically produced to regulate the use of signs and images related to mega-events began in Australia. In addition to regulating the use of the images belonging to the IOC or the SOCOG for commercial ends, the *Sydney 2000 Games (Indicia and Images) Protection Act 1996* (Cth) also protected words, expressions, or combinations of words relating to the Olympic Movement or the 2000 Olympic Games. However, this act allowed for possible exceptions for certain uses, such as those intended for purposes of information or critical analysis, and guaranteed the right to defense and indemnity against unwarranted threats from judicial processes.

The Athens 2004 Organizing Committee for the Olympic Games (ATHOC) submitted eight legal projects to the Greek government, as well as other ad hoc legal measures to guarantee that the IOC's demands for hosting the Games would be met (ATHOC 2005). Among other issues, these laws established tax and security regulations as well as special regulations regarding the entrance and presence of foreigners on Greek territory and special authorizations for work. They also guaranteed protection of the Olympic brand; control of the circulation of cruise ships, land vehicles, and parking spaces; and the prohibition of unauthorized publicity in central Athens as well as in areas near official competition and non-competition venues. Violations were subject to severe administrative sanctions and criminal charges (ibid.).

In China, different spheres of public administration established specific legal measures for the organization of the 2008 Olympics in addition to previously existing legislation establishing rigorous protections for intellectual property (BOCOG n.d.). Beijing's municipal government issued the *Regulations on Protection of Olympic Intellectual Property Rights in Beijing 2002* (Bj), while China's State Council created the *Regulations on Protection of Olympic Symbols 2002* (PRC) and the *Regulations on Reporting Activities in China by Foreign Journalists during the Beijing Olympic Games and the Preparatory Period 2006* (PRC) (BOCOG n.d.). An educational publicity campaign aimed to teach the entire population the punishments detailed in these laws. In addition, teams were trained to repress "ambush marketing" at competition venues and in surrounding areas (ibid.).

The British government chose to create a single law – the *London Olympic Games and Paralympic Games Act 2006* (UK) – establishing legislative measures relating to the 2012 London Olympics, including protection of the Olympic brand, alterations in the city's public transportation plans, regulations to prevent ambush marketing, restrictions on street commerce, and the creation of the Olympic Delivery Authority (ODA). In relation to protecting the Olympic brand, a significant part of the Act's text was dedicated to establishing exceptions, limits, and restrictions. Among these restrictions, special emphasis was placed on the use of protected words and symbols, including exceptions to the IOC's exclusive ownership rights for informative, artistic, or literary usages.

In Brazil, the *Olympic Act 2009 – Law nº 12.035/2009* – (RFB) was published one day before Rio de Janeiro's official selection as the host city for the 2016 Olympic and Paralympic Games; the Act's authors argued that the law would guarantee commitments made in the city's candidature. The *Olympic Act* created tax breaks and eased barriers to migration for those responsible for the 2016 Olympics, as well as for service providers and athletes. In addition, the Act prohibited the use of symbols related to the Rio 2016 Games for commercial and non-commercial purposes without the previous authorization of the IOC or the Organizing Committee of the Olympic and Paralympic Games Rio 2016 (Rio 2016). It extended this prohibition to the utilization of terms and expressions that were sufficiently similar to those reserved by the Rio 2016 Olympics or the Olympic Movement, even if these were not explicitly mentioned in the text of the law. In order to prevent ambush marketing, the Act suspended contracts governing publicity in airports or in federal areas of interest to the Rio 2016 Olympics in the period leading up to and including the Games. The mayor's office also issued Municipal Decree Number 30.379–2009 (CRJ), the content of which was similar but more detailed.

Organizers of the 2020 Tokyo Olympics relied exclusively on existing Japanese legislation to guarantee intellectual property rights related to the Games (Tokyo 2020 Candidate City n.d.; Tokyo 2020 2017). The country's *Patent Act 1959* (Jpn), *Trademark Law 1959* (Jpn), the *Design Law 1959* (Jpn), and *Copyright Law 1970* (Jpn) establish some of the world's most rigorous intellectual property protection. These laws already protected most symbols belonging to the IOC, whereas specific symbols for the 2020 Games were registered immediately upon their creation (ibid.). The *Unfair Competition Prevention Act 1993* (Jpn), amended in 2017, was already sufficiently robust to prevent ambush marketing. Paris and Los Angeles, host cities for the 2024 and 2028 Olympics, also limited intellectual property protection for the Games to pre-existing legal framework in France and the United States, respectively (Paris 2024 Candidate City n.d; Los Angeles 2024 Candidate City n.d).

In relation to migration, the Tokyo 2020 Bid Committee communicated to the IOC that "permission to work" does not exist in Japan and that, instead, foreign workers must solicit "resident status" (Tokyo 2020 n.d, 2017). The Bid Committee also pledged to cooperate closely with the IOC and other authorities in order to produce and accelerate the concession of resident status to people with work credentials for the organization and execution of the Games (ibid.).

Despite the lack of clear rules in relation to the Football World Cup, FIFA also produces political-institutional ruptures in organizing its signature mega-event.

According to the German federal government's official report on the 2006 World Cup (Stab WM 2006 2006), Germany granted work visas to FIFA employees and service providers without hindrance in addition to facilitating the concession of entry visas for fans from 11 countries who required them. In order to guarantee this service, German consulates had to adopt other exceptional measures, such as increasing the hours they were open to the public, restricting staff vacation days in the months before the Cup, changing consular procedures, and increasing the number of staff. In addition, between May 1 and July 20, 2006, the German government allowed FIFA employees to work nights and weekends, sometimes surpassing federally mandated limits of 60 hours per week, without demanding prior communication to or authorization from the responsible authorities as required under German law. According to this same report (ibid.), Germany adopted legislative measures to exempt FIFA from taxes, reduce customs controls, and allow for unrestricted currency transfers. Additionally, various host states and cities, including Berlin, adopted the Federal Council Resolution on Shop Opening Times During the *2006 World Cup 2005* (FRG), which relaxed Germany's normally rigorous regulation of store opening times. For areas surrounding stadiums where matches were to be exhibited, including the FIFA Fan Fest, the Ordinance on Noise Protection in Public Outdoor TV Shows for the *2006 World Cup 2006* (FRG) allowed loud noises beyond normally permitted hours. The sale of all brands of beer in Fan Fest locations only became authorized after a long standoff between FIFA and German authorities. Inside stadiums, however, only Budweiser – the World Cup's official sponsor brand – could be sold (Stab WM 2006 2006).

In South Africa, the *2010 FIFA World Cup South Africa Special Measures Act 2006* (RSA) addressed migration issues and established procedures for the commercial control of public spaces and thoroughfares designated by the Local Organizing Committee (LOC). General Notice n° 683/2006 (RSA) declared the World Cup to be an event protected under the rigorous terms of the *Merchandise Marks Act 1941* (RSA) amended in 2002.

The organization of the 2014 World Cup in Brazil resulted in a series of new juridical measures in addition to those already established for the 2016 Olympics. *Provisional Measure 49/2010* (RFB), later adopted as Federal *Tax Benefit Law 2010 – Law n° 12.350/2010 –* (RFB), exempted FIFA, its Brazilian subsidiaries, and broadcasters responsible for distributing television rights from all federal taxes. In addition, the law freed all transactions related to events promoted by FIFA, its commercial partners, and associated service providers from taxation.

Meanwhile, *Law Lei n° 12.663/2012 – General Law of the Cup –* (RFB) established exceptions to the juridical order for four specific situations relating to the 2014 World Cup and the 2013 Confederations Cup: the protection and exploitation of commercial rights related to the event; the flexibilization of entry and work visa concessions; Brazil's federal government's responsibility for any damages caused to FIFA or to third parties during the preparation and execution of the event; and ticket sales. In addition, the *General Law of the Cup* also covered the regulation of volunteer work for the Cup and related events; the restriction of event transmission rights to the press; and the polemical, exceptional suspension of Brazilian legislation that, under normal circumstances, prohibits alcohol sales in stadiums and guarantees half-priced tickets for students. The General Law address four central aspects of commercial rights: property rights relating to FIFA's brand; rights to images, sounds, and radio transmissions; areas of commercial restrictions and access roads; as well as the definition of crimes and subsequent penalties related to these areas. Such penalties included fines, restitutions, or imprisonment for periods ranging from three months to one year.

Laws that limit the commercial use of certain territories to restricted groups of companies not only restrict these companies' competitors, they also impede street vendors. This has an especially noteworthy impact in countries like Brazil and South Africa where informal work serves as a primary source of income for a significant part of the population. Meanwhile, increasingly flexible migration is a violation of the constitutional apparatuses and, as such, the juridical sovereignty of the majority of countries that host sport spectacle. Finally, laws that establish tax exemptions for the IOC, FIFA, and their partners waive a source of funding that may be essential to recuperating some of the vast sums of public resources invested in venues and infrastructure for these mega-events.

Measures regarding security and control of public space

Arguments involving public security and the valorization of urban spaces are frequently used to legitimize measures that restrict civil liberties in public spaces and promote other kinds of human rights violations. This is especially true in cities that host sport spectacle. I will discuss these kinds of restrictive measures here in terms of their relation to FIFA and the IOC's demands, but it is worth noting that they tend to exercise a double function, inasmuch as valorizing the image of a city also favors the valorization of capital and, consequently, locally acting coalitions.

Among the most common of these types of measures are those that criminalize society's most vulnerable groups. Criminalizing peoples' lack of housing was a fundamental aspect of preparations for the 1996 Atlanta Olympics. Atlanta began adopting so-called "Quality of life ordinances" in 1988 with the objective of establishing measures to facilitate the criminalization of homeless populations, prohibiting people from entering unoccupied buildings, panhandling, or even loitering in parking lots in which they did not own a car (COHRE 2007; Burbank, Andranovich & Heying 2001). Based on these ordinances and as part of the clean-up promoted for the 1996 Games, police issued 9000 citations to homeless people in Atlanta's city center between 1995 and 1996. According to COHRE (2007), this represented an increase of more than four times the usual number of citations. The persecution of homeless people was so intense that it led to a court order prohibiting their arrest without probable cause (ibid.).

Bluden (2007) denounces laws in Sydney that aimed at controlling the behavior of people in public space. He holds that – in addition to functioning as a means to remove homeless people – such legislation also served to repress protest during the period leading to and including the 2000 Olympics. The *Homebush Bay Operations Act and Regulation 1999* (NSW) and the *Sydney Harbour Foreshore Authority Regulation 1999* (NSW) gave police and forest rangers the power to approach people or remove them from public spaces in the Homebush Bay and Harbour Foreshore areas on subjective bases, including the use of "indecent, obscene, insulting or threatening language" (12.a) or "behav[ing] in an offensive or indecent manner" (12.b).

Both laws prohibited specific activities in public spaces in these areas, including: "sell[ing] or offer[ing] for sale, any article . . . (3.a); or "provid[ing], or offer[ing] to provide, any services for fee, gain or reward" (3.b). The *Sydney Harbour Foreshore Authority Regulation* went further, prohibiting the "use [of] facilities for sleeping overnight" (4.j), and establishing that "a person must not, except as authorised by the Authority, conduct or participate in any public assembly in a public area" (5.2). The *Olympic Arrangements Act 2000* gave authority to OCA to move unwelcome people along immediately and operated across all city during the Games. All ranger personnel, City of Sydney, Sydney Harbour Foreshores Authority, and Darling Harbour Authority were authorized officers under the Olympic Arrangements Act (SOCOG 2001, p. 179).

Stavrides (2017) highlights the security apparatus created for the 2004 Athens Olympics, the first Games held after the terrorist attacks of September 11, 2001, in the United States. According to Stavrides (ibid.), Greece bowed to anti-terrorist hysteria in the IOC by accepting the guidance of an Olympic Security Consulting Team with members from seven countries – the United States, United Kingdom, Spain, France, Israel, Germany, and Australia – which led to US$1.5 billion in costs and to the naturalization of hypervigilance in peoples' daily lives. Stavrides and COHRE (2007) point to the confinement of drug users and homeless people as well as the expulsion of Roma communities from their settlements as legacies of the 2004 Games.

Leaders in Beijing adopted 16 legislative measures for the 2008 Olympics addressing public security and anti-smoking initiatives among other issues (BOCOG n.d.). Through the *2007 Resolutions on Strengthening the Legal System for Preparing and Hosting a Successful Beijing Olympic Games*, the Standing Committee of Beijing's Municipal People's Congress authorized the city's Municipal Government to stipulate temporary rules, regulations, and administrative orders to maintain public order before and during the Beijing Olympics (ibid.). In addition to legislative measures, some of the government's actions made greater control of public spaces possible. Broudehoux (2007, 2012) believes that, in addition to reforming the city, Beijing's leaders also sought to "reform" residents through "civilizing" programs that encouraged the local population "to conform to the image of China as a friendly, enduring civilization embracing modernity" (ibid., p. 390). Broudehoux highlights messages in the press, on television, and on public billboards that ranged from teaching the proper use of public restrooms to encouraging residents to smile more, learn English, not spit, and wear shirts in the summer heat. To Broudehoux, these campaigns were aimed primary at the masses of migrant workers who are subject to intense exploitation by the construction industry, lack basic rights, and are most vulnerable to Beijing's modernization projects. Beyond these exceptional measures, the repressive force that the People's Republic of China exercises in public spaces and in its control of the press – even in normal times – renders any possibility of protesting or questioning consensus impossible.

The criminalization of homeless people was also characteristic of preparations for the 2014 World Cup and the 2016 Olympics in Brazil. Among the measures adopted to this end, it is worth highlighting the 2011 resolution issued by the Secretary of Social Assistance for the City of Rio de Janeiro establishing a "protocol for approaching homeless people," creating a policy of "compulsory containment and hospitalization" of drug addicts, especially children and adolescents crack users. The Rio de Janeiro State Legislature's Commission for the Defense of Human Rights and Citizenship (CDDHC-ALERJ) (CDDHC-ALERJ 2012a, 2012b) criticized (among other factors): the lack of consultation between those charged with implementing this protocol and public health institutions; violent practices in approaching homeless people; the utilization of outdated clinical methods for treating drug addiction; the unconstitutional character of the law which violated Brazil's 1990 Statute on Children and Adolescents (ECA – RPF) and numerous health policies; uncontrolled practices of isolation, incarceration, and medication; and a return to asylum models. Rio de Janeiro's municipal "Shock of Order" policy, enacted on January 5, 2009, aimed to implement "urban clean-up" by repressing people who worked and lived on the city's streets as well as by cracking down on irregular buildings and unauthorized publicity. Complaints of the persecution of homeless people, drug users, street vendors, and sex workers were also common in other Brazilian cities hosting the 2014 World Cup (ANCOP n.d.).

During the 2013 Confederations Cup, police forces across Brazil violently repressed millions of protestors who took to the streets in cities across the country to challenge the neoliberal consensus. Protestors denounced the precariousness of Brazil's public transportation, education, and healthcare while vast quantities of public funds were being invested in constructing mega-event venues of questionable use to society. Dilma Rousseff,[8] Brazil's president at the time, intensified police repression so as to assuage the IOC and FIFA's nervousness regarding Brazil's capacity to maintain "public order" during the 2014 World Cup and the 2016 Olympics. The passage of the *Criminal Organizations Law 2013 – Lei n°12.850/2013 –* (RFB) and *Terrorism Law 2016 – Law 13.260/2016 –* (RFB) reinforced previously existing legal instruments that served to criminalize and constrict Brazil's social movements.

In any examination of the production of exceptional legal measures to support sports spectacle, Rio de Janeiro's security policies are worth mentioning. Some of the measures associated with these policies precede Brazil's selection as host country of the 2014 World Cup and Rio de Janeiro's selection as host city for the 2016 Olympics; they were adopted from the first moments in which Rio established a development strategy based on attracting mega-events. Bringing this project to fruition depended on gaining the world's confidence in Brazilian institutions' capacity to control the territory Rio de Janeiro so as to offer security to the athletes, politicians, and tourists visiting the city over the course of these events. It also justified intense police repression, especially of poor people, carried out with the objective of valorizing areas for the benefit of investment capital. Countless initiatives were carried out to these ends, but I will cite three representative instances. First, the "Pan American Massacre" in the Alemão complex of favelas, which took place over two months in 2007 on the eve of the Pan American Games, leaving 44 dead and 78 wounded (Alvarenga Filho 2010). Second, the actions of Rio de Janeiro's Police Battalion of Special Operations (BOPE) in the Maré complex during the 2013 Confederations Cup, which besieged residents, invaded houses, and left ten dead and several more wounded.[9] Third, then-mayor Eduardo Paes' failed attempt to institute Police Pacification Units (UPPs) in select favelas, intended to create a sort of "security belt" around the area in which mega-events would be held. The UPPs did not represent a public security policy for the city; the state's presence in these communities was restricted to ostentatious police actions completely disconnected from social policies and public participation. Instead, UPPs represented an exercise of police power with the goal of maintaining control over specific areas of the city that – like many others – were marked "by the presence of the 'parallel state' [drug trafficking cartels] and heavy armaments" (CDDHC-ALERJ 2012a, p. 50). Denunciations of human rights violations in communities occupied by UPPs were frequent. Many of these were related to police procedures like abuse of authority, unlawful arrests, repression of informal workers, restrictions on residents' social lives, and precarious labor conditions for police assigned to UPPs. In addition, as Rio de Janeiro CDDHC-ALERJ (2012a) noted, ostentatious and permanent police occupations reinforced the stigmatization of favelas as violent enemy territories requiring constantly monitoring in order to maintain peace.

The use of exceptional measures and laws – legitimated by arguments for the necessity of guaranteeing order and public security – that make the social control of public spaces and the police repression of vulnerable groups viable is a noteworthy characteristic of the contemporary production of sport spectacle. However, the approaches of these actions and the level of violence with which they are applied vary depending on the correlation of forces within each territory's dominant coalition at any given moment. It is worth highlighting, in agreement with Stavrides (2017), that the significant recurrence of these measures and their justification through subjective arguments – such as "necessity" – tends to create a naturalization of exception. In extreme cases, this leads to situations in which, as Agamben puts it, the exception "becomes the rule" (Agamben 2005, p. 86).

Legal frameworks to suit local and localized interests

Taking Logan and Molotch's (1987) concept of the growth machine as a methodological reference point, Chapter Four studied the principal agents behind the adhesion of cities' elite groups to pro-growth coalitions formed around a strategy of attracting sport spectacle. This section focuses on exceptional measures, justified through the production of sporting mega-events, that satisfy these locally acting groups' interests. To the extent that business management models for the city drive such groups' competitive practices, they also determine their main agendas of demanding exceptional legal measures. Such measures tend to be organized in accordance with four thematic areas: fiscal benefits, changes in zoning laws and parameters, special structures of public management, and measures relating to land ownership and social clean-up in urban space.

Tax benefits

Places aiming to attract the types of investments most sought after under neoliberal thinking frequently adopt strategies that involve conceding significant fiscal incentives. In addition to granting benefits to the IOC, FIFA, and their partners, certain mega-event host cities give tax breaks to locally acting private businesses in order to stimulate their interest in the coalition. For example, during preparations for the 1992 Barcelona Olympics, the Spanish government created the *Tax Benefit Law 1988*, establishing tax breaks for companies and people who made donations or investments, or implemented infrastructure, in support of the event. The Barcelona '92 Olympic Organizing Committee (COOB'92) also benefitted from these same incentives (COOB'92 1992).

In this sense, the organization of the 2016 Olympic Games and the 2014 World Cup were emblematic. When Brazil's federal government issued *Provisional Measure 49/2010*, which later became *Tax Benefit Law 2010*, conceding fiscal benefits to FIFA and its partners, it took the opportunity to insert RECOPA – the Special Tax Regime for the Construction, Growth, Renovation, or Modernization of Football Stadiums – into Section IV of the law. Through RECOPA, construction firms responsible for projects in football stadiums scheduled to be used for official matches in the 2013 FIFA Confederations Cup or the 2014 FIFA World Cup were exempted from many of the taxes on the importation or domestic acquisition of goods utilized in the stadiums construction.

In Rio de Janeiro, almost all of the sectors active in the pro-growth coalition that formed around the 2016 Olympics received some sort of financial benefit. The urban requalification project known as *Porto Maravilha* (the "Marvelous Port" – cf. Chapter Four) established, through Municipal *Law Number 5.128–2009* (CRJ), tax benefits for people or companies that chose to construct or establish businesses within the limits established by the urban operation of Rio de Janeiro's Port District. Meanwhile, Municipal *Law Number 716/2010* (CRJ), part of the so-called *Olympic Package*, established fiscal incentives for the hotel industry, as well as for construction firms working in service of hotels and all companies directly providing services to members of FIFA and the Olympic Movement.

The cases examined here, along with many others, accommodate perfectly the cross-scale articulation of interests. While they attend to the IOC and FIFA's demands and to other international interests, these exceptional measures also benefit local groups (active on both country- and city-wide scales) involved in pro-growth coalitions (cf. Chapter Five).

The flexibilization of zoning legislation

Coalitions that sustain market-oriented urban policies usually demand increased flexibility of zoning laws. In addition to being agile, the competitive city must be flexible (Vainer 2000); within this logic, it must also free itself from the bonds of legislation that threaten the viability of business opportunities. In cities that host mega-events, the urgency of commitments made to bodies like FIFA and the IOC have legitimated the creation of laws that permit flexibility on greater or lesser scales depending on the structural context both in and outside of these coalitions.

Seoul's *Urban Redevelopment Law 1982* (RK), created under exceptional circumstances to facilitate urban redevelopment by removing earlier administrative obstacles, eased limits on the height and size of construction projects in certain central commercial districts of the city. However, these changes led to widespread negative reactions, even among certain members of dominant groups (COHRE 2007).

In Athens, political leaders introduced multiple exceptions to existing legislation in order to appease the interests involved in the project of modernizing the city. Among these exceptions, Stavrides (2017) highlights the alteration of the city's *Master Plan – Law Number 1515/1985* – (HR). Athens' Olympic project, a business-oriented proposal for development, conflicted directly with the Master Plan that established control over urban growth and protecting the city's coastline against unrestricted urbanization. Other legislative changes, which were quickly approved, directly benefitted real estate promotors. Among the most noteworthy of these changes was the flexibilization of zoning and environmental restrictions for construction associated with the Games (ATHOC 2005). In order to compensate for some of the extra costs associated with Athens' Workers' Housing Organisation (OEK), which was responsible for building the Olympic village, the city government made additional lands available and promoted changes in rules regarding construction and permission of use (ATHOC 2005).

In Rio de Janeiro, Municipal *Law nº 44/2010* (CRJ), also part of the so-called *Olympic Package*, altered zoning parameters as well as usage and occupation norms throughout the city for the exclusive benefit of the hotel industry. Meanwhile, the package of laws included with the *Porto Maravilha Project 2009 – Law nº 101/2009, Law nº 102/2009 and Law nº 15.128 /2009* – (CRJ) altered all zoning parameters – limits on height, usage, and urban usage – in the city's port district, thereby completely reconfiguring the urban fabric of Rio de Janeiro's historic center. In addition, the *Urban Structuring Plan for the Vargens District 2009 (PEU Vargens) – Law nº 104/2009* – (CRJ), also promoted a total transformation of the zoning parameters of the Vargens district, which includes multiple neighborhoods in Rio de Janeiro's west zone, including part of Barra da Tijuca, significantly increasing the density allowed in this environmentally vulnerable area.

Olympic competitions do not always occur in areas targeted for urban intervention. Frequently, the speculation of construction of an Olympic venue is enough to legitimize a project, as was the case with *Porto Maravilha*.[10]

In general, the main beneficiaries of this flexibilization of zoning laws are real estate promotors, hotel and entertainment industries, and construction firms. It is worth emphasizing the urgency with which these oftentimes extensive and complex legal projects are implemented. For example, the *PEU Vargens* project was submitted by Rio de Janeiro's executive branch and voted on in the municipal legislature within the space of a single week. In the case of *Porto Maravilha*, the process took a month. These changes are also frequently implemented through executive decree without being submitted to legislative bodies.

The expansion of executive power in legislative functions – whether through provisional measures, decrees, or laws issued during states of emergency – establish an imbalance in the democratic order, with a preponderance of institutional power exercised by one branch of government at the expense of the others. In these cases, the condition of anomie that Agamben (2005) defines as characteristic of the state of exception becomes clear, inasmuch as the legislature is reduced "to ratifying measures that the executive issues through decrees having force of law" (Agamben 2005, p. 7).

Special management structures

If, as Vainer (2017) posits, the entrepreneurial city depends on quick and agile decisions and actions in order to be competitive, the rigorous timeline that mega-events impose on cities confers legitimacy to even more radical demands for agility. In democratic countries, legislation that applies under normal conditions establishes rules rigorous enough to guarantee that the state's acquisition and disappropriation of goods – as well as contracts for public works established with construction firms – will be carried out according to the principles of free and open competition. Under these conditions, the speed that the city-business demands – especially when involved in the production of sport spectacle – becomes unviable. In order to steer through these obstacles, political leaders tend to resort to laws of exception.

Generally, exceptional models of governance created to meet the demands of the IOC and FIFA – bestowing attributes that both institutions demand be enshrined into law – also fulfill the function of easing the movement of public resources, bypassing inherent bureaucracy, and other state actions. The Sydney 2000 OCA, the London 2012 ODA, and certain Organizing Committees for the Olympic Games (OCOGs) have also played this role, as have COOB '92, Beijing Organizing Committee for the Games of the XXIX Olympiad (BOCOG), Athens 2004 Organizing Committee for the Olympic Games (ATHOC), and Tokyo 2020. The official report of the 2000 Sydney Olympics illustrated this condition perfectly.

> Legislation was enacted to facilitate the management of the Common Domain. The *Homebush Bay Operations Act* provided OCA with the powers necessary to manage and control the Common Domain before, during and after the Games. Under the terms of the legislation, OCA had all rights as an owner of the land, including rights of use, occupation and enjoyment, and rights for trade and commerce. OCA was also the legal consent authority in respect of all building and planning approvals under local government legislation.
>
> (SOCOG 2001, pp. 187–188)

In other places, similar structures have been created on smaller scalar levels. Examples include Olympic Village S.A., a subsidiary company that OEK created while constructing the Olympic Village in Athens in order to guarantee a "more flexible structure for the timely implementation of the Project" (ATHOC 2005, p. 161), or the creation of the Urban Development Company of Rio de Janeiro's Port Region (CDURP) to make the transference of public resources in the city's Port District to private enterprise viable.

In other instances, special strategies have been established within already existing management structures. Such is the case of Rio de Janeiro's *Porto Maravilha* project, examined in Chapter Four. The passage of a law approving a project presented by the same private companies that later won bids to implement it involved a maneuver that disassembled the entire structure of the Instituto Pereira Passos (IPP), an institution run by the city government, and substituting some of its employees with consultants from the McKinsey firm under the coordination of Felipe Góes,[11] a former McKinsey owner.

In some places, legislative measures have increased the agility of mechanisms used to create contracts for public works. One example worth highlighting is the *Differentiated Public Contracts Regime* (RDC) – *Law nº 12.462 2011* – (RFB), passed by Brazil's federal Congress in 2011 to establish special conditions for bids and contracts linked to the 2014 World Cup and the 2016 Olympic Games. In these exceptional cases, this law took the place of the *Bid Law 1993 – Law nº 8.666/1993* – (RFB), which establishes oversight for public contracts throughout Brazil under normal circumstances. Among other conditions established for such contracts, the *Differentiated Public Contracts Regime* (RDC) created the possibility of the government transferring responsibility for projects to construction firm executives. The Regime, which was intended to streamline construction projects, withdrew the state's ability to establish technical requirements guaranteeing political and civic leaders control and oversight into the costs and quality of construction techniques and materials. In an opinion issued in May 2010, Brazil's Federal Public Ministry, a government oversight body, alleged that the Differentiated Contracts Regime was unconstitutional. Among the Public Ministry's arguments for this unconstitutionality was the implicit subjectivity of criteria established under the law as well as the definition of these criteria's application according the "necessity" of a given development to mega-events. Still, Brazil's Congress approved the law. However, strong social pressure led to the rejection of one article of the law that freed companies from adding to the total cost of contracts so as to meet the demands of international institutions. After its passage, the Differentiated Contracts Regime was amended until its terms could be applied to any construction in Brazil whose execution was deemed to occur under "emergency" conditions. This constitutes an exemplary case in which an exception became the rule.

The IOC and FIFA have often been receptive to authoritarian forms of exercising power; in occasional moments of carelessness, these institutions' leaders have admitted as much. The IOC's Evaluation Commission for the 2000

Games held that China's candidature to host the 2008 Olympics presented a favorable situation.

> The overall presence of strong governmental control and support is healthy and should improve operational efficiency of the Games organisation through the OCOG. However, care should be taken to ensure that the OCOG would not be restricted by unnecessary bureaucracy.
>
> (IOC 2001, p. 74)

Jérôme Valcke, FIFA's former secretary general, expressed similar sentiments to São Paulo's *Estadão* newspaper, albeit in a much less subtle tone.

> I am going to say something that is crazy, but less democracy sometimes is better for organizing a World Cup. . . . When you have a very strong head of state who can make decisions, maybe like Putin might make in 2018. . . [i]t's easier for us organizers.
>
> (*Estadão* 2013)

According to this perspective, denying space to politics – a clear goal of theories that inspire market-oriented management models – can be best realized through its convergence with the field of production of sport spectacle.

Land ownership and strategies of social clean-up

Disputes for urban land ownership tend to take on a central role in processes of capitalist valorization that depend on territories free of any sign of poverty. Within this context, removing people and small businesses has become an increasingly common strategy in cities that seek to implement planning projects according to business logic. In the case of sport spectacle mega-events, the visibility afforded to host cities, along with the rigor of the timeline they impose, legitimizes the intensification of both the quantity and brutality of these removals.

Already in Chapter Four, I noted the regularity of forced relocation in mega-event host cities. Here, I will examine how such processes take place in different territories, often with the objective of accelerating the disappropriation of lands or buildings so as to allow urban restructuring project to proceed. To these ends, governments introduce certain special apparatuses in their legislation.

Some authors attest to eviction processes that have been negotiated by, and even occasionally proven advantageous for, removed persons in Olympic host cities like London (Raco & Tunney 2010), Barcelona (COHRE 2007; Sánchez 1992), and Athens (Stavrides 2017; COHRE 2007). It is worth highlighting that, in Athens, only ethnic Greeks received preferential treatment, whereas the Roma population suffered violent persecution.

In other cases – such as in Seoul (COHRE 2007), Atlanta (COHRE 2007; Burbank, Andranovich & Heying 2001), Beijing (COHRE 2007; Broudehoux 2007), and Rio de Janeiro and other Brazilian cities in the run-up to the 2014 World Cup and 2016 Olympic (de Oliveira 2016a; de Oliveira et al. 2017) – eviction processes were accompanied by generalized abuse. Removals in these places, justified as "collateral damage" to the "benefits" afforded by mega-events, obeyed a systematic progression: a lack of information, together with coercive attempts to convince residence to accept eviction; the expulsion of the first people to be "convinced" and the demolition of their homes, or expulsion and demolition of entire communities with no prior notice; threats to those who resisted; the creation of inhospitable and unhealthy environments created by debris from destroyed homes and cuts in essential services; and, finally, the complete destruction of communities slated for removal. During initial "negotiations," political leaders tend to offer two alternatives: relocation to places without infrastructure and located far from a community's original location or restitution payments far below the cost necessary for resettling in nearby areas.

Depending on a country's tolerance for dissident voices and freedom of expression, measures taken against attempts at resistance can be violent. Occasionally, professionals who offer support to threatened people also suffer from repression. In Rio de Janeiro, lawyers from the city's Public Defender's Nucleus for Land and Habitation were all transferred to cities elsewhere in the state due to their support of communities threatened with removal. In Beijing, many lawyers were arrested and, after a period of imprisonment, told not to represent housing rights cases (Broudehoux 2007; COHRE 2007).

Forced relocations reveal the most perverse side of the city of exception because they involve the most vulnerable segments of society. Groups most affected by evictions for Olympic projects include: ethnic minorities (like the Roma population of Athens); older people (especially in Barcelona, Sydney, and Tokyo); street vendors and people with physical or mental disabilities (such as in Seoul, Athens, Beijing, and Rio de Janeiro); sex workers (such as in Barcelona and throughout Brazil); and migrant workers (as in Beijing). In all cases, populations targeted by mass evictions tend to be poor and without historic access to public aid.

Partial considerations

The imperative of carrying out mega-events in accordance with the interests of FIFA and the IOC justify exceptional juridical measures in cities that host sport spectacle, which activate certain legal mechanisms in order to guarantee results. The combination of a sophisticated system of regulations in the candidature process and a powerful network of consultants creates conditions that standardize candidature offers according to the logic and limitations determined by these institutions. After the choice of host cities for the World Cup and the Olympic Games, contracts and other guarantees assure that nothing about the events will stray from these standards. Meanwhile, the legitimations that these events confer allows leaders to impose new measures. Although the IOC and FIFA do not demand these measures, political leaders annex them to their hosting bid with the objective of attending to locally active interests.

The ruptures and realignments in cities' and countries' judicial-institutional limits that result from this process reveal the recognition that entities who control the field of production of sport spectacle have conquered for themselves. This recognition is based, on the one hand, on the massive symbolic, political, and juridical capital that they have accumulated over the course of more than a century and, on the other hand, on discourses of technique and competency.

Although the field of production of sport spectacle claims for itself a universal application of the regulatory apparatus that it produces to steer its relation with the field that produces the city, this does not occur uniformly across all territories. The macrostructural context and the correlation of forces that exist within the coalitions of dominant groups define the peculiarities, gravity, and limits of this application in every individual case.

In general, by making decisions regarding mega-events and associated actions more agile, special governance structures allow urban management to grow more authoritarian in character. However, the perceptions of these possibilities vary according to place. In certain territories, legislation establishes limits on its own actions, as is the case of Sydney's OCA and London's ODA. In other territories, political leaders see these institutional spaces as offering the opportunity for authoritarian actions and a lack of transparency, and as making the interests of locally active coalitions viable. Such was the case, for example, with Atlanta's MAOGA, later absorbed by ACOG – an institution controlled by private enterprise – and with the APO in Brazil, which was eventually the object of disputes among rival claims to power.

Similar territorial variations can be seen in all exceptional measures created to satisfy the demands of the production of sport spectacle. Most cases allow for the adoption of one of three options, as seen in the examples elucidated here. The first of these options is the use of pre-existing legislation linked to the search for mechanisms that provide adequate exceptions to the standard rules, as in candidature bids for the 2020 Tokyo, 2024 Paris, and 2028 Los Angeles Olympics. The second option is the institution of laws or measures of exception, together with the definition of limits guaranteeing basic rights, as in Sydney and London's Olympic brand protection laws. Finally, there is the option of ceding completely to the impositions of exception and, in certain cases, even taking advantage of its legitimacy to accommodate the interests of locally acting coalitions, as has been the case almost everywhere in terms of security regulations and control of public spaces.

The territorial repercussions of each of these exceptional measures on different cultural, political, and economic realities cannot be minimized. For example, the effects of prohibitions of informal labor in London or Sydney cannot be taken to be equal to their effects on cities in Brazil or South Africa, where informality is a structural social characteristic. On the other hand, noisiness, the violation of labor laws, or restrictions on brands of beer sold in stadiums would not have the same repercussions in Brazil as they had in Germany during the 2006 World Cup.

In any event, variations in the application of rules established by FIFA and the IOC reveal the limits of these institutions' power in each individual country.

Certain factors can be determinant in defining these limits. The capacity of politicians to defend their own sovereignty is one example. The degree of commitment that a country's political leadership has assumed – whether in the interests of a majority of the country's residents or with locally active economic groups – can also play a significantly determining role.

In addition to frequent recurrences of legal decrees and urgent votes on exceptional measures, processes of instituting laws of exception can be identified by an absence of juridical determination of the limits between public and private interest. In his first examination of the genealogy of *iūstitium*, Agamben (2005) presents the anomie of juridical determinations – especially in terms of distinction between public and private spheres – as one of the most important characteristics of the state of exception.

As Swyngedouw (2010) notes, the idea of a modern, competitive city requires a reconfiguration of public order that includes private actors and other non-state agents in the act of governing. As such, the proposal to overcome the rigid separation between the public and privates sectors (Borja e Castells 1998) becomes a clear and visible reality.

The political-institutional framework that the production of sport spectacle justifies in many places establishes exceptions through the content of juridical and political orders and in the political practices that carry out such orders. In addition to establishing themselves at the margins of existing legal frameworks, laws of exception are frequently implemented through the executive branch's non-management of the act of legislating.

While states of exception have historically been closely linked to war, battle metaphors are also frequently invoked in times of relative peace to stir the voluntary creation of a "permanent state of emergency," which, even if not explicitly declared, "has become one of the essential practices of contemporary states, including so-called democratic ones" (Agamben 2005, p. 2). Periods that, like times of war, present symptoms of economic, political, or social crisis suit this situation quite well.

The metaphor of "war against the crisis" in all or part of a city has established the bases on which inter-urban competitions for funding are converted into a "war between cities" to attract investments, following terms established by market-oriented management models. As such, the metaphor of war serves to justify exceptional measures. Mega-events, meanwhile, function as effective catalysts in this process.

Candidature files promote a perfect coordination of the cross-scale articulation of interests that sustain sport spectacle. By justifying the "necessity" of exceptional measures to guarantee projects committed to meeting the IOC or FIFA's demands, they also support local elites in their demands for parallel, agile forms of exercising power so as to satisfy their own interests. When candidature commitments show gaps in their quests for legitimization, a great coalition of forces works to build new mechanisms that – with the later support of FIFA or the IOC – show themselves to be equally effective. Such was the case, for example, of the coalition established through the transfer of Olympic venues to Rio de Janeiro's port district, which I discussed in Chapter Four.

The significant overlap between public agents and private interests, as seen in major companies' influence in defining public policies, is not exclusively the domain of the production of sport spectacle, much less of recent neoliberal policies. In Brazil, this functional articulation between private enterprise and state actions – seen, for example, in the creation of the city of Brasília or in the Trans-Amazonian highway, both of which made the expansion of heavy construction viable in the mid-twentieth century – represents a case study of bureaucratic-business accords defining and executing public policies within the capitalist system.

This lack of definition of limits between public and private, which has marked the functioning of capitalism under "normal" circumstances, finds an ideal context for more radical, amplified manifestations in the convergence between neoliberal thinking and the production of sport spectacle. By making the inclusion of a significant number of segments of the dominant classes viable across a number of different scales and within the bureaucratic-business pact, sport spectacle offers sufficient legitimacy to define a new legal structure, albeit still contained under the aegis of exception.

On the one hand, the content of these new institutional frameworks reveals political realignments linked to neoliberal planning models, privileging exceptional measures of governance. On the other hand, such processes reveal inter-scalar coalitions and disputes within the bloc of power responsible for mediating between these ideas and the rest of society. Once again, they reinforce my earlier argument that only a cross-scale perspective can allow us to understand social phenomena or strategies established for political action.

Generally speaking, the facts I have presented here point to a correlation of forces favorable to pro-growth coalition members, but it is important to note that, in certain cases, an effectively mobilized civil society can guarantee its rights and force regimes of exception to retreat. As Payne (2012) puts it, rules are not synonymous with principles, and they can be softened depending on specific situations. Such is the case of situations in which rules are broken when a correlation of forces is not favorable to the Olympic Movement, as occurred in the choice of Los Angeles – the sole candidate – to host the 1984 Games. This also seems to be the case in instances of solutions that are less aligned with laws of exception, as in the choices of Tokyo, Paris, and Los Angeles to host the 2020, 2024, and 2028 Olympics after the negative repercussions of laws of exception related to mega-events in Brazil. The ability to mobilize and control society may therefore produce surprising results that lessen the perverse consequences of a development strategy based on the primordial presupposition of preserving the interests of capital.

Notes

1 Portions of this chapter first appeared in the book *O Poder dos Jogos e os Jogos de Poder: Os interesses em campo na produção da cidade para o espetáculo esportivo* (Oliveira 2015), published by Editora UFRJ. The English translation is by Raphael Soifer.

2 An expression coined by Foucault (2009) to describe "government tactics" that, according to him, are responsible for defining, in every instant, the competencies of public and private spheres.

3 For over a century, the IOC has sought to link celebrations of sport to the promotion of universalist ideals so as to strengthen its symbolic capital. The symbolic elements it invokes have included "union among peoples," solidarity, health, gender equality (de Oliveira 2016b), and environmental causes (see Chapter One).

4 Marketing strategies adopted by the organizers of the 1996 Atlanta Olympics did not appeal to the IOC's partners. To understand this crisis better, see Chapter One.

5 These mechanisms include the need to submit plans to the ministry and to create a committee consisting of government officials and members of the SOCOG to whom the Authority would issue periodic reports.

6 Eduardo Paes began his political career serving as sub-mayor of the Barra da Tijuca and Jacarepaguá neighborhoods from 1993–1996, under then-mayor César Maia. He served on Rio de Janeiro's city council from 1997–1998, as a federal congressperson for two terms (1999–2006), and as mayor of Rio de Janeiro for two terms (2009–2016). Over the course of his political career, he was a member of center-right, centrist, and center-left parties. Although he was initially a fierce opponent of Luis Inácio Lula da Silva, Lula da Silva supported his election as mayor, although they continued to dispute the political capital that the Olympics represented.

7 For further details of the APO's creation, see de Oliveira (2015).

8 Dilma Rousseff joined the armed struggle against Brazil's military dictatorship soon after the 1964 coup d'état. She was a member of the Palmares Armed Revolutionary Vanguard (VAR-Palmares) and was arrested in 1970. During her imprisonment, which lasted from 1970–1972, she was a victim of torture. She reconstructed her life in the state of Rio Grande do Sul, where she was active in both municipal and state governments. After working as the Minister of Mines and Energy and the Chief of Staff under Lula da Silva, Rousseff was elected President in 2010 and reelected in 2014. On May 12, 2016, she was temporarily removed from office due to impeachment proceedings; she was definitively removed in August 2016.

9 A supposed mass robbery during a protest on the Avenida Brasil highway served as justification for the action, and the death of an official in the BOPE unit (analogous to American SWAT teams) during the operation led to an intensification of the violence.

10 See Chapter Four.

11 In various public events, mayor Eduardo Paes presented Felipe Góes as the man responsible for the sale of the city of Rio de Janeiro. In addition to serving as president of IPP, Góes was Extraordinary Secretary for Development, a role created specifically for him. After leaving IPP at the end of 2010, Góes remained connected to the Secretary of Development until May 2011, when he announced that he had already completed his task (namely, selling the city) and returned to private enterprise, after which the role of Secretary of Development was extinguished.

References

Agamben, G 2005, *State of Exception*, University of Chicago Press, Chicago.

Alvarenga Filho, JR 2010, "A 'chacina do Pan' e a Produção de Vidas Descartáveis na Cidade do Rio de Janeiro: 'não Dá Pé Não Tem Pé Nem Cabeça. Não Tem Ninguém Que Mereça. Não Tem Coração Que Esqueça'", masters dissertation, Universidade Federal Fluminense, Niterói, viewed 10 May 2019, <https://app.uff.br/slab/index.php/busca/formulario_completo/743>

Articulação Nacional dos Comitês Populares da Copa (ANCOP) n.d., *Megaeventos e violações de direitos humanos no Brasil: Dossiê da Articulação Nacional dos*

Comitês Populares da Copa, viewed 5 January 2019, <https://apublica.org/wp-content/uploads/2012/01/DossieViolacoesCopa.pdf>

Athens 2004 Organising Committee for the Olympic Games S.A. (ATHOC) 2005, *Official Report of the XXVIII Olympiad: Homecoming of the Games*, vol. 1, ATHOC 2004, Athens.

Barcelona'92 Olympic Organising Committee S.A (COOB'92) 1992, *Official Report of the Games of the XXV Olympiad Barcelona 1992*, vol. 2, COOB'92, Barcelona.

Beijing Organising Committee for the Games of the XXIX Olympiad (BOCOG) n.d., *Official Report of the Beijing Olympic Games*, vol. 3, BOCOG, Beijing.

Blunden, H 2007, *The Impacts of the Sydney Olympic Games on Housing Rights: Background Paper*, COHRE, Geneva.

Borja, J & Castells M 1998, *Local y global: la gestión de las ciudades en la era de la información*, Taurus, Madrid.

Bourdieu, P 1991, *Language and Symbolic Power*, trans. G Raymond & M Adamsom, Polity Press, Cambridge.

Bourdieu, P & Wacquant, LJD 1992, *An Invitation to Reflexive Sociology*, The University of Chicago Press, Chicago.

Broudehoux, AM 2007, "Spectacular Beijing: The Conspicuous Construction of an Olympic Metropolis", *Journal of Urban Affairs*, 29.4, pp. 383–399.

Broudehoux, AM 2012, "Civilizing Beijing: Social Beautification, Civility and Citizenship at the 2008 Olympics", in G Hayes & J Karamichas (eds) *Olympic Games, Mega-Events and Civil Societies*, Palgrave Macmillan, London, pp. 46–67.

Burbank, M, Andranovich, G & Heying, C 2001, *Olympic Dreams: The Impact of Mega-Events on Local Politics*, Lynne Rienner Publishers, Boulder.

Centre on Housing Rights and Evictions (COHRE) 2007, *Fair Play for Housing Rights: Opportunities for the Olympic Movement and Other*, COHRE, Geneva.

Cidade do Rio de Janeiro (CRJ 1996), *Plano Estratégico da Cidade do Rio de Janeiro – Rio sempre Rio*, Imprensa da Cidade, Rio de Janeiro.

Comissão de Defesa dos Direitos Humanos e Cidadania da Assembleia Legislativa do Estado do Rio de Janeiro (CDDHC-ALERJ) 2012a, *Relatório 2009–2012*, ALERJ, Rio de Janeiro.

Comissão de Defesa dos Direitos Humanos e Cidadania da Assembleia Legislativa do Estado do Rio de Janeiro (CDDHC-ALERJ) 2012b, *Relatório de visitas aos "abrigos especializados" para crianças e adolescentes*, ALERJ, Rio de Janeiro.

de Oliveira, FL, Sánchez, F, Tanaka, G & Monteiro, P (eds) 2017, *Planejamento e Conflitos Urbanos: Experiências de luta*, Letra Capital, Rio de Janeiro.

de Oliveira 2015, *O poder dos jogos e os jogos de poder: interesses em campo na produção da cidade para o espetáculo esportivo*, Editora UFRJ, Anpur, Rio de Janeiro.

de Oliveira, NG 2016a, "Les méga-événements au Brésil et la réinvention du spectacle sportif", *Problèmes d'Amérique Latine*, 103, pp. 17–36, April.

de Oliveira, NG 2016b, "Jumping Hurdles: Women in Sports Spectacle", in D Bartelt, M de Paula & M Vianna (eds) *Dossier: Olympic Games 2016 in Rio de Janeiro*, Heinrich-Böll-Stiftung, Rio de Janeiro.

Estadão 2013, "É mais fácil organizar uma Copa com menos democradia, diz Valcke", *Estadão*, 24 April 2013, viewed 26 April 2013, <http://esportes.estadao.com.br/noticias/futebol,e-mais-facil-organizar-uma-copa-com-menos-democracia-diz-valcke,1025076>

Forn y Foxá, M 1993, *Barcelona: estrategias de transformación urbana y econômica*, Mimeo, s.l.

Foucaul, M 2009, *Security, Territory, Population: Lectures at the College De France, 1977–78*, Palgrave Macmillan, New York.

Gramsci, A 1957, "The Modern Prince: Essays on the Science of Politics in the Modern Age", in A Gramsci (ed) *The Modern Prince and Other Writings*, Lawrence and Wishart LTD, London.

Gramsci, A 1971, *Selections from the Prison Notebooks*, eds. Q Hoare & GN Smith, International Publishers, New York.

International Olympic Committee (IOC) 1999a, *Olympic Charter: In Force as from 17th June 1999*, IOC, Lausanne.

International Olympic Committee (IOC) 1999b, *Olympic Charter: In Force as from 12th December 1999*, IOC, Lausanne.

International Olympic Committee (IOC) 2001, *Final Report of the IOC Coordination Commission: Games of the XXIX Olympiad Beijing 2008*, IOC, Lausanne.

International Olympic Committee (IOC) 2010, *Report of the IOC Evaluation Commission for the Games of the XXIX Olympiad in 2008*, IOC, Lausanne.

Logan, J & Molotch, H 1987, *Urban Fortunes: The Political Economy of Place*, University of California Press, Berkeley.

Payne, M 2012, *Olympic Turnarounds: How the Olympic Games Stepped Back from the Brink of Extinction to Become the World Best Known Brand*, Infinite Ideas Limited, Oxford.

Poulantzas, N 1974, *Fascism and Dictatorship: The Third International and the Problem of Fascism*, Verso, London.

Raco, M & Tunney, E 2010, "Visibilities and Invisibilities in Urban Development: Small Business Communities and the London Olympics 2012", *Urban Studies*, 47, pp. 2069–2091, September.

Rancière, J 2007, "Ten Theses on Politics", *Theory & Event*, 5.3.

Sánchez, A 2007, *Barcelona 1992: International Events and Housing Rights: A Focus on the Olympic Games*, COHRE, Geneva.

Schmitt, C 1921, *Die Dictatorship*, Duncker &Humpblot, München- Leipzig, translated by M Hoelzl & G Ward 2014 as *Dictatorship: From the Origin of the Modern Concept of Sovereignty to Proletarian Class Struggle*, Polity Press, Cambridge.

Schmitt, C 1922, *Politsche Theologie: Ver Kapitel zur Lehre von Souveranitat*, Duncker &Humpblot, München- Leipzig, translated by G Schwab in 1985 *as Political Theology: Four Chapters on the Concept of Sovereignty*, University of Chicago Press, Chicago.

Stab WM 2006 2006, *Bundesministerium des Innern. Fußbal-WM 2006: Abschlussbericht der Bundesregierung*, vol. 1, Presse- und Informationsamt der Deutschen Bundesregierung, Berlin.

Stavrides, S 2008, "Urban Identities: Beyond the Regional and the Global. The Case of Athens", in *Regional Architecture and Identity in the Age of Globalization: Proceedings of 2nd International Conference of CSAAR*, CSAAR, Tunis, pp. 577–588.

Stavrides, S 2017, "Athens 2004 Olympics: An Urban State of Exception Which Became the Rule", in C Vainer, AM Broudehoux, F Sánchez & FL Oliveira (eds) *Mega-Events and the City: Critical Perspectives*, Letra Capital, Rio de Janeiro.

Sydney Organising Committee for the Olympic Games (SOCOG) 2001, *Official Report of the XXVII Olympiad*, vol. 2, SOCOG, Sydney.

Swyngedouw, E 2010, "Post-Democratic Cities for Whom and for What", in *Regional Studies Association Annual Conference*, Pecs, Hungary, May.

Tokyo 2020 Candidate City n.d., *Tokyo 2020: Discover Tomorrow*, Tokyo 2020 Candidate City, Tokyo.

Tokyo Organising Committee of the Olympic and Paralympic Games (Tokyo 2020) 2017, *Brand Protection Tokyo 2020 Games*, ver. 3.3, Tokyo 2020, Tokyo.

Vainer, C 2000, "Pátria, empresa e mercadoria: notas sobre a estratégia discursiva do planejamento estratégico urbano", in O Arantes, C Vainer & E Maricato (eds) *A cidade do pensamento único: desmanchando consensos*, Petrópolis, Vozes, pp. 75–103.

Vainer, C 2017, "Rio de Janeiro's Strategic Plan: Olympic Construction of the Corporate Town", in L Albrechts, A Balducci & J Hillier (eds) *Situated Practices of Strategic Planning*, Routledge, Abingdon and New York.

Žižek, S 1999a, *The Ticklish Subject: The Absent Centre of Political Ontology*, Verso, London.

Žižek, S 1999b, "Carl Schmitt in the Age of Post-Politics", in C Mouffe (ed) *The Challenge of Carl Schmitt*, Verso, London.

Legislation

2006 World Cup Act 2005 (FRG)
2006 World Cup Act 2006 (FRG)
2010 FIFA World Cup South Africa Special Measures Act 2006 (RSA)
APO Federal Law – Law 12.396 of 2011 (RFB)
APO Municipal Law – Law 5.260/2011 (CRJ)
APO Municipal Law – Law 5.272–2011 (CRJ)
Bid Law – Law n° 8.666/1993 (RFB)
Constitution of the Federative Republic of Brazil 1988 (RFB)
Copyright Law 1970 (Jpn)
Criminal Organizations Law 2013 – Lei n° 12.850/2013 (RFB)
Design Law 1959 (Jpn)
Differentiated Public Contracts Regime (RDC) – Law n° 12.462 2011 (RFB)
General Law of the Cup – Law Lei n° 12.663/2012 (RFB)
General Notice n° 683/2006 (RSA)
Homebush Bay Operations Act and Regulation 1999 (NSW)
London Olympic Games and Paralympic Games Act 2006 (UK)
Master Plan – Law Number 1515/1985 (HR)
Merchandise Marks Act 1941(RSA)
Olympic Act 2009 – Law n° 12.035/2009 (RFB)
Olympic Arrangements Act 2000 (NSW)
Olympic Co-Ordination Authority Act 1995 (NSW)
Olympic Package – Law n° 716/2010 and Law n° 44/2010 (CRJ)
Patent Act 1959 (Jpn)
Porto Maravilha Project 2009 – Law n° 101/2009, Law n° 102/2009 and Law n° 15.128 /2009 (CRJ)
Provisional Measure 489/2010 (RFB)
Provisional Measure 49/2010 (RFB)
Quality of Life Ordinances 1998 (Atl)
Regulations on Protection of Olympic Intellectual Property Rights in Beijing 2002 (Bj)
Regulations on Protection of Olympic Symbols 2002 (PRC)
Regulations on Reporting Activities in China by Foreign Journalists During the Beijing Olympic Games and the Preparatory Period 2006 (PRC)
Sydney 2000 Games (Indicia and Images) Protection Act 1996 (Cth)

Sydney Harbour Foreshore Authority Regulation 1999 (NSW)
Tax Benefit Law 1988 (RE)
Tax Benefit Law 2010 – Law nº 12.350/2010 (RFB)
Terrorism Law 2016 – Law 13.260/2016 (RFB)
Trademark Law 1959 (Jpn)
Unfair Competition Prevention Act 1993 (Jpn)
Urban Redevelopment Law 1982 (RK)
Urban Structuring Plan for the Vargens District 2009 (PEU Vargens) – Law nº 104/2009 (CRJ)

Final considerations[1]

The convergence between the field in which the city is produced and the field in which sport spectacle is produced engenders forms of exercising power and organizing public administration that radicalize the already familiar authoritarianism inherent in neoliberal urban management practices.

When the production of sport spectacle is converted into a development strategy linked to management models for the city, it reveals itself to be capable of causing significant mobilizations of economic, political, and symbolic capital. This, in turn, results in profound ruptures and realignments in diverse dimensions and across multiple scales of social space within the territories in which these forms of capital are mobilized. This research has sought to demonstrate – from a perspective that privileges the effects produced within a political-institutional dimension – that by constituting a social universe relatively independent of external pressures, the field in which sport spectacle is produced functions as a means of submitting the city and its inhabitants to the pressures of the economic field to which sport spectacle is also subject.

Some evidence of the adequacy between these two fields' dominant commercial strategies – the imperative of valorizing Olympic or football-related brands in the field that produces sport spectacle and the axiom of capitalist businesses in the field in which the city is produced – make it possible to formulate this hypothesis. In these final considerations, I will aim to point to such evidence while being mindful of the ever-present risk of oversimplification.

In relations between these two fields, sport spectacle offers the entrepreneurial city valorization of its urban brand within the worldwide market of cities as well as the legitimation conferred on projects that prioritize business and profits. In return, the field of sport spectacle seeks to execute grandiose events in favorable environments so as to sustain the value of Olympic or football-related brands; in other words, to keep sponsors and broadcasters – its paying clients – satisfied.

The relatively autonomous constitution of the field in which sport spectacle is produced has occurred over the course of more than a century, from the foundation of the International Olympic Committee in 1894 to the present day. Through disputes within the field as well as its relations with other fields, it has managed to emerge as an autonomous social universe and, "through the logic of its own specific functioning, to produce and reproduce a juridical corpus relatively independent of exterior constraint" (Bourdieu 1987, p. 815). Within the context of the rules established within it, the field has guaranteed not only its own autonomy but also its ability to impose certain constraints on the functioning of other fields, especially the juridical field of territories that receive its events.

A genealogy of the historical conditions of this field's formation allows us to identify three crucial stages in its relation to the economic field: amateurism, professionalism, and spectacularization. In each of these, sport spectacle has also reconfigured its relations with other fields.

During the first stage, the emphasis on the symbolic values of amateurism and fair play – both of which served the formation of bourgeoise morals and the distinction between the bourgeoisie and other social classes – created the basis for the modern production of sport spectacle to emerge as an autonomous field. In alignment with the idea of regulatory control over the market, which prevailed within the economic field until the 1970s, the hegemonic discourse of the Olympic movement did not accept the existence of any pressures from economic structures. At that time, although the production of internal sporting events was dependent on external financing and showed significant advances in mobilizing spectators and economic capital, it did not participate in the process of capital reproduction, whether as a means of accumulation or a product to be accumulated.

Sporting events became increasingly complex at the end of the 1940s, creating new possibilities for political and commercial power through television broadcasting and vertiginous growth in the number of countries and athletes involved in competitions. As a result, the IOC began to introduce reforms into its Olympic Charters. In addition to emphasizing the construction of symbols, which had previously dominated these regulatory instruments, the IOC began to focus on demanding commitments from cities interested in hosting sporting mega-events.

Beginning in the 1970s, as a result of internal disputes and macrostructural pressures relating to the emergence of neoliberal thought in the system of capitalist production, a gradual and irreversible professionalization process began to change the bases for the functioning of modern sport. This configured a second stage of the field of the production of sport spectacle's relation to the field of economics: the stage of professionalism. As market-oriented discourses began to take hold over all spheres of social life and spectacle began to emerge as a valuable commodity, there was no longer space for the discourse of sport practiced purely for the pleasure of those involved in competitions. The commodified idea of income generating sport-business, already predominant in the production of football-related spectacle since the beginning of the twentieth century, began to gain strength, becoming institutionalized within the Olympic Movement's leadership. From this moment forward, we can refer to a "field of production" of major sporting events. However, tensions persisted with idealist symbols that sustained the rhetoric of modern sport's autonomy.

At the end of the 1970s, a variety of factors led the Olympic Movement to enter into political and economic crises that challenged the continuity of its primary events and, therefore, its very existence. At the beginning of the 1980s, with the rise of neoliberal hegemony in the global economy, ideas of spectacularization offered a solution to these crises. The guiltless adoption of such ideas in all of their magnitude marked a new stage in the history of modern sport, which henceforth assumed the quality of sport spectacle.

This radical change in the Olympic Movement's posture was made possible through the implementation of a daring marketing program that equalized contradictions between the Movement's idealistic and universalist principles, thereby commercializing its symbolic capital. This program, created and implemented through the decisive actions of actors both within and outside of the field, transformed what had previously been seen as a conflict into a hypothetical equilibrium.

The commodity that the International Olympic Committee (IOC) sold to sponsors and television networks through this marketing program was the right to be associated with the Olympic Movement's supposedly non-commercial symbolic values. The need for financial support for the world's greatest and most grandiose events was the main argument behind the complete and definitive conversion of major sporting events into commodity-spectacle. On the one hand, the universalist ideals linked to the field of production of sport spectacle produced symbolic capital that became economic capital through the transformation of symbols into commodities. On the other hand, this same symbolic capital, transmuted into political capital, made new economic currents possible in its interactions with the field of production of the city.

The sophisticated system of rules that currently reign over the field of production of sport spectacle – as expressed through the Olympic Charter, the Statutes of the Fédération Internationale de Football Association (FIFA), and a complex tangle of recommendations, candidature guidelines, codes of conduct, guarantees, and contracts – attends to the interests and strategies of hegemonic players within this field, especially institutions involved in promoting it across different scales (the IOC, FIFA, and their affiliates) and those responsible for its commercialization (i.e., broadcasters and sponsors).

This normative system enjoys relative autonomy and is capable of imposing its constraints on juridical order, the legitimized symbolic violence on which a state holds a monopoly (Bourdieu 1987, p. 838). It achieves these constraints through its position outside of the state's apparatus, a positioning dependent on its indisputable and universal recognition. However, this recognition is sustained through a logical paradox. On the one hand, it is based on the discourse of equality of principals, political neutrality, and autonomy in relation to economic interests. On the other hand, the system arrives at the pinnacle of its sophistication by denying these bases. In other words, by attending to structural pressures from the economic field, the field of production of sport spectacle intensifies and complexifies its own normatization.

The regulatory apparatus that controls the field of production of sport spectacle in its relation to other fields has the principle function of guaranteeing the satisfaction of the IOC, FIFA, and their affiliates and partners. In order to bring these interests into line with the ever-changing political and economic global orders, this regulatory apparatus exists in a state of permanent metamorphosis driven principally by processes of innovation or crisis. A group of autonomous tribunals instituted by the IOC and FIFA guarantee compliance with this legal system. Thus, dominant agents within the field of production of sport spectacle, who hold a monopoly of the power to determine norms capable of satisfying their own interests, are also the only ones who hold the power to define the body of specialized professionals authorized to interpret the codified proceedings of these norms and to put the resolutions of related conflicts into practice.

The functioning of the gearwork that sustains the production of sport spectacle – which broadcasters and sponsors, in their disputes for partnerships, are responsible for moving – depends above all on the control of other gears (namely, local pro-growth coalitions). By producing spaces that are adequate for executing grandiose mega-events, such coalitions also move the gearwork of production of the city so as to satisfy their own interests. The regulatory system within the field of production of sport spectacle legitimates the production of exceptional measures to make major urban development projects viable, thereby satisfying the interests of locally acting coalitions. These, in turn, sustain the dispute between cities for the privilege of hosting sport spectacle, thereby helping to keep the gearwork in motion.

Although, under these conditions, relations between the field of production of sport spectacle and the field in which the city is produced seem to be mechanically rigid, they also present fluid possibilities that depend on structural conditions as well as on changes in subjects' positions and strategies. Thus, the concept of the field (Bourdieu 1991) is an analytical tool that is well suited to understanding reciprocal effects of relations between two distinct universes. The concept of a field of forces and disputes steers analysis toward privileging interactive processes between these two universes, thereby supplanting narratives that merely describe their historical processes. Observing these universes from this perspective has made it possible to understand certain forms of power outside of the governing-coercive device of the state (Gramsci 1957),[2] that utilize this apparatus as a vehicle for their own realization.

Projects that ignore the necessities of the majority of a city's population in favor of the interests of elites cannot materialize if they are confronted with other possibilities and priorities through an ample political discussion involving multiple segments of society. Therefore, the viability of elites' interests depends on a negation of political space that can only be carried out through liberal-democratic consensus. As Žižek (1999), Rancière (2001), Swyngedouw (2010), and Vainer (2017) note, this consensus holds within itself its own authoritarian inverse.

Executing this type of project during preparations for sporting mega-events can be guaranteed through exceptional juridical measures and special forms of organizing public management. This proves that the success of the field of production of sport spectacle resides in being recognized, making itself valuable, and imposing constraints on the autonomy of other relatively independent universes in relation to external pressures. It achieves these ends through the bureaucratic apparatus of countries and cities which, according to Bourdieu (1991, 1987), hold a monopoly on legitimate symbolic violence.

The constraints that the regulatory system of the field of production of sport spectacle and its exclusive interpreters impose on the juridical order of countries and cities are only effective to the extent to which agents of state bureaucracy – who are also subject to structural pressures from the field of economics – are willing to accept this system as legitimate and to embody this discourse of legitimacy, thereby causing other members of society to accept it. To these ends, such agents rely on those who hold cultural capital, especially consulting firms and the media which, through the prestige of their supposedly unquestionable competency, create bases for consensus.[3]

In the system of objective relations between mega-events and the city, the field of production of sport spectacle functions as a means through which the city is molded to capitalist production across multiple scales from the local to the global. The constraints that this field imposes on cities limits their autonomy, transforms hierarchies within social space, reorganizes forces in dispute, and legitimizes authorities.

Although the project of attracting sport spectacle is demanding, it also unites dominant groups in the exercise of hegemony, creating a context in which different class segments within these groups can unite while using consent to establish their domination over subordinate groups (Gramsci 1957, 1971). In other words, two conditions necessary for attracting sporting mega-events can also be made viable through mega-events: namely, the constitution of an urban regime (Stone 2008) or a pro-growth coalition (Mollenkopf 1983) among dominant groups and the consolidation of social consensus in support of the project. Meanwhile, civic patriotism and consciousness of a crisis – either throughout the city or in parts of it – are elements that sustain the construction of this consensus. The progressive and daring strategy of creating commitments during the candidature period establishes the idea of a "fait accompli" that impedes society from debating the effects of these commitments in time to decide whether or not to accept them, thus eliminating the possibility of dissensus.

Although articulating local forces is a necessary component of such projects, it alone is not enough to guarantee success. A winning bid to host a sporting mega-event depends on cross-scalar articulations of forces capable of unifying local, national, and global interests. This reinforces my methodological hypothesis of the impossibility of understanding these phenomena through a perspective based on a single scale of observation.

Although the production of political-institutional ruptures has become an inherent characteristic of the production of sport spectacle – inasmuch as it constitutes a necessary condition for cities that seek to become hosts or even to submit a candidature – historical, economic, political, social, and cultural differences confer specificities to the ways in which these ruptures occur in any given place and the ways in which the parts of society affected by these ruptures accept or reject them.

Cases observed here allow us to identify an exceptional character in the political-institutional ruptures that sporting mega-events produce, both in their relations to the established juridical order and to processes that institute this order. Certain characteristics of these processes operate in ways that are very similar to the propositions that Poulantzas (1974) and Agamben (2005) use to identify the state of exception, including: the suspension of the state's normal ideological apparatuses, especially those instituted through participatory processes, such as master plans and public assemblies; an intimate connection between public agents and private interests, which is especially evident in public-private partnerships; and a centralization of power in the executive branch, expressed through decisions relating to public policies, the use of provisional measures and decrees, and legal projects sent to legislatures under urgent circumstances.

Empirical data indicates that coalitions created around the organization of sporting mega-events include a majority of actors already identified in other pro-growth coalitions by authors such as Logan and Molotch (1987), Stone (2008), and Mollenkopf (1983). In general, we can also observe the recurrence of certain groups – such as state bureaucrats, real estate developers, and service industry representatives – who benefit when these coalitions adopt the goal of attracting sporting mega-events. However, territorial specificities demonstrate the effects that place has on the production of sport spectacle.

One of these singularities of place can certainly be observed in the weight of the federal sphere in South Korea, Brazil, and China, which shows the central role that the policy of attracting mega-events played in these places' national political cal processes. In Brazil specifically, it is also crucial to understand the obvious disputes between different spheres of public administration, especially between municipal and federal governments.

Although all cities that organize mega-events have carried out evictions, the levels of violence associated with these removals differ in every territory. In Atlanta, where city leaders were completely left out of decision-making processes in the organization of the Olympic Games, evictions took on a more violent character, as they did in countries like Brazil, South Korea, and China whose societies do not possess effective means of exerting control over their political leaders. Greater tolerance for dissent in Brazil than in South Korea and China – as well as Brazilian social movements' organizational capacity – led to some success in combatting processes of mass removal during the lead-up to the 2014 World Cup and 2016 Olympics. In Brazil, negotiations that took place later in the planning process were more advantageous for people threatened with removal; some residents avoided being evicted, especially after social movements managed to draw international attention to their plight. However, the quantitative magnitude of these processes largely attained the aims of pro-growth coalitions.

Within relations between capital and the state, the power accumulated by construction firms within some of the coalitions that support sport spectacle stands out. In certain cities, these companies have managed to define the priorities of planning processes and the implementation of public policy, as was the case in Seoul, Barcelona, and Rio de Janeiro as well as in other Brazilian host cities for the 2014 World Cup.

Although I recognize the existence of past forms of relationships between private capitalist interest and the state, I note the existence of specific forms of articulation between capital, the bourgeois state, and society in the era of "globalized competition." While the production of sport spectacle does not necessarily create these forms, it helps facilitate their existence. In this new context, the mechanisms of the representation of capital are also new and introduce new dimensions that question traditional forms of political representation. The bourgeois state functions in specific and unfamiliar ways.

Within these new mechanisms, the generalized institutionalization and naturalization of old – but previously clandestine – forms of articulation between the public sector and capitalist interests stands out. This institutionalization challenges traditional forms of mediation between the state and private interests.[4] One example is the annihilation of legislatures' traditional power over legislation. Through the use of provisional measures, decrees, and urgent voting, the executive branch of government has increasingly taken over this function. Relations that might be considered scandalous under other circumstances now take appear virtuous and even commendable.[5]

The production of sport spectacle does not create exception; instead, in an inverse way, exception establishes itself as a paradigm of government linked to neoliberal economic models, thereby creating conditions in which attracting sporting mega-events serves as a development strategy. This strategy allows for a radicalization of exception that can extend beyond the execution of mega-events.[6] The market-oriented nature of this strategy, and its utilization of authoritarian forms of management disguised as consensus have, since the 1980s, become hegemonic within the field in which the city is thought of and produced. However, we must not ignore the radicalization that these practices assume when they are legitimated by constraints from the field of production of sport spectacle.

In moments of crisis, the IOC and FIFA's capacity to impose constraints on the juridical order of countries that seek to host mega-events can be challenged. This occurred twice in Los Angeles, in its candidatures to host the 1984 and 2024 Olympics (this second bid resulted in hosting rights for the 2028 Games), and once in Paris, in that city's winning bid to host the 2024 Games.

These two most recent bids to host the Olympic Games demonstrate a certain autonomy on the part of cities in relation to constraints imposed on their juridical, political, and urban order, whether by the IOC – which ultimately saw fit to frame its exceptional demands within existing legislation – or by local coalitions, inasmuch as the aforementioned Olympic bids did not present opportunities for major urban restructuring projects. Certainly, the possibility of an embarrassingly limited selection process with only one candidate – or worse, with none at all – weighed on the IOC's decision to grant hosting rights for the 2028 Olympics to Los Angeles. In addition, the significant attrition that the IOC suffered thanks to abuses of the "city of exception" established in Rio de Janeiro during the run-up to the 2016 Olympics[7] led the organization to be more cautious with exceptional rules and measures. Naturally, the cost of postponing the 2020 Tokyo Olympic Games could expose the IOC to an even more vulnerable financial situation. However, such costs should be easy to overcome should the event occur successfully in 2021.

These facts established a challenge for my research inquiries. Will Paris, Los Angeles, and the IOC manage to sustain the relative autonomy of the field of production of the city in the context of its convergence with the production of sport spectacle in the time that elapses between candidature bids and the realization of the Games? Or will relations with the field of economics lead to new challenges, resulting in contradictions and tensions to which both sport spectacle and the production of the city will be forced to submit? If the aforementioned pact holds, will a period of eight years without dissonance during the preparations for two editions of the Olympic Games be capable of restoring all of the symbolic capital that the IOC lost in the lead-up to the 2016 Olympics? And, if so, would this be enough to restore the golden age of fierce disputes for hosting rights?

Given that none of the changes made to the IOC's regulatory framework through 2019 suggest a structural transformation in relations between the production of sport spectacle and the production of the city, it is worth articulating one final inquiry here: does the pact established for the 2024 and 2028 Olympic Games mark an era of new relations in the convergence between the production of sport spectacle and the production of cities? Or does it simply represent another circumstantial adjustment to a moment of crisis, like that which occurred during the 1984 Olympics?

Any effort to find the answer to these questions must not ignore the splits and conflicts that take place within the blocs of power constituting both fields, within these fields' hegemonic groups, or between these groups and subaltern social classes. Observing political-institutional ruptures and realignments determined by the interests of capital and mediated by the organization of sport spectacle in places throughout the world reveals the emergence of new social subjects committed to actions – some of which have been successful – that aim to hinder the supposed inexorability of these authoritarian processes.

At the same time that it is capable of producing profound spatial, economic, political, and institutional restructuring within the city, the convergence of these two fields also helps to intensify contradictions of class and to open gaps in which forces and subjects capable of challenging hegemonic thought may arise. The visibility of these subjects' actions creates opportunities to build new worldviews that take into account the social damages and authoritarian character that sport spectacle can produce in public management. Under these conditions, citizens of different parts of the world have dared to dissent, refusing the possibility of hosting this type of event.

Constructing new categories that can offer support to these subjects in creating proposals that substitute the incessant search for economic development with guarantees of democracy and social justice necessitates discovering new gaps and identifying moments and conditions suited to action. For this to occur, it is important to know how to organize, who the subjects participating in this field are, what coalitions and disputes exist within hegemonic blocs, what strategies and mechanisms these blocs use, and – especially – how they construct the discourses used to justify their actions. This is how my research aims to contribute.

Notes

1 Portions of this chapter first appeared in the book *O Poder dos Jogos e os Jogos de Poder: Os interesses em campo na produção da cidade para o espetáculo esportivo* (Oliveira 2015), published by Editora UFRJ. The English translation is by Raphael Soifer.
2 Gramsci (1957) understands governing-coercive devices of the state as hegemonic devices at the base of the state, formed by social groups organized either contractually or voluntarily and that exert relative or absolute dominance over the rest of the population (or civil society).
3 Here, it is worth noting the double function of specialists who represent two chains of interests. On the one hand, they validate the strategies of interests acting in the field of production of sport spectacle (such as FIFA, the IOC, sponsors, and broadcasters), to the extent to which these groups hold the power to enunciate standards for the perfect execution of sport spectacle. On the other hand, by establishing urban planning models driven by attracting major economic investments, they legitimate the dispute among cities for hosting rights for these spectacles.
4 In this sense, the demands imposed by the IOC fit perfectly.
5 Here, it is worth citing the example of Public-Private Partnerships (PPPs), spread by the World Bank and other multilateral agencies.
6 This capacity for extending the effects of exception beyond mega-events is very evident in the case of the Law of Differentiated Contractual Regimes (RDC), which was applied to any project in Brazilian territory for which construction was considered to be an emergency. The rigorous legislation established by the European Union to guarantee the principal of open competition impeded measures like the RDC from being adopted in host cities located within EU territory, such as London, Barcelona, or Athens.
7 See de Oliveira 2016.

References

Agamben, G 2005, *State of Exception*, University of Chicago Press, Chicago.
Bourdieu, P 1987, "The Fore of Law: Toward a Sociology of the Juridical Field", *The Hastings Law Journal*, 38, July.
Bourdieu, P 1991, *Language and Symbolic Power*, trans. G Raymond & M Adamsom, Polity Press, Cambridge.
de Oliveira, NG 2016, "Les méga-événements au Brésil et la réinvention du spectacle sportif", *Problèmes d'Amérique Latine*, 103, pp. 17–36, April.
Gramsci, A 1957, "The Modern Prince: Essays on the Science of Politics in the Modern Age", in A Gramsci (ed) *The Modern Prince and Other Writings*, Lawrence and Wishart LTD, London.
Gramsci, A 1971, *Selections from the Prison Notebooks*, eds. Q Hoare & GN Smith, International Publishers, New York.
Logan, J & Molotch, H 1987, *Urban Fortunes: The Political Economy of Place*, University of California Press, Berkeley.
Mollenkopf, JH 1983, *The Contested City*, Princeton University Press, Princeton.
Poulantzas, N 1974, *Fascism and Dictatorship: The Third International and the Problem of Fascism*, Verso, London.
Rancière, J 2001, "Ten Theses on Politics", *Theory & Event*, 5.3.
Stone, C 2008, "Urban Regime and the Capacity to Govern: A Political Economy Approach", *Journal of Urban Affairs*, 15.1, 28 June.

Swyngedouw, E 2010, "Post-Democratic Cities for Whom and for What", in *Regional Studies Association Annual Conference*, Pecs, Hungary, May.

Vainer, C 2017, "Rio de Janeiro's Strategic Plan: Olympic Construction of the Corporate Town", in L Albrechts, A Balducci & J Hillier (eds) *Situated Practices of Strategic Planning*, Routledge, Abingdon and New York.

Žižek, S 1999, *The Ticklish Subject: The Absent Centre of Political Ontology*, Verso, London.

Index

Printed in the United States
By Bookmasters